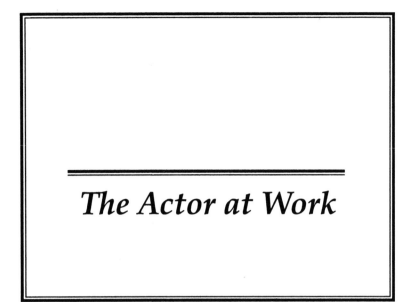

*The Actor at Work*

# The Actor at Work

## SIXTH EDITION

## ROBERT BENEDETTI

PRENTICE HALL, Englewood Cliffs, New Jersey 07632

*Library of Congress Cataloging-in-Publication Data*

BENEDETTI, ROBERT L.
  The actor at work/Robert Benedetti.—6th ed.
     p.   cm.
  Includes bibliographical references and index.
  ISBN 0-13-035452-X
  1. Acting.   I. Title.
  PN2061.B39   1994
  792′.028—dc20                          93-16737
                                              CIP

Editorial/production supervision,
  interior design, and electronic page makeup: Kari Callaghan Mazzola
Acquisitions editor: Steve Dalphin
Cover design: Maureen Eide
Prepress buyer: Kelly Behr
Manufacturing buyer: Mary Ann Gloriande

 © 1994, 1990, 1986, 1981, 1976, 1970 by Prentice-Hall, Inc.
A Simon & Schuster Company
Englewood Cliffs, New Jersey 07632

Printed in the United States of America
10  9  8  7  6  5  4  3  2  1

ISBN 0-13-035452-X

PRENTICE-HALL INTERNATIONAL (UK) LIMITED, *London*
PRENTICE-HALL OF AUSTRALIA PTY. LIMITED, *Sydney*
PRENTICE-HALL CANADA INC., *Toronto*
PRENTICE-HALL HISPANOAMERICANA, S.A., *Mexico*
PRENTICE-HALL OF INDIA PRIVATE LIMITED, *New Delhi*
PRENTICE-HALL OF JAPAN, INC., *Tokyo*
SIMON & SCHUSTER ASIA PTE. LTD., *Singapore*
EDITORA PRENTICE-HALL DO BRASIL, LTDA., *Rio de Janeiro*

# Contents

# Exercises

# *Foreword*

## TED DANSON

I met Bob Benedetti twenty-four years ago, when I was in his second-year acting class at Carnegie Tech. As long as I have known him, he has been exploring, discovering, and sharing what it means to act.

His classes filled me with the kind of excitement athletes must feel when they are in full stride. He taught me how to get acting out of my mind, out of theory, and into my body, into action; he gave me a point of concentration, so that my mind would not be censoring every impulse that came up.

He was also fun to be around, and he planted in me the thought that acting, performing, could be joyous. I will cherish him always for that, because as far as I'm concerned acting, if it is nothing else, had best be joyous, both in the childlike spirit of play and as a profound celebration of life. For me, acting is a wonderful excuse to live life as fully as possible.

My mother had a prayer that has always stayed with me: "Dear Lord," she would say, "please help me to become fully human." The job of all of us in life is to experience the human condition and our own humanity fully; your job as an actor is to reflect what you have experienced in a way that clarifies and enhances people's lives.

As an actor, you are a pleader of causes. The characters you play have a cause, a purpose, and it is up to you to plead it with utmost integrity and commitment, as if a life depended on it—for in fact, it does.

To be able to do this, you must master the techniques of acting. You stretch your body, your voice, your thoughts and feelings so as to encompass as much of the human condition as possible; you must develop the capacity to reflect it all, not just that small portion with which you feel comfortable.

You must also live the same way: You must push past the comfortable, easy answers and explore the scary side of life and of yourself, for finally you have nothing to offer but yourself, your insights, your truth, your slice of the human condition. As you grow and expand, remember that at any moment in your personal journey as an actor, you have only yourself to offer: Who you are at that moment is enough.

As you work to master technique, then, keep your attention focused outward. Don't worry about yourself, think about everybody else; don't worry about being interesting, just be interested in everybody else, in life itself. All the technique in the world will be meaningless unless you have something worth sharing through it; technique is the tool you will use to communicate whatever you have to say, through the characters you choose to play, about the human condition.

To me, acting has itself become a life process. Whatever is next in my development as a human being will happen either through my everyday life or through my acting; they are completely intertwined. This blending of acting and living is never more obvious to me than when I am working on a film (or a play or any other creative group effort); when everyone is aligned toward the common purpose, then there are no more "accidents"; everything that happens at home, on my way to work, in front of the camera, all contributes to our creative purpose. Only when you hold your acting separate from your life do they interfere with each other; when they are aligned, they feed each other. You can become a better actor by becoming a more complete human being, and you can become a more complete human being by becoming a better actor.

Back to technique!

# *Preface*

In 1989, after twenty-six years of teaching acting, I changed careers. I still teach on a part-time basis, but I now spend most of my time in the maddening world of film and television production.

Although I had spent many years acting part-time in film and TV, my producing experience in the past four years has changed my perspective on acting. Those changes are reflected in this sixth edition of *The Actor at Work*, which I hope is more practical and direct and less "academic." The preparatory work in Part One has been reworked but retains the same focus; the rest has been extensively expanded, reorganized, and rewritten. Most of the scholarly detail of the section on text has been dropped in favor of a clearer and fuller exploration of action and character.

You may wonder why, given my present occupation, I have not included a separate section on acting for the camera. Certainly, the actor of the future will have to be capable of both stage and camera acting if he or she is to make a living. This means that camera technique should not be a separate study; instead, *all* our basic acting principles should be taught for both stage and camera. Therefore, I've referred to the camera whenever appropriate throughout this edition. I have placed emphasis on *action* partly because this concept is at the heart of successful camera—as well as stage—acting.

I'm grateful that I have had the chance to clarify my evolving understanding of the acting process by producing a new edition of this book every four years or so over the more than twenty years that it has been in print. I thank all of the teachers and students who have given me their reactions to the book over the years, and I thank the reviewers of this edition, Dr. William F. Hutson, *Creighton University*; J. Lauren le Lowenstein, *Brookdale Community College*, and George W. Sorensen, *Texas Tech. University*.

Robert Benedetti

# Lesson One

## The Actor in You

You are already an actor. You "play a role" every time you adjust your behavior to achieve some desired goal: to get someone to do something, to persuade someone of something, to win love or respect. In various circumstances, in various relationships, you pursue your needs by behaving in certain ways, doing things to other people and reacting to the things they do to you. It is this interaction with your world, this-give-and take of acting and reacting, that shapes and expresses your personality, your *character*, in everyday life.

In his book *The Presentation of Self in Everyday Life*, social psychologist Erving Goffman analyzed social behavior as if it were a stage performance. He found that most of us have a highly developed capacity to play our social roles successfully:

> It does take deep skill, long training, and psychological capacity to become a good stage actor. But...almost anyone can quickly learn a script well enough to give a charitable audience some sense of realness....This is so because ordinary social intercourse is put together as a scene [in a play] is put together, by the exchange of dramatically inflated actions, counteractions, and terminating replies. Scripts even in the hands of unpracticed players can come to life because life itself is a dramatically enacted thing....In short, we all act better than we know how.[1]

The fact that you are acting most of the time does not mean that you are insincere: To behave in a way that will achieve your objectives in a given circumstance is a natural and necessary way of coping with life. You adapt your social behavior to the demands of your situation automatically and unconsciously. In fact, you play several characters every day—student, son or daughter, friend, employee— each with its own appropriate behavior, speech, thought, and feelings—your own little repertory company.

To this extent, then, you already know how to act. As an art, however, acting requires that these everyday abilities must be heightened and purified. As Brian Bates of the Royal Academy of Dramatic Art says in his book *The Way of the Actor*:

> Almost everything that actors do can be identified with things we do in less dramatic form, in everyday life. But in order to express the concentrated truths which are the life-stuff of drama, and to project convincing performances before large audiences, and the piercing eye of the film and television camera, the actor must develop depths of self-knowledge and powers of expression far beyond those with which most of us are familiar.[2]

It is the development of your everyday acting skills into the greater power of artistic technique that is the aim of this book. You will work on three types of skills as you develop your acting techniques: physical, intellectual, and spiritual. The physical skills involve the development of the body and voice as expressive instruments. The intellectual skills involve recognizing how plays work, analyzing the script, and identifying the purposes for which your character was created by the author. The spiritual skills involve your ability to observe and focus, to be aware on several levels at once, and to experience transformation.

Each of these types of skill requires different learning processes. Physical skills are developed through regular repetition over a period of time and cannot be hurried; intellectual skills require shorter but intensely focused periods of study, preferably motivated by a real need for the information; the spiritual skills are partly a byproduct of the other two and partly a result of life experience, but can also be heightened by a variety of techniques, some of which will be contained in the exercises you will do here.

The study of acting is a journey of personal discovery. As you make this journey you will have many experiences, make many discoveries. Explorers have always found it valuable to record their journeys: Begin now to keep a journal. Writing things down as they happen can help you to clarify your experiences and will let you see how far you have come as a way of deciding where you might go next.

### Exercise 1:
### An Acting Journal

Keep a journal as you work; record thoughts, observations, and experiences that relate to your development as an actor. The discipline of writing things down can help you to clarify and intensify your experiences. Make it a regular discipline.

## ACTING AND YOUR PERSONAL GROWTH

The development of what Bates called the actor's "depths of self-knowledge and powers of expression" is an unending process of personal as well as artistic growth. It is exactly this opportunity for ongoing personal growth that attracts many people to the profession of acting. Even if you do not commit to the profession, your study of the acting process can enrich you in many ways. Bates, who is both an acting teacher and a psychologist, lists some of the ways in which the study of acting can contribute to personal growth:

> Finding our inner identity. Changing ourselves. Realizing and integrating our life experience. Seeing life freshly and with insight into others. Becoming aware of the powers of our mind. Risking and commitment. Learning how to concentrate our lives into the present, and the secrets of presence and charisma. Extending our sense of who we are, and achieving liberation from restricted concepts of what a person is.[3]

Buddhists describe the process of personal growth as the "threefold way." It begins with preparing the *ground*, in the way a gardener cultivates the soil to make it ready to accept the seed. Next a *path* is opened, as when the gardener plants the seed and waters the young plant. Finally, the *fruition* follows naturally, as when the gardener perfects the plant by pruning and tending, always with respect for its own nature.

We will use this idea of the threefold way of *ground*, *path*, and *fruition* to organize our study of acting. The first part of this book will begin with *you*, your body, voice, thoughts, and feelings. You are the "ground," the instrument of your work as an actor. The second part will open the "path," which is the concept of *action*. Here we will explore your ability to experience the needs and thoughts of the character within his or her circumstances, and to experience for yourself the things the character does to try to satisfy those needs. The "fruition" of this process will make up the third part of the book, the *characterization*. Building on the experiences discovered in action, you develop an artistically heightened creation that serves the purpose intended by the author.

Your task will be to recognize, focus, and strengthen the natural actor you already are. Only you can do this, but this book can help. What I can supply here are physical, intellectual, and spiritual techniques that can help you to realize yourself within the demands of the theatrical art, not just for your own sake but also for the contribution you may someday make through the theater. That is why I have written this book: to provide experiences and insights that may help you to fulfill your talent so that you, the theater, and the world may benefit.

## STARTING OUT: WHY YOU ACT

There are nearly as many reasons to study acting as there are acting students. For some of you, acting seems like an easy or enjoyable way to fulfill an academic credit (and it is); some of you think it might be a way to meet interesting women or men (and it is). Some of you may have serious career intentions. And some of you may even feel that acting might offer the possibility of satisfying some deep personal needs, even if you are unaware of those needs. These last are the ones who have the best chance for a professional life, for acting is a dreadful way to earn a living, and only very deep needs can provide sufficient motivation to sustain a career.

Many great actors have spoken of their inescapable need to act in spite of many misgivings about it. As Sir Laurence Olivier once told some reporters, "It does seem sometimes that acting is hardly the occupation for an adult....I can't stand it any more....But without it I would die, I suppose."[4]

For those who, like Olivier, have made acting not just a career but their way of life (and this includes all of our greatest actors) it is clear that acting fulfills needs far deeper than the desire for attention or material success. These actors often speak of the release that playing a role gives them from what Alec Guinness called "my dreary old life"; for them, acting gives them permission to have experiences they would never dare have in real life. For many, the special position of the actor provides compensation for a sense of personal unworthiness.

Whatever the needs that are urging you to act may be, they are the source of your personal satisfaction as an actor, as well as a source of tremendous power on stage. Acting turns you on, so let yourself go for it.

**Exercise 2:**
**Your Motives for Acting**

A. Below are a number of phrases. Working with a partner, take turns repeating and completing each phrase spontaneously. Answer from your feelings; tell the truth.

The theater experience I remember most vividly is...
Some of the actors I admire most are...
The thing I think I'd like most about being an actor is...
The thing I think I'd hate most about being an actor is...
The kind of acting I'd most want to do in the future would be...
The thing I want most out of acting is...
Some of the things I would rather do than act are...
What I would need for a career in the theater would be...

B. Relax and recall your earliest memory of theater. Imagine yourself there again.

How did you come to be here?
What are you thinking?
How is it making you feel?
Are you making any choices or coming to any conclusions, conscious or unconscious, that have affected you since?
Why do you think you will remember this?
Is there anything about this that relates to studying acting later in life?

C. Review the results of these experiments. Do you see a pattern? Did you uncover anything that surprised you? What seemed the most true? Record your thoughts in your journal.

This exercise may have helped you to recognize why you're interested in acting; the answer may even have surprised you. In any case, remember that one reason is no better, no more noble, no more effective than another. Your motives and needs will probably change as you grow, and you may outgrow these early motives. As you work, you may discover new reasons for acting that are even stronger than those with which you began.

What is important is that you have *your* reasons now, and they motivate you to take this journey of discovery. Let them!

## THE EXERCISES AND READINGS

As you have seen, there are exercises in each lesson in this book. They are a program of self-discovery and self-development and are arranged roughly according to a "natural" acquisition of skills and insights. These exercises have no "right" outcome, so try not to anticipate the results; just follow the instructions and see what happens.

The experiences provided by the exercises are essential to a true understanding (in the muscles as well as in the mind) of what this book is about, so please be sure to read each exercise, even if you do not do the exercise. At the very least, there can be some benefit from imagining yourself doing it.

In addition to the exercises, later lessons will contain examples of various kinds taken from plays. These examples will be especially important to your understanding of the work. I have drawn most of my examples from five popular plays, and if you will take time to read these plays now, you will benefit much more from the examples themselves. The plays are Brecht's *Mother Courage*, Miller's *Death of a Salesman*, Williams' *The Glass Menagerie* and *A Streetcar Named Desire*, and Albee's *The Zoo Story*.

## DISCIPLINE

Before you begin your preparation of yourself in the following lessons, think about the one skill that will make all others possible: *discipline*.

Real discipline is not a matter of following someone else's rules: In the best sense it is *your acceptance of the responsibility for your own development through systematic effort*, not because you are ordered to do so by someone else or compelled by some external criteria, like a grade or a good review or landing a job, but because you choose to become all that you can be in order to contribute as much as you can to your world through your work.

Discipline is rooted in your respect for yourself, your respect for your fellow workers, for your work, and for the world you serve through that work. Poor discipline is really a way of saying, "I'm not worth it" or "What I do isn't worth it" or "People are not worth the effort." Discipline will come naturally if you can acknowledge the importance and seriousness of your work and the great need for it in the world. The director Eugenio Barba put it this way in a letter to an undisciplined actor:

> First of all, one gets the impression that your acts are not dictated by that interior conviction or undeniable need which would show itself in the execution of an exercise, or of an improvisation or a scene....You have not proven to yourself the importance of what you want to share with the spectators. How, then, can you hope that the spectator will be captivated by your actions?...
>
> The second tendency which I see in you is the fear of considering the complete seriousness of our work: You find the need to laugh, to snigger, to pass humorous remarks upon whatever you and your classmates happen to be performing. It is as if you wanted to flee that responsibility which you sense is joined to our work and which consists of establishing a communication with other men and of facing up to the consequences you discover thereby....
>
> I believe you have never considered that all you are doing, delivering, shaping in your work belongs to the phenomena of life and that as such it deserves consideration and respect.[5]

Discipline also involves regularity. Your work, especially on technical skills, must be a daily affair. Stanislavski, looking back late in his life, had this to say:

> Let someone explain to me why the violinist who plays in an orchestra on the tenth violin must daily perform hour-long exercises or lose his power to play? Why does the dancer work daily over every muscle in his body? Why do the painter, the sculptor, the writer practice their art each day and count that day lost when they do not work? And why may the dramatic artist do nothing, spend his day in coffee houses and hope for the gift [of inspiration] in the evening? Enough. Is this an art when its priests speak like amateurs? There is no art that does not demand virtuosity.[6]

You must have the patience to work each day, to let your techniques and understanding develop slowly. Learning to act is the development of patient, persistent self-discipline.

Patience and a sense of striving together—being able to accept the momentary failure for the sake of the long-range success—are the attitudes that you must nurture. The pressures of our educational system and of the commercial theater are against these attitudes, as is the normal desire of all of us to be "successful" right now. Resist your desire to be an overnight star and instead explore a variety of approaches and experiences. Most of your explorations will lead up blind alleys, but it is better to suffer momentary disappointments now than to commit yourself to an approach or an attitude that may limit you later. Your discipline is dedicated to the whole of your career. As playwright David Mamet says:

> Those of you who are called to strive to bring a new theatre, the theatre of your generation, to the stage, are set down for a very exciting life.
>
> You will be pulling against an increasingly strong current, and as you do so, you will reap the great and priceless reward of knowing yourself a truly mature man or woman—if, in the midst of the panic which surrounds you, which calls itself common sense, or commercial viability, you are doing your job simply and well.
>
> If you are going to work in the true theatre, that job is a great job in this time of final decay; that job is to bring to your fellows, through the medium of your understanding and skill, the possibility of communion with what is essential in us all: that we are born to die, that we strive and fail, that we live in ignorance of why we were placed here, and, that, in the midst of this we need to love and be loved, but we are afraid.[7]

## SUMMARY OF LESSON ONE

You are already an actor. You "play a role" every time you adjust your behavior to achieve some desired goal. In this sense, you play several characters every day—your own little repertory company.

As an art, however, acting requires that these everyday abilities must be heightened and purified. It is the development of your everyday acting skills into the greater power of artistic technique that is the aim of this book.

There are three types of skill involved in becoming an actor: physical, intellectual, and spiritual; each requires different learning processes.

The development of your acting skill is an unending process of personal as well as artistic growth. Even if you do not commit to the profession, your study of the acting process can help you to grow in many ways. Buddhists describe the process of personal growth as the "threefold way." We will use this idea of *ground, path,* and *fruition* to organize our study of acting. The first part of this book will begin with *you* as the "ground," the instrument of your work as an actor. The second part will open the "path," which is the concept of *action.* The "fruition" of this process will make up the third part of the book, *characterization*. Your task will be to recognize, focus, and strengthen the natural actor you already are.

For many actors, acting fulfills needs far deeper than the desire for attention or material success; for many, acting provides compensation for a sense of personal unworthiness. Whatever your reasons, they motivate you to take this journey of discovery.

As you begin this journey, remember that one skill makes all others possible: discipline. Real discipline is not a matter of following someone else's rules; *it is your acceptance of the responsibility for your own development through systematic effort*. Discipline will come naturally if you can acknowledge the importance and seriousness of your work and the great need for it in the world.

You must have the patience to work each day, to let your techniques and understanding develop slowly. Resist your desire to be an overnight star and instead explore a variety of approaches and experiences.

# Lesson Two

## Relaxing and Breathing

"Mister Duffy lived at a little distance from his body." This description of one of James Joyce's characters applies to many of us in our everyday lives; we go through life largely unconscious of our physical existence. Many of us are also distanced from our intellectual and emotional lives; there are certain feelings and thoughts that we block out, certain experiences that we avoid, and certain forms of expression that we do not permit ourselves to use.

To be an actor, you can no more maintain this distance from yourself than could a violinist refuse contact with the violin. Your job requires that you make all aspects of your self—body, voice, thoughts, and feelings—available and controllable. They are the tools of your trade.

As you study acting, you will sometimes work separately on various aspects of your self: your body, your voice, your emotional and conceptual skills. When you act, however, you must see, hear, think, move, speak, and feel as one action of your whole self. You must be *integrated*.

Unfortunately, many of you, like most people in our culture, have grown up in a way that has *dis*integrated you. Partly because of the impact of television, we have become a nation of "talking heads" and there is sometimes little connection between our minds and our lower bodies. Your work as an actor requires that you rediscover the natural integration of mind and body that you enjoyed as a child.

You will do this not so much through effort as through the ending of effort: Since integration is our natural state, you don't need to *do* anything to reintegrate yourself; you need only to *stop* doing whatever it is that you are doing to disintegrate yourself. For this reason, the first step in preparing yourself to act is *to relax*.

## RELAXATION

When we speak of relaxation for the actor, we do not mean it in the ordinary sense of reduced energy or slackness; rather, we mean that all unnecessary tensions have been removed, the remaining energy has been purposefully focused, and awareness is acute. The kind of relaxation you want is a state in which you are *most ready to react*, like a cat in front of a mouse hole. Tensions that would inhibit movement are gone, and you are in a state of balance that leaves you free to react in any way required.

The best description of the relaxed actor's state is what meditators call "restful alertness." You are already capable of restful alertness: You don't need to do anything to achieve it; you only need to become still enough to experience it. You can do this right now, through a simple meditation.

### Exercise 3:
### A Meditation

Sit comfortably in your chair, both feet flat on the floor, back and neck straight but not rigid, hands resting on your thighs. Look at a spot on the floor eight feet in front of you. Focus your awareness on your breath flowing in and out of your nose. Allow any thoughts that come up to play across your consciousness; then simply return your awareness to your breath. Nothing is to be resisted. If you like, close your eyes. Sit for as long as you are comfortable. Whatever experience you have is correct as long as you keep good physical form.

Your meditation is focused on your breath for a very good reason: The breath is life. The word psychology means "study of the soul," and the word for soul, *psyche*, originally meant "vital breath." A common superstition is that the expiring breath of a dying person is the soul leaving the body.

Your breath constantly reflects your relationship to your world. It is through the breath that you literally bring the outside world into your body and then expel it again; the way you feel about your world will be expressed in the way you breathe it in and breathe it out. This is why your natural voice, which is profoundly affected by your breath, is so expressive of your inner state. You can see sobbing, laughing, gasping, sighing, and all the other forms of breathing as tangible reflections of your relationship to your world.

Unfortunately, our cultural disintegration between mind and lower body has caused many of us to lose touch with our natural breathing and therefore also with our natural voice. Bundles of chronic tension may stand in the way of your natural responses. Now that you have begun to experience restful alertness, however, you can begin to identify and rid yourself of these chronic muscular tensions, some of which may have become so familiar that you have lost consciousness of them. In the next two exercises you will take time to inspect the tensions within your body; invade your own privacy.

### Exercise 4:
### Playing Cat

Lie on the floor comfortably in a surrounding that is not too distracting. Stretch yourself out face up, hands at your sides. Put yourself at rest by yawning and stretching.

*To see yawning and stretching at their luxurious best, watch a cat just awakening from a siesta. It arches its back, extends to the utmost legs, feet, and toes, drops its jaw, and all the while balloons itself up with air. Once it has swelled until it occupies its very maximum of space, it permits itself slowly to collapse—and then is ready for new business.*[1]

Act like a cat. Stretch, arch your back, extend all your limbs to their utmost, drop your jaw, wiggle your arms and hands, and breathe deeply (not once, but many times); each time taking in more and more air. When a real yawn comes, encourage it; let the full natural sound of the yawn pour out. Then settle back with your knees raised enough to make the small of your back touch the floor. Place your toes, heels, hip joints, and shoulders on two imaginary parallel lines (see Figure 1). We will call this our *floor alignment*.

Using your cat stretching as a preparation, you will now take systematic inventory of your body, looking for any residual bundles of tension. The following exercise was developed by a pioneer in the field of relaxation, Dr. Edmund Jacobson. The exercise is more effective every time you repeat it, so that you develop your "relaxation

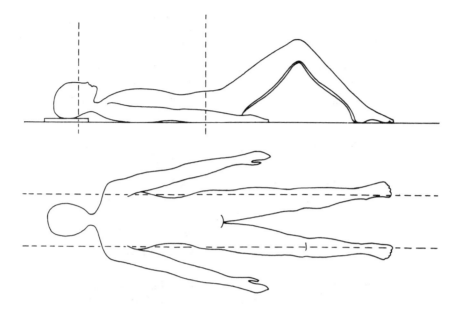

**FIGURE 1**   Floor Alignment. The head is level (a small pad should be placed under it); the waistline is also level. The knees are raised to avoid any strain on the lower back.

response." As you do, bundles of chronic tensions will surface and be dissolved by the natural wisdom of the body.

Remember that you are dealing with habits and structures that have formed over a lifetime; have the patience and discipline to adopt a long-term program of correction and maintenance; Jacobson's Phasic Relaxation Exercise can be the foundation of such a program. (Though this exercise can be quickly learned, a tape recording of these instructions with the necessary pauses would be useful at first.)

### Exercise 5:
### Phasic Relaxation

Begin in floor alignment. Breath is again the focus of your awareness: Imagine that each inhalation is a warm, fresh, energy-filled fluid flowing into your body. Each exhalation carries away with it tension and inhibition, like a refreshing wave. Breathe deeply and easily in a slow, natural, regular rhythm; don't "act" your breathing or artificially exaggerate it.

Each successive breath will be sent into a different part of the body, awakening that area. As the breath flows into a new area, let the muscles there contract as much as they can; then, as the breath flows out, the muscles release and the breath carries all the tension away with it, leaving the area refreshed and at ease. *Exhaling is letting go.*

The sequence of breaths will move from the top of the body downward, and the regular rhythm of your breathing should make the muscular contractions and relaxations flow smoothly down the body like a slow wave. Allow only one area at a time to be involved:

*The forehead and scalp,* furling the brow, then releasing it;

*The eyes at rest,* closed and turned slightly downward;

*The jaw,* clenching, then falling easily downward until the teeth are about one-half inch apart;

*The tongue,* extending, then lying easily in the mouth;

*The front of the neck,* with the chin extending down to touch the chest, stretching the back of the neck—then rolling the head easily back down;

*The back of the neck,* with the top of the head rolling under to touch the floor, stretching the front of the neck—then rolling the head slowly down and lengthening the neck;

*The upper chest,* swelling outward in all directions so that the shoulders are widened—then easily subsiding, feeling the shoulder blades spread and melt into the floor, wider than before;

*The arms and hands,* becoming stiff and straight like steel rods; the hands clenching into fists, then easily uncurling and melting into the floor, uncurling;

*The pit of the stomach,* clenching, becoming a small, hard ball—then, with a sigh, releasing;

*The buttocks,* clenching, then releasing and widening so that the hips are wider than before;

*The knees,* stiffening as the legs straighten, the feet being pushed downward by this action—then releasing the legs and feeling them melt into the floor;

*The toes,* reaching up to touch the eyes (but the heels remain on the floor)— then releasing and falling into a natural position;

*The heels and the shoulder blades,* simultaneously pushing downward into the floor so that the whole body lifts in a long arch—then, with a sigh, you slowly fall, the body lengthening as it relaxes, melting deep into the floor.

Now take ten deep, slow, regular breaths, and with each breath move more deeply into relaxation, remaining alert and refreshed. The flow of breath is a continuous cycle of energy that is stored comfortably in the lower body; with each breath this store of energy is increased. If a yawn comes to you, enjoy it fully; vocalize the exhalation, letting the sound of the yawn pour out.

As you repeat this exercise on successive days, you can begin to give yourself the instructions silently, reminding yourself of the specific activities in each phase. Keep a steady rhythm that follows the tempo of deep, relaxed breathing. Gradually the action of the exercise will become natural, and you will no longer need to think of the instructions, giving your full awareness to the flow of contractions and relaxations that follow the breath as it travels down the body like a wave, awakening, refreshing, and relaxing it, making you ready for work.

You can use this exercise as an easy, quick preparation for all future work. Over a period of time, it will help chronic bundles of tension within your body to break up and dissolve.

Did you notice, by the way, that relaxation in the sense of being ready to react required you to immerse yourself in the present instant, in the *here and now*? It is only now that you exist, and only now that you can act. In everyday life you rarely achieve complete contact with the present: You prefer to create a sense of comfortable continuity by blurring the lines that separate the present from the past and future. The past, in memory, and the future, in expectation, can be controlled by your consciousness; but the present can be met only on its own terms. Although you can never specifically isolate it, you can put yourself in touch with the unending flow of the present. As the psychologist Fritz Perls put it:

> The wish to seize the present and pin it down—to mount it, as it were, like a butterfly in a case—is doomed to failure. Actuality forever changes. In healthy persons, the feeling of actuality is steady and continuous but, like the view from a train window, the scenery is always different.[2]

When you act, you must work in the here and now. Even though your character may be lost in memory, consumed with desire for the future, or dreaming of being far away, in Moscow, the Yukon, or on the high seas, you will perform all this here and now.

## MINIMIZING EFFORT

Acting, like all creative activity, arouses anxiety. This can be both pleasurable (in the quest for creative discovery) and unpleasurable (in the fear of failure and ridicule). In either case, this arousal tends to disrupt your breathing and to raise the level of your bodily tension. In turn, this tension interferes with your readiness to react; it "freezes" you and reduces your creativity.

When you find yourself scared or "stuck" in this way, you may attempt to compensate by "trying harder," putting more effort into the work, and trying to "muscle" your way through your difficulty. Unfortunately, this is exactly the wrong thing to do. It only *increases* your tension and further reduces your freedom of creative response. It is common to see students in beginning acting classes who make the mistake of "trying harder," and the harder they try, the worse they get.

This kind of excessive effort makes you self-aware, obscures your own experience of what you are doing, and reduces your control. Movement therapist Moshe Feldenkrais uses the example of trying to open a sticking drawer: If you tug indiscriminately at it, chances are that it will let loose all at once and go flying out, spilling the contents. Because you were using excessive force, you failed to perceive the exact moment when the drawer loosened; you had ceased to experience the drawer and were experiencing *only your own effort.*

Unfortunately, many actors are driven to excessive effort; in their desire to deliver an acceptable performance, they do too much. Their assumption seems to be that they are unworthy of the audience's attention unless they *do* something extraordinary to earn it; the option of doing nothing, of simply allowing themselves to "be there," is terrifying. They feel naked, exposed, and they become desperate to do something—anything! As a result, they have difficulty experiencing what is really happening on stage and instead experience only their own effort.

Do you feel unworthy of our attention? Can you let your simple, unadorned presence be enough, or do you feel that you must do something extraordinary to earn our attention? See if you can let go of this need so that your stage choices will not be compensations for a sense of unworthiness.

### Exercise 6:
### Being There

Take turns standing in front of the group. Place yourself in restful alertness and simply "be there." Let go of your need to do something until you are quite still.

Fully experience stillness both as actor and as audience; support one another with quiet attention. See how interesting the simple, unadorned presence of a human being can be.

## SUMMARY OF LESSON TWO

Acting requires that you make all aspects of your self—body, voice, thoughts, and feelings—available and controllable. These aspects are the tools of your trade. Also, when you act you must see, hear, think, move, speak, and feel as one action of your whole self. You must be *integrated*. Your work as an actor requires that you rediscover the natural integration of mind and body that you enjoyed as a child.

You needn't *do* anything to reintegrate yourself, you need only to *stop* doing whatever it is that you are doing to disintegrate yourself. For this reason, the first step in preparing yourself to act is *to relax*.

The kind of relaxation you want is a state in which you are most ready to react, the state meditators call "restful alertness." The breath is deeply involved with relaxation, since it constantly reflects your relationship to your world. Unfortunately, our cultural disintegration has caused many of us to lose touch with our natural breathing.

Remember that you are dealing with habits and structures that have formed over a lifetime; have the patience and discipline to adopt a long-term program of correction and maintenance; Jacobson's Phasic Relaxation Exercise can be the foundation of such a program. Over a period of time, it will help chronic bundles of tension within your body to break up and dissolve.

Relaxation in the sense of simply "being there," ready to react, requires you to immerse yourself in the present instant, in the *here and now*. It is only now that you exist, and only now that you can act.

Acting, like all creative activity, arouses anxiety, which disrupts your breathing and raises the level of your bodily tension. In turn, this tension "freezes" you and reduces your creativity. When you find yourself "stuck" in this way, you may attempt to compensate by "trying harder." Unfortunately, this only *increases* your tension and further reduces your freedom of creative response; excessive effort also makes you self-aware.

Unfortunately, many actors are driven to excessive effort; they feel unworthy of the audience's attention unless they *do* something extraordinary to earn it. See if you can let go of this need so that your stage choices will not be compensations for a sense of unworthiness.

Movement therapists like Moshe Feldenkrais say that *there is no new thought where there is no new movement*; your capacity to "see the world" in a new way is reflected in your capacity to move within that world in a new way. Perhaps this is because when you were an infant you explored the world mainly through movement, and your "self" began to develop during this movement-oriented exploration. Researchers have found, for instance, that infants who are bound, like those of some tribal cultures, have greatly reduced personality development during the period of their confinement.

Your ability to move is critical to you as an actor, then, not only because you will eventually express your character partly through movement, but because your ability to move is a necessary part of the process by which you will discover and develop the character itself.

So, having begun to remove unwanted tensions from the body through the techniques of relaxation, you will now proceed to loosen the body and make it more limber, more free in its capacity for movement, and more *ready to respond*.

## LIMBERING

You begin limbering with an expanding of the joints. Like any mechanism your skeletal structure produces friction and requires a certain degree of looseness and lubrication that permits the parts to slide easily against one another: Your muscles are housed in sheaths of smooth tissue that permit them to slide easily against each other; your joints have spaces filled with viscous fluids that lubricate. Distorted posture or muscular habit may compress the joints or hold them rigid, or cause the sheaths of tissue around the muscles to shrink into permanent misalignment. When this happens, your capacity and readiness to move are reduced and you become less responsive, both physically and mentally. Your voice will also be affected.

Sometimes such bodily distortions or areas of rigidity may be so severe as to require forceful intervention through massage techniques like Rolfing or Shiatsu; more gradual and gentle, though also powerful, is the Alexander Technique (which is of special interest to us, since it was developed by an actor). In all such cases, of course, only the most qualified professionals should provide treatment.

For most of us, however, it is sufficient to direct the energies of our own bodies toward the release of misalignments, or to engage in a gentle, pleasurable massage by a caring and careful partner. The following exercises will begin to lengthen and widen your torso, expanding your joints and opening your body to maximum size.

### Exercise 7:
### Massage for Size

Have your partner assume floor alignment while you gently and steadily lengthen and widen his or her torso according to the following instructions. During the exercise, the partner on the floor gives full awareness to your actions by imagining breathing into your hands.

1. The head is cupped gently in the hands from above and is rolled and rocked while being gently pulled directly upward along the axis of the spine; do not pull the head in such a way that the chin lifts (see Figure 2).
2. Placing one hand palm up under the center of your partner's back and the other palm down just below the base of the neck, massage and pull slowly outward toward the side. You will see the shoulder visibly widen and flatten. Repeat with the other side (see Figure 3).
3. Massaging the whole arm, beginning in the armpit, draw the arm steadily downward, continuing through the hand and into the fingers. Repeat with the other arm.
4. Repeat this same action with each leg.
5. Trade roles and repeat the exercise.

After you have done this exercise a few times with a partner, you can do it alone by taking floor alignment and remembering the

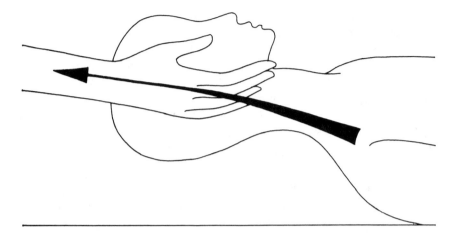

**FIGURE 2**   Stretching the Neck.

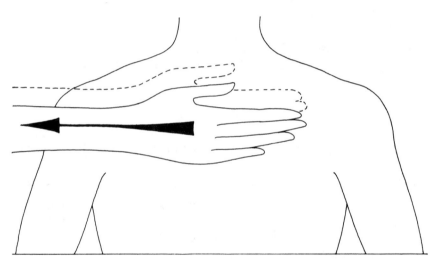

**FIGURE 3**   Opening the Shoulders.

actions of your partner's hands, telling yourself to "lengthen" and "widen"; your body can be taught to massage itself. The following exercise does not require a partner.

### Exercise 8:
### Lengthening and Widening

1. In floor alignment, slowly rock your pelvis upward; feel the thrust as a curving motion indicated by the arrow in Figure 4. The motion is a flowing undulation; one after another, each vertebra is lifted until the back is raised as far as the midback (dotted line); then it is

rolled back down vertebra by vertebra in a steady motion; the back is longer when it comes down than when it went up. Leave the arms relaxed and the head free to roll from side to side. Breathe out on the way up and in on the way down, counting aloud seven counts up and silently seven counts down. Release completely between each series; begin with four repetitions.

2. Now stretch in all directions at once, again playing cat, and then fall easily back into the floor alignment position. Let the noise of your stretches be full and natural. Again, encourage any yawn that occurs spontaneously, letting the sound freely pour out. The yawn is a good friend to us in our work.

As you begin to experience your own physical being fully, you experience also the natural wholeness of your body and consciousness. The actor strives to maintain this sense of wholeness because the stage demands total responsiveness simultaneously from all the aspects of the self; only an integrated, limber organism can supply such responses.

## YOUR RELATIONSHIP TO GRAVITY

As our species evolved, we became gradually more and more erect, standing within the field of gravity (though this adaptation is far from complete; our common lower back problems may be partly

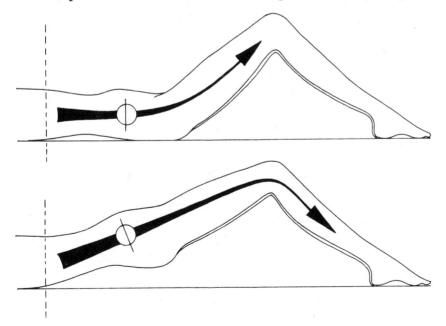

**FIGURE 4** Lengthening the Back.

due to an incomplete adaptation to being erect). Your relationship to gravity is continuous; even when lying down, you are making constant adjustments within the field of gravity.

The way in which you experience gravity, like your breathing, is a fundamental expression of your relationship to your world. Some days it seems that we wake up pounds heavier, with "the weight of the world" on our shoulders. At such times, we speak of feeling "down," and at the saddest times we say we have a "heavy heart." On the other hand, sometimes we feel "light as a feather," "floating on cloud nine," and the most "light-hearted" moments are often expressed by a physical action that ignores gravity, skipping. Try to imagine a sad tap dance!

A person's attitude toward gravity can be seen in his or her posture. When Arthur Miller opens *Death of a Salesman* with Willy Loman crossing the stage, back bent under the weight of his sample case, Willy's sense of defeat and hopelessness is directly expressed in the way he is losing his fight with gravity.

We also seem to receive strength from gravity when we feel at one with it; at such times we speak of "knowing where we stand" or "holding our ground." One of the qualities of some classical heroes like Oedipus or Electra, for example, is their oneness with the earth and the way the power of nature flows up through the earth and into them. Perhaps for this reason I have noticed that it is impossible to play a strong character if the feet are kept too close together. Not only does such a character need a wide, stable base, but also the character needs to be open to receive the flow of energy that is coming upward from the earth.

## STANDING ALIGNMENT

In the course of human evolution, the skeleton has begun (and is still) adapting itself to an erect posture so that we can stand against the force of gravity with a minimum of muscular strain. Imagine the bones as building blocks; if each is set properly above the one below, they can almost stand erect by themselves.

Bringing each part of your body into the proper position to permit its weight to flow directly downward through the body into the ground will not only give you stability, but will also give you the most responsive alignment from which to move or sound in any direction.

The following sequence of exercises will give you a direct experience of this alignment and centeredness. We will begin by examining the structure of the body as it relates to movement.

**Exercise 9:**
**Finding the Joints**

A. With a partner, stand and face each other. Help each other to find the two joints in the spinal column; one is high in the head, inside the valley that runs up the back of the neck, underneath the bony ridge that can be felt at the top of this valley. The joint itself is inside the head roughly level with the eyes. The other joint is at the base of the spine, roughly on a level with the hip joints. Find the hip joints by lifting each leg and feeling for them; they are higher than you may suppose, roughly level with your center.

It is common to think of the spine as having many "joints," but in fact only these two, at top and bottom, are true joints. The rest of the spine is capable of considerable flexibility, of course, but too often we try to make small areas of the spine do the work of joints; for instance, we commonly behave as if the back were jointed at points A and B in Figure 5, while it is actually jointed only at points X and Y.

This widespread misuse of the spine produces the back and neck problems so common in our culture. For the actor, however, the bad effects of this misuse are even more severe; you can see immediately how bending the back at point B causes the abdomen to be constricted, severely limiting the action of the diaphragm and thus limiting breath support. Likewise, bending the neck at point A causes you to crush the voice box, disturbing the natural production of vocal tone. You can experience this for yourself by sounding and moving the head from the real joint, and then from the false joint. Try it.

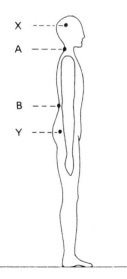

**FIGURE 5**   The Spine.

In the next section of the exercise, try to loosen and expand the true joints in your spine and feel yourself moving more fluidly. Notice also how your sound can remain full and free when you move in this way.

B. With the partners again facing each other, one partner reaches out and cups the other's head in his or her hands, as in Figure 6. Gently lift the head slightly upward along the central axis of your partner's body. The partner being lifted hangs loosely, like a medical student's skeleton on a spring. As your partner slowly moves the head in many directions, the hanging partner allows his or her body to respond easily and makes sound, experiencing the voice through a variety of motions.

C. Change roles and repeat. After you have experienced these exercises with a partner, you may repeat them alone by remembering the feeling of your partner's lift; the remainder of the exercise does not require a partner.

D. Moving on your own with the memory of your partner's lift, explore the balance of your body when it moves as a single system hinged at the real joints.

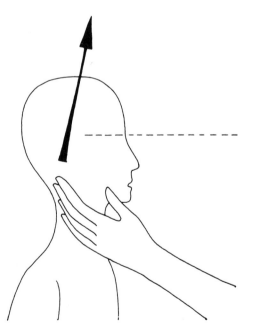

**FIGURE 6**   Lifting the Head. Be sure that the head remains level as it is lifted.

**Exercise 10:**
**Sitting and Standing**

A. Sit comfortably in a plain, straight-backed chair while your partner gently cups your head and lifts up and forward. Feel your weight shift forward, then up as you stand, maintaining continuous balance between the system formed by your ankles, knees, hips, and head. (See Figure 7.) Notice that the back needn't bend and that your effort can be greatly reduced when you maintain the balance of your system.

B. Repeat the experience on your own, remembering the touch of your partner's hands. Let your energy originate deep in the center of your body and flow effortlessly up the spine and out the top and front of your head as if your partner were still lifting you.

In Exercise 10, energy flows upward through your spine and out of the top of your head. Become aware of the point at which your spine would protrude from the scalp if it were extended upward; for most of us it is also the center of the whirlpool-like swirl in our hair. You and your partner can help each other to determine this point. When you are lifted upward from this point, your head remains perfectly level with your chin, neither lifting toward the ceiling nor dropping toward your chest.

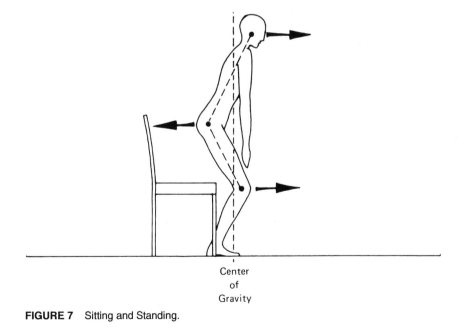

Center
of
Gravity

**FIGURE 7**  Sitting and Standing.

In the next exercise, we translate this upward lift along the central axis of your body into an "unfolding" motion that produces good standing alignment.

### Exercise 11:
### Hanging Yourself Up

Stand, then bend at the hip joint and let the entire top half of your body fall forward and downward so that you are folded like a rag doll hanging from a string tied to the base of its spine. Don't strain; simply hang as limply as you can with knees locked (but not tense). If necessary your partner may hold you at first.

Imagine now that the string has been moved up one vertebra, and you are now hanging from a point a few inches farther up your back. Steadily, the "string" moves up your back, vertebra by vertebra; your head and arms hang loosely as you straighten up until the head at last floats upward as the "string" reaches the last of the small vertebrae in your neck and comes out the top of your head.

The overall movement is of an undulation or wave motion as you "uncurl" into standing alignment (see Figure 8). You will feel taller and

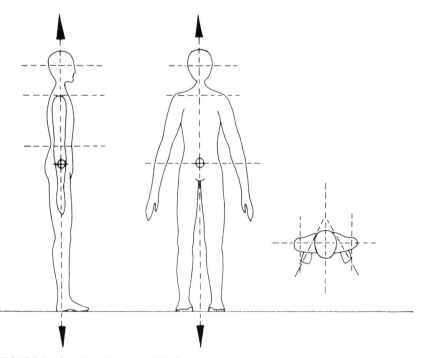

**FIGURE 8**   Standing Alignment. The feet are spread to shoulder width, the knees pointing out directly over the toes.

lighter, you will have a sense of openness, and the distance from your ears to your shoulders will be greater. Avoid "pushing" up from below; try to feel yourself being "pulled" up from above.

Feel how little effort is required to move from this properly aligned position.

These exercises may have revealed misalignments and distortions in your body of which you were not aware. Everyone has some habitual, unconscious way of holding the tensions of everyday life in the muscles; over a long period of time the tendons and connective tissue within the body may become distorted under the influence of these habits, resulting in an actual change in the shape of the body. Part of the way we read "body language" in real life is through our unconscious recognition of these patterns, and this is an important aspect of the expression of dramatic character in the theater.

We will return to this relationship between the structure of the body and personality in Part Three. For now, realize that your habitual physical patterns are part of your personality, and it will be helpful to your development as an actor to bring these patterns within your conscious artistic control. If you do not, you may carry your uncontrolled physical habits and body structure into every character you play, appropriate or not.

### Exercise 12:
### Your Body Structure

Working with a partner or before a large mirror, assume standing alignment and check yourself: Is one shoulder higher or wider than another? Does your pelvis rock to one side as you stand? Perhaps your chest is somewhat sunken, drawing your shoulders forward; or, in the other extreme, the shoulder blades are pinched together and the shoulders drawn back. As you move, do you see parts of your body that are being held? Everyone has symptoms of this kind; find yours.

You can use these symptoms to trace habitual bundles of tension or to identify misused areas of your body; try to relate each of your alignment symptoms to the habitual posture or inhibition that produced it.

Do not be overly concerned with your findings; everyone has some distortion from "perfect" alignment, and such distortion is not in itself a major obstacle to your development as an actor unless it is extreme. As you continue your daily exercise program, remain aware of the structures you have noticed; and in your daily life as well, "catch" yourself when you notice yourself falling into the old habits. A "trigger" word that you say to yourself, like "lengthen" or "level," can be valuable. Do not, however, *force* yourself into a new alignment; merely try to stop doing whatever you are doing to mis-align yourself, and let the body's natural structure reassert itself. This is a very gradual process of *undoing*, and over a period of months you may begin to notice change.

These suggestions pertain only to common and mild misalign-ments. If you have a severe problem, or wish to pursue this work further, you may want to consult an expert therapist. The Alexander Technique is one of several good therapies that help to align and lib-erate the body; other recommended techniques include Structural Integration (Rolfing), Patterning, Bioenergetics, and even deep mas-sage such as Shiatsu. You should consult only licensed, reputable practitioners by contacting state or national accreditation centers for each type of therapy, or by conferring with your physician. Avoid home remedies.

### Exercise 13:
### Let's Get Big!

As a continuation of the preceding exercises, stand easily in good alignment with the eyes closed:

A. Let your conscious awareness roam at random throughout the body.

B. Mentally measure the distances within the body from point to point; are you as big as you can be in a relaxed way? Again, what is needed is not that you *do* anything, but rather that you *stop doing* whatever it is that is distorting your natural condition.

C. Become aware of all kinds of paired relationships within the body; explore the connections between various sensations and parts of the body. What does the stomach do when you breathe, what does your tongue do when you clench your buttocks, and so forth?

D. Finally, breathing very easily and feeling the warm energy of the breath flowing into and out of the body, make a neutral sound without effort or change in the breath stream; simply "let" a sound be there for a moment. What bodily activities support the sound? Do you see that a tiny change is required to produce sound? Did you truly experience sound as an aspect of the breath, and the breath as an aspect of the wholeness of your mind and body?

For all its dynamism and seeming complexity, the body is at any moment a single, unique, harmonious entity. All of the activities you are capable of, even your very consciousness, express this same wholeness and spring from the same source.

This sense of a common source, or center, from which all your life energy springs, can help you to experience wholeness. When your center becomes felt and fully energized, you will begin to move, sound, and even think in a more integrated way, with greater continuity and effectiveness. The next lesson will help you to enjoy your center as you begin to move and produce sound.

## SUMMARY OF LESSON THREE

Your ability to move is critical to you as an actor, not only because you will eventually express your character through movement, but because your ability to move is part of the process by which you will develop the character itself. You want to develop a limber body, free to move and ready to respond.

Distorted posture or muscular habit may compress the joints or hold them rigid, or cause the sheaths of tissue around the muscles to shrink into permanent misalignment, making you less responsive, both physically and mentally. For most of us, luckily, it is sufficient to direct the energies of our own bodies toward the release of misalignments, or to engage in a gentle, pleasurable massage by a caring and careful partner.

As you begin to experience your own physical being fully, you experience also the natural wholeness of your body and consciousness. The actor strives to maintain this sense of wholeness because the stage demands total responsiveness simultaneously from all the aspects of the self.

The way in which you experience gravity, like your breathing, is a fundamental expression of your relationship to your world. Bringing each part of your body into proper alignment will not only give you stability, but will also give you the most responsive alignment from which to move or sound in any direction.

Everyone has some habitual way of holding the tensions of life in the muscles; over a long period of time these habits can distort our connective tissue, resulting in an actual change in the shape of the body. Part of the way we read "body language" in real life is through our unconscious recognition of these patterns. Such distorted alignment may create impediments in your work as an actor, making it harder to move freely and may even prejudice you to certain kinds of emotions, psychological qualities, or relationships.

# Lesson Four

## Centering and Moving

Incarnation: bodying forth. Is this not our whole concern? The bodying forth of our sense of life?... We body forth our ideals in personal acts, either alone or with others in society. We body forth felt experience in a poem's image and sound. We body forth our inner residence in the architecture of our homes and common buildings. We body forth our struggles and our revelations in the space of theater. That is what form is: the bodying forth...[1]

This thought is from a book called *Centering* by Mary Caroline Richards, a poet and potter. As a potter she knows how the centering of the clay upon the wheel is essential to creation of a pot, for only from perfectly centered clay can the motion of the wheel and the potter's hands bring the pot's shape freely and naturally toward its ultimate form. As a poet she also knows how the experiences of one's life must touch a personal center before they can, in turn, flow outward and be embodied in the form of a poem. As an actor you must also center yourself so that your energy, like the clay, will flow outward into the new form of yourself demanded by your role.

This idea of a personal center is not just a metaphor; it has a tangible physical dimension. Finding and activating your bodily center are necessary first steps in laying a foundation for good stage movement and voice; the sense of center can integrate your responses and give you strength by involving your total organism in your actions.

Developing your physical center is also a way of developing a psychological and spiritual centeredness as well, because at this deep level your energy exists simultaneously in physical and psychological forms; movement, feeling, thought, and the beginnings of sound, all intermingle here. This deep *psychophysical* energy is the raw material of the acting process; like the potter's clay, you must gather it, make it responsive, and center it so that it can be shaped easily into new forms.

As you work on a role, this psychophysical energy flows outward into new forms of behavior demanded by your character's actions and the style of the play. As this happens, you begin to experience yourself anew. As you come to experience this new form of yourself more fully, you begin to enter into a new state of being, which in turn summons new energies from you; this is the creative cycle of the acting process.

Having begun the unending task of developing relaxation and limbering your body, then, you will now explore the experience of centering. In this lesson you will explore the physical dimension of centering; later you will see how its psychological dimension can be a primary tool of characterization.

Here is an exercise to help you localize a specific sense of your physical center.

### Exercise 14:
### Finding Center

Place yourself in standing alignment, clear your mind, and witness your body as it performs the following activities:

A. Move either foot out to the side about two feet; rock from foot to foot, feeling your center of gravity moving from side to side. Quickly make your rocking smaller and smaller, like a bowling pin that almost falls down; come to rest on center.

B. Move either foot forward about two feet; find your center with front-to-back motions as described above.

C. Move your center around rotationally, exploring the limits of various stances. Feel the weight of your body flowing into the ground and out of your center through the legs.

D. Point into your body at the spot you feel is your center; don't be concerned about where it "ought" to be; sense where it really is.

E. Explore how your center is involved in moving and speaking.

As you become aware of your center over a period of days, you will notice that it moves within the body as your mood changes; frequently, your center will rise upward when you are in an excited or fearful state or downward in states of well-being or determination. You will notice, too, that different people have different characteristic centers and that the locations of their centers are very appropriate to their personalities. Such diversity can be found in people who have a "lot of guts," who "follow their nose," "lead with their chins," are "all heart," "drag their feet," "have their heads in the clouds," and so on.

This sense of centeredness is, for the actor, rooted in a literal, specific recognition of a physical center from which all impulses to move or make sound flow outwardly and into the external world.

## THE PURE CENTER AND THE VOICE

The martial arts teach that a "pure" sense of center is the natural biomechanical center of an undistorted body. This "ideal" center is deep within the body, in an area roughly three finger-widths below your navel. It is here that the breath (and therefore the voice) originates, as well as all large motions of the body. This area is the literal center of gravity of your body, as shown by Leonardo da Vinci's famous drawing (see Figure 9).

You will want to develop a sense of your pure center, for it is from this center that your deepest impulses spring. If you are operating instead from some higher center (such as the chest, or even the head) you will inevitably look and sound "stiff" and "superficial"; the movements and sounds you will produce will not be deeply motivated or complete, because they will not be originating from the true center of your being, and your voice in particular will not have the fullness and expressiveness required for good stage speech.

The committed worker is often the noisy one, humming, singing, laughing, or grunting; all action usually flows into the world through sound as well as motion. The student of karate learns this—the outward flow of energy from our deepest center naturally carries the breath, and hence the voice, with it. Unfortunately, we sometimes inhibit this natural flow of sound out of fear or because our upbringing has taught us to restrain our natural impulse to move, breathe, and make sounds.

The following exercise will give you an experience of the breath flowing from your center, carrying sound and motion with it.

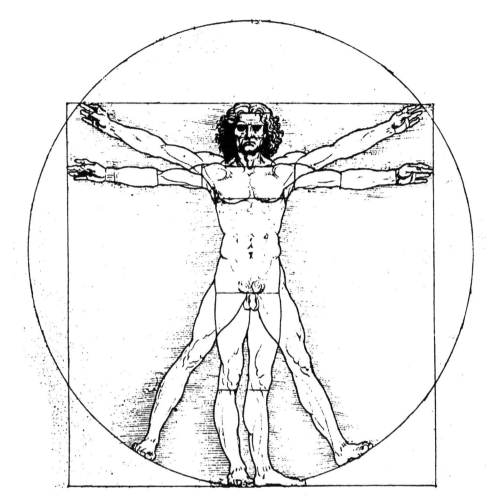

**FIGURE 9**  The Bodily Center According to Leonardo.

### Exercise 15:
### Moving and Sounding from Center

A. Align and center yourself as in the previous exercises.

1. Breathe easily and slowly, feeling the breath as an expansion and a release of the center. As you breathe in, the center becomes larger and you feel yourself expanding in all directions; as you breathe out, the center is effortlessly released, and it draws to itself the energy of the breath you have just taken. Feel each breath as a gathering of energy into your center.

2. Become aware of the breath rising and falling in the body from the center.
3. As the breath travels outward, make sound lightly. Do not disturb the breath; just allow it to vibrate. This is your voice: your vibrating breath carrying energy from your center into the outside world.
4. Reach effortlessly with your vibrating breath into the world around you.

B. Put yourself, at random, into a new position; sit, bend over, or lean to one side. Repeat the above exercise in this new position and experience the breath flowing through this newly shaped pathway. What changes are there in the voice? Explore a variety of positions, but avoid strain; simply let the breath vibrate as it flows out of the center in each new bodily composition.

C. Begin moving from your center, allowing the breath to vibrate so that the energy of each motion is the same energy that produces your vibrating breath. Your sound should become an audible symptom of your motion so that it flows as easily as the motion flows, and takes on all the changing qualities of the motion and breath.

D. Come gradually to stillness and let each breath vibrate. As you continue to produce sound, feel the vibrations of that sound spreading into every part of your body: out of the neck into the head and chest, into the back, the stomach, the buttocks, into the arms and hands, into the legs and feet, and into the scalp. As each area of the body opens to the vibration, let the easy energy of the sound lift you and open you so that you rise first to your knees, then to a standing position. Feel the sound radiating from every part of your body.

E. Remain standing and vibrate; check every surface of your body with your fingertips. Are there "dead spots" that are not participating in the sound?

Examine your experience during sounding: Were there parts of your body that did not join in the vibration? Did you have a new sense of the capacity of your entire body to join in the act of sounding? Did you feel more in touch with yourself, and with the space around you, as if your sound were literally reaching outside yourself in a tangible way? Are you now more alert, refreshed, and relaxed?

Those areas of your body that are not available for sounding will relate in some way to the distortions and chronic tensions that you identified during your phasic relaxation work; examine each and find the relationship. A disused abdomen will cause a shallow, unsupported tone because the breath is not flowing freely from the center. A rigid or pinched chest and shoulders will withhold the chest from sound, robbing the voice of the deep resonances that give it richness; a tense neck and jaw may pinch the tone and force it into a narrow channel, causing a strident or sharp quality.

Whatever your findings, you see that vocal and physical qualities are integral with one another because the breath, body, and voice are all integral with one another. As you begin to gain freedom and ease in one, you will enhance the other; enhancing, too, a quality of mind important to your work, for your consciousness is itself a partner in this same wholeness.

## THE ACTOR'S USE OF CENTER

Just as we experienced relaxation as a readiness to react, so our aim in aligning and centering the body is to put ourselves in the most responsive physiovocal condition. The "pure" center is an undistorted condition from which we begin our work so that we may develop in any direction required by the role without the impediment or bias of our personal distortions.

While we *begin* from a pure center, however, we certainly do not *end* there. We are not interested in "correct" posture and voice for performance, for there are no "correct" voice and posture for the actor until they are determined by the demands of the role. Each character you play will have his or her own center, which functions as the source of that character's breathing, motion, and sound.

In fact, any dramatic characterization is *a set of distortions* created to express the particular nature of that character. Whole and healthy people are rare in plays; dramatic characters are usually caught in difficult situations, driven by neurotic needs, or in other ways bent out of "normal" shape. It will be a major aspect of your work to discover the particular "abnormalities" that comprise the unique nature of each role you play.

In order to do this, you begin from as undistorted or "neutral" a base as you can, exploring and testing the particular qualities useful in creating the role. In truth, of course, you will never eradicate *all* your personal idiosyncrasies, nor should you; they give your work special and individual qualities that enable you, when at your best, to bring special insights and qualities to the roles you play. But those personal misalignments, inhibitions, and unconscious mannerisms—like regional dialects, unnatural postural or breathing habits, repetitive gestures—must be brought within the control of your conscious artistic discipline, or they may forever limit the roles and qualities you can play.

And note that we wish not to *eliminate* these habits and qualities, but rather to bring them within our control. We actors shouldn't throw anything away; any quality, mannerism, way of speaking, or experience might be needed someday. But we must hold all these in such a way that *we are controlling them instead of them controlling us.*

In these lessons we are working to achieve a neutral but energized condition where you are ready to move in any way necessary to fulfill your dramatic task.

## THE CYCLE OF ENERGY

You are preparing yourself as the "ground" of your work. Your relaxed and aligned body is ready to move and your energy is ready to flow spontaneously from your deepest center. This energy, flowing into the outside world, may take a variety of external forms: Its visible aspects are movements; its audible aspects are sounds and words; its psychological aspects are emotions. All of these are only different modes of the same energy; any impulse may flow into any of these forms or into all of them simultaneously. All of these forms—movement, sound, and feeling—are as integral to one another as you are to yourself. To whatever degree your movement, sound, and feelings are not integral with one another, you are less whole and less accessible to yourself in your work—your work will inevitably exhibit this same fragmentation.

We turn next to consider the *cycle* of energy that flows from our center outward toward the world *and back again*. Whenever we try to do something, to achieve some objective—in short, whenever we *act*—we send energy flowing out from our center into forms of sound, speech, or gesture in the outer world. We then receive a *reaction* to our action, and this energy flows into us and touches our center, in turn eliciting a further reaction from us, and so on. As this cycle flows out, then in, then out again, we see that there is no truly unilateral action; we do not *do* unless we have been *done to*, and vice versa. In the theater, we like to say that *acting is reacting!*

This sense of a cycle of energy is central to the Oriental martial arts (for example, T'ai Chi Ch'uan), and the study of these arts can greatly benefit the actor. Developing this sense of the cycle of energy can also help to open and free the passageway through which the voice naturally flows.

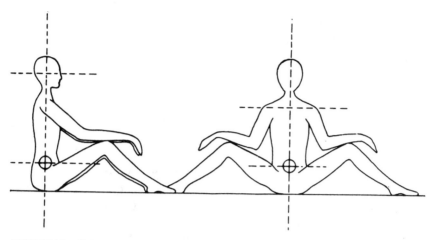

**FIGURE 10**   Sitting in Balance.

### Exercise 16:
### The Cycle of Energy

Sit up, directly on the bony points you can feel just below the surface of each buttock; spread your legs as wide as is comfortable, with the knees slightly raised (see Figure 10). Feel lifted from your center out of the top of your head so that your back and neck are long and wide. The head is level, eyes ahead, and the waist is level as well. You should do this exercise as a continuous flow, not as a series of positions; the tempo and flow of the exercise are determined by slow, deep breathing, and each cycle uses one complete breath.

A. Breathing out, reach forward and down, keeping your back and neck long and shoulders wide. Imagine that you are bowing to someone sitting at the back of a theater.

B. As you begin to breathe in, draw the breath into the lower part of your body by drawing the small of your back to the rear and scooping "energy" into the funnel formed by your legs with your hands.

C. As the breath begins to fill you, feel its warmth and power flowing up within you. Follow its upward movement with your hands.

D. As the breath rises in your body, it lifts you, straightening and lengthening the upper torso and neck, lifting the head, widening the shoulders and the throat as it flows upward like a wave moving you in a slow undulation. You unfurl like a fern opening.

E. The breath then flows into the outer world, with the feelings and sound of a yawn; you are giving this sound to those people sitting at the back of the theater, and you accompany it with an unfolding gesture of the arms toward them. Your eyes are alive; you "see" the people.

F. As the power of the breath begins to diminish, you easily close your mouth so that the "ah" sound of the yawn becomes an "m," and you experience a tingling sensation in your mouth and nose areas. The smooth flow of the sound produces a trisyllable word, "ah-oh-m" or *om*.

G. As the breath and sound begin to die away, your body again bows forward and down, your back is still long and wide, and your arms are reaching forward to scoop in a new quantity of breath energy.

H. As the breath and sound are completely used up, your body has sunk low in its bow, and the cycle begins again. At no time do you strain or pinch the voice, for the breath always lifts the head, widens and relaxes the throat, and pours easily out with the feeling of a yawn.

I. Repeat the entire cycle: As the breath enters and leaves your body, feel the continuity of inward and outward breaths as two aspects of one cycle; change over easily from one to the other so that the entire exercise becomes one unbroken, flowing experience with no "sharp corners," only smoothly curving patterns of time, energy, motion, and sound.

J. When you have completed enough cycles of this exercise to feel the full integration of breath, motion, and sound in an unbroken pattern, hold in the erect position and begin to produce a continuous tone, pausing easily for breath. (If you are in a group, the entire group should produce one continuous, harmonious sound, and each member of the group should feel part of the group sound and the group sound a part of them.)


## BEING GROUNDED

As you begin to sense your physical center more acutely, also begin to feel the way your energy interacts with gravity. Your energy flows downward into the ground as well as upward, and there is also energy coming up into your center from the earth. We can speak, therefore, not only of being "centered," but also of being "grounded."

There is great power in being grounded, and several contemporary theater makers have placed special emphasis on developing this quality, most notably the Japanese director Tadashi Suzuki, whose actor training system is based on a series of walks, many of which attack the earth as if to penetrate it. At the same time, some types of characters can be best expressed by a *lack* of grounding, by a floating or even flying quality.

Here is an exercise to help you experience the various ways in which we can experience gravity.

### Exercise 17:
### Roots

Imagine yourself standing on a mirror. Below you is your other self with its own center; imagine a bond between your center and that in your mirror image. This imaginary bond of energy is like a root, giving you stability, strength, and nourishment.

As your energy flows into your root, it also flows upward, so that your rootedness permits you to stand taller, to be stronger. As you move, your rootedness moves with you; you "detach" your rooted center, and at your destination you "plant" or ground yourself again.

A. Select a destination; lift your rooted center, move to the destination, and *plant* yourself there.

B. Now move to a destination without lifting the root; *plow* yourself there. Don't act this out; simply experience moving with this image and feel what it is like to *plow*. Extend this feeling so that you are pushing your way through the air itself, as if you are *molding* space as you move through it.

C. Now lift your root and leave it dangling all the time, whether moving or still: *Float.* Again, give yourself time to experience *floating.*

D. Now imagine the root being drawn upward, still attached at your center, but now lifting your center upward and out of the top of your head. Move with the sense that you have to reach down to touch the floor: You are *flying!*

There is a distinct difference between the experiences of *molding, floating,* and *flying,* though each state offers numerous possibilities: Molding, for instance, can feel like dejection or defeat, but it might also feel like determination or commitment; floating can feel like joy or enthusiasm, but it might also feel like confusion or vulnerability. The particular emotional quality of any one of these states can be determined only by *context,* and our bodily expression cannot be understood according to any sort of fixed or abstract system (though in the past, particularly in the nineteenth century, there were attempts to construct such systems and a few, notably the Delsarte system, in which various body centers were related to emotions and qualities of thought, were temporarily popular).

## ARTICULATING MOVEMENT

In the last exercise you began to move through space by "lifting" your rooted center, moving, then "planting" your rooted center again at your destination. Review this experience; did it give you a heightened sense of clarity and purposefulness in your movements?

An actor moving from one point to another on stage goes through much the same process as the musician playing a note on an instrument. The actor chooses a destination, just as the musician selects a note to play. Then, deep within the body where the largest muscle systems intersect, the first energy of the movement is initiated, just as the musician begins to breathe and finger the instrument. Finally, the movement, like the sound of the instrument, erupts into the outside world in all its fullness. When the destination has been reached, the energy that initiated the entire process is expended and the movement ceases, just as the musician's note dies away when the breath stops.

Like the musician's music, and like your speech on stage, your stage movement needs to be well *phrased* and *articulated*, with a clear beginning, middle, and end to each phrase.

### Exercise 18:
### Articulating Movement

As in Exercise 16, begin by creating the experience of your own rooted center in relationship to your mirror image beneath the floor. Now make a movement by following each of these steps:

A. Select your destination: Locate a specific spot with your eyes and let your face turn toward it so that your movement "follows your nose."

B. Begin to move by *lifting* the root; exaggerate this motion at first.

C. Carry your root to your destination and "land" there.

D. As you land, "spear" your root into the floor to complete your movement.

| Motion Quality | Effort Quality | | Appearance |
|---|---|---|---|
| | *Firm* | *Gentle* | |
| Dynamic | Molding | Floating | Resistant or Effortless |
| Flow | Bound | Free | Stopping or Releasing |
| Charge | Strong | Weak | Fighting or Yielding |
| Speed | Sudden | Sustained | Quick or Slow |

**FIGURE 11**   Effort Shape.

E. Repeat this action several times, paying special attention to the sense of beginning, middle, and end to each movement phrase.

F. Now begin to play with variations of this cycle, extending them beyond realistic movement. For instance, try lifting the root slowly and heavily; then drag it to the destination and *dump* it there so that it "plops" into the ground. Or make your lift light and high, moving *away* from your destination, then *throw* your root toward your destination and *fly* there, landing with a light jump. These are the kinds of "stylized" movement we associate with *commedia dell'arte*.

The states we have named *molding, floating,* and *flying* are different bodily *dynamics* and are adapted from the analysis of "effort shape" made by Rudolf Laban (who developed the system used for notating dance choreography). In addition to the dynamic quality of physical energy, he spoke of three other qualities: *flow*, which was either "bound" or "free," *speed*, which was either "sudden" or "sustained," and *charge*, which was either "weak" or "strong." Let's extend this exercise to explore these additional qualities.

**Exercise 19:**
**Effort Shape**

A. As you move, be aware of the quality of energy flowing from your center into that movement: Is it *weak* or *strong*? Experiment with each.

B. As your energy leaves your body and enters the outside world, how does it contact others? Is it *bound* or *free*? Experiment with each.

C. Now randomly select qualities from Figure 11 and experience various effort shapes: For instance, try molding with a strong charge, fast speed, and a direct flow, and then try floating with a weak charge, slow speed, and an indirect flow, and so on.

Virtually any quality of movement can be created by using these variables. On stage, your performance is partly a dance that, without appearing to be dancelike, is nevertheless composed, intensified, and purified through repeated testing and rehearsal (even if this process is rarely a conscious one). Your aim here is *not* to become self-consciously controlling of your movements, but rather to begin to experience the almost limitless range of movement qualities of which we are capable: This is one of the "palettes" from which you will "paint" as an actor, and you want to be sure that you have a wide choice of colors available to you.

**SUMMARY OF LESSON FOUR**

A potter knows how the centering of the clay upon the wheel is essential to the creation of a pot; as an actor you must also be centered so that your energy, like the clay, will flow outward into the new form of the role.

This idea of a personal center is not just a metaphor; it has a tangible physical dimension. Finding and activating your bodily center are necessary first steps in laying a foundation for good stage movement and voice and can integrate your responses and give you strength.

Developing your physical center is also a means of developing a psychological and spiritual centeredness, because at this deep level your energy exists simultaneously in physical and in psychological forms.

The center moves within the body as your mood changes; also, different people have different characteristic centers that are appropriate to their personalities.

There is an "ideal" center deep within the body, roughly three finger widths below your navel. It is here that the breath (and therefore the voice) originates, as well as all large motions of the body and all your deepest impulses.

The "pure" center is an undistorted condition from which we begin our work so that we may develop in any direction required by the role without the impediment or bias of our personal distortions. However, we are not interested in "correct" posture and voice, for there are no "correct" voice and posture for the actor until they are determined by the demands of the role. Any dramatic characterization is *a set of distortions* created to express the particular nature of that character.

Our energy moves as a *cycle* that flows from our center outward toward the world *and back again*. It also flows downward into the ground, and there is also energy coming up into your center from the earth. We can speak, therefore, not only of being "centered," but also of being "grounded."

Various kinds of energy states produce different experiences. There is a distinct difference between *molding, floating,* and *flying,* though the particular emotional quality of any one of these states can be determined only by *context*. These states are different bodily *dynamics* and are adapted from the analysis of "effort shape" made by Rudolf Laban. Any quality of movement can be created by using these variables.

Your aim here is *not* to become self-consciously controlling of your movements, but to be sure that you have a wide choice of movement available to you.

# Lesson Five

## Body Gesture

When you have an impulse, feeling, or idea it arouses an energy at your deep center that naturally flows outward, reaching the outer world in many forms: words, sounds, motions, or postures. Broadly speaking, any such external sign of a feeling or thought may be called a *gesture*.

In fact, the word "express" literally means "to move outward." When you have a feeling or idea, it is natural to externalize it, to "move it outward" through gesture and speech. Although this expressive behavior communicates your feelings and ideas to others, it is an automatic part of your thought process itself and goes on even when you are alone. Watch people driving alone on the highway, for instance; you will see some amazingly animated conversations.

This lesson examines gestures of the body; the next lesson will explore gestures of the voice, which are both verbal (the speaking of words) and nonverbal (the many sounds we make other than words).

### GESTURE AS COMMUNICATION

Our culture has a large vocabulary of body gestures that we use to augment and often to substitute for verbal communication. While our verbal language communicates fairly precise meanings, our ges-

44

tural language provides information about feelings and action greater expressiveness than words alone. Simply put, words can best say *what we mean*, and gestures can best tell *how we feel* about what we mean.

Psychologists have for years been interested in body language, and this area of study has been given the name "kinesics" by Professor Raymond Birdwhistle. He defines kinesics as "the study of body motion as related to the nonverbal aspects of interpersonal communication." Several of his basic premises are of interest to you as an actor: First, body gestures are socially learned; second, no gesture carries meaning by itself, so that all gestures must be interpreted in context; third, it is the physiological similarity of our bodies and the generally similar influences of our environment that cause some gestures to develop roughly standardized meanings within our culture.

Here is a brief example of nonverbal expression at work as observed by Birdwhistle. He recorded this scene from real life and describes the nonverbal action just as a playwright would give "stage directions."

[*The situation is that a guest of honor at a party arrives forty-five minutes late. Three couples besides the host and hostess have been waiting. The door-bell rings.*]

HOSTESS: Oh! We were afraid you weren't coming; but good. [*As the hostess opened the door to admit her guest, she smiled a closed-toothed smile. As she began speaking she drew her hands, drawn into loose fists, up between her breasts. Opening her eyes very wide, she then closed them slowly and held them closed for several words. As she began to speak, she dropped her head to one side and then moved it toward the guest in a slow sweep. She then pursed her lips momentarily before continuing to speak, nodded, shut her eyes again, and spread her arms, indicating that he should enter.*]

GUEST: I'm very sorry; got held up you know, calls and all that. [*He looked at her fixedly; shook his head, and spread his arms with his hands held open. He then began to shuffle his feet and raise one hand, turning it slightly outward. He nodded, raised his other hand, and turned it palm-side up as he continued his vocalization. Then he dropped both hands and held them palms forward, to the side and away from his thighs. He continued his shuffling.*]

HOSTESS: Put your wraps here. People are dying to meet you. I've told them all about you. [*She smiled at him, lips pulled back from clenched teeth, then, as she indicated where he should put his coat, she dropped her face momentarily into an expressionless pose. She smiled toothily again, clucked and slowly shut, opened, and shut her eyes again as she pointed to the guests with her lips. She then swept her head from one side to the other. As she said the word "all" she moved her head in a sweep up and down from one side to the other, shut her eyes slowly again, pursed her lips, and grasped the guest's lapel.*]

GUEST: You have! Well, I don't know....Yes....No....I'd love to meet them. [*The guest hunched his shoulders, which pulled his lapel out of the hostess' grasp. He held his coat with both hands, frowned, and then blinked rapidly as he slipped the coat off. He continued to hold tightly to his coat.*][1]

As you reconstruct this scene in your mind's eye, it is obvious that the nonverbal behavior is very eloquent; you can deduce a great deal of specific information from the gestures. The "logic of the body" has, within our culture, provided some gestures with conventionalized meanings: The clenching of the teeth beneath the smile, the making of fists, the shuffling of feet, all tend to have similar meanings when they appear in similar situations.

Moreover, many of the gestures tend to express feelings that run *counter* to the surface meaning of the words being spoken. This is an extremely important aspect of nonverbal expression: It often "counterpoints" or even contradicts our verbal expression and "safely" expresses feelings that would otherwise be impolite or embarrassing. For example, while the guest and the hostess are being very polite to each other, what is going on physically is that she is grabbing him and pulling him into the room against his will. To the very end, he continues to clutch his coat as a way of saying "I want to run away!" even while his words are saying "I'd love to meet them."

In acting terms, these nonverbal gestures are conveying a *subtext*, feelings that run beneath the surface of the dialogue and that are different from those being expressed on the surface of the scene. (Subtext will be examined in greater detail in Part Two.)

Though most of us read "body language" on an almost unconscious level all the time, the actor needs to heighten this skill through observation and analysis. You will need to become an expert, like the famous detective Sherlock Holmes:

He had risen from his chair and was standing between the parted blinds, gazing down into the dull neutral-tinted London street....On the pavement opposite there stood a large woman with a heavy fur boa around her neck, and a large curling red feather in a broad-brimmed hat which was tilted in a coquettish Duchess of Devonshire fashion over her ear. From under this great panoply she peeped up in a nervous, hesitating fashion at our window, while her body oscillated backward and forward, and her fingers fidgeted with her glove buttons. Suddenly, with a plunge as of the swimmer who leaves the bank, she hurled across the road and we heard the sharp clang of the bell. "I have seen these symptoms before," said Holmes, throwing his cigarette into the fire. "Oscillation upon the pavement always means an *affair de coeur*. She would like advice, but is not sure that the matter is not too delicate for communication. And yet even here we may discriminate. When a woman has been seriously wronged by a man she no longer oscillates, and the usual symptom is a broken bell wire. Here we may take it that there is a love matter, but that the maiden is not so much angered as perplexed, or grieved. But here she comes in person to resolve our doubts."[2]

In his book *The Silent Language*, Edward Hall comments on this passage by saying that Sherlock Holmes "made explicit a highly complex process which many of us go through without knowing that we are involved. Those of us who keep our eyes open can read volumes into what we see going on around us."[3] The actor has special need to engage in this kind of acute observation. As Brian Bates reports in his book *The Way of the Actor*:

> Liv Ullmann regards observing other people as an essential path to "becoming other people" more fully and truthfully....Actors have been observers for centuries, for without this keen attention to others, performances are limited to the prison of one's own personal life.[4]

To see how explicit a playwright can be about such details of nonverbal behavior, read the scene from *The Glass Menagerie* in Appendix A now, and pay special attention to Williams's stage directions.

### Exercise 20:
### The Science of Deduction

A. Through observation over the next few days, find for yourself a brief real-life scene involving subtext, and record it in the same way as the hostess/guest scene recorded by Birdwhistle.

B. Analyze it as if you were Sherlock Holmes. Re-create as completely as you can the reasons for the behavior of the characters and create a personality profile for each.

C. With a partner, re-create the scene for the group. Let everyone develop their own ideas about the subtext; then compare your accounts to see what similar deductions you have made. What areas were the most commonly agreed upon, and what evidence was the most persuasive? Be specific: Why did you draw the conclusions you reached from each bit of evidence?

While the scientific study of body language is fairly new, our interest in it is very old. One of the first studies of the "silent language" (which may have been influential on the style of acting of its time) was John Bulwer's *Chirologia and Chironomia*, written in 1644. The book calls itself a study of "the Speaking Motions, and Discoursing Gestures, the patheticalle motions of the minde." The book discussed and illustrated an enormous number of feelings as expressed by nonverbal gestures (see Figure 12). Similar attempts to categorize physical gestures for the performer were made throughout the seventeenth, eighteenth, and nineteenth centuries. Even a few modern systems of acting use, in a very modified form, a formalized approach to the physical expression of emotion by locating "emotional centers" in the body, an idea borrowed from Oriental acting and medicine.

## THE GENESIS OF GESTURE

As we have seen, some of our body gestures have developed a common meaning within similar situations; these form a sort of gestural subvocabulary. This is because these gestures have a common origin.

Some of these gestures derive their meaning from the structure of the body itself. For example, a man hitching up his pants is usually asserting his masculinity, since this action refers attention to his genitals. Likewise, a woman covering her cheeks with her hands is probably expressing embarrassment, and her gesture is a *substitute blush* as the hands rise to the face in the same way that the blood would have risen to the cheeks in a real blush.

Other gestures derive their meaning by being leftovers of animal behavior that we would have used at an earlier, more primitive stage of our evolution as a species. These vestiges of animal behavior live on as symbolic activity long after the action has ceased to be practical. This idea was developed by Charles Darwin as part of his theory of evolution in *The Expression of Emotion in Man and Animal*. Darwin's ideas are expanded on here by my teacher, the late Robert S. Breen:

> Consider the expressive value of behavior that was once in our human history adaptive, but is no longer so except in a vestigial sense—for example, the baring of teeth in the preparation for attack

**FIGURE 12** From *Chirologia and Chironomia*, 1644.

or defense. In primitive experience, the use of the teeth for tearing and rending an enemy was common enough, and a very effective means of adapting to an environmental necessity. Today, the use of teeth in this primitive fashion is rare, but the baring of the teeth is still very much with us. In an attitude of pugnacity, men will frequently clench their teeth and draw back their lips to expose their teeth. This action is a reinstatement of the primitive pattern of biting, though there is no real intention of using the teeth in such a fashion. The "tough guy" talks through his teeth because he is habituated to an attitude of aggressiveness. When he bares his teeth, it is a warning to all who see him that he is prepared to attack or to defend himself. His speech is characterized by a nasality because his oral cavity is closed, and his breath escapes primarily through his nose. Lip action in speech is curtailed because the jaw is held so close to the upper jaw that there is little room between the lips for even their normal activity. Restriction of the lip action results in the tough guy's talking out of the corner of his mouth.

When we see a person bare his clenched teeth, curl his lip, narrow his eyes, deepen his breathing, etc., we conclude that he is angry. These are the signs of attack in our ancestors which have become for us *social symbols expressive of an emotional state* known as *anger*.[5]

### Exercise 21:
### Animal Gestures

A. Select a strongly physical action directed toward another, such as intimidation, seduction, rejection, or approval. Adopt the characteristics of an ape or prehistoric man performing the same function. When you have begun to experience the activity on a purely physical, "animalistic" level, begin gradually to "civilize" the behavior. Do not premeditate; let the activity itself lead you as it gradually becomes less and less practical and more and more "symbolic."

B. Using the hostess/guest scene, or your own subtext scene, work with a partner to develop the scene as it might have happened between two animals.

You will probably notice that the "animalized" version of your scene brought the subtext to the surface, since the purposeful suppression of feelings is an almost exclusively human ability. You also noticed that the animal version involved a great deal more overt movement of the lower body than its civilized offspring. Consider, however, that all these same impulses are at work in the original; they are felt as muscular arousal even though they may not result in observable movement, and will affect your voice and movement quality no matter how polite and symbolic your character is trying to be.

For this reason it is useful for you to reawaken a sense of the animal origins of expressive behavior. Even as you perform the "polite" contemporary behavior, your memory of its animal origins can serve as a source of power and deep involvement.

## FUNCTIONS OF GESTURE

We can divide the language of gestures into four broad functional categories, though almost every gesture we make serves a combination of two or three of these functions simultaneously:

1. Illustrative, or imitative
2. Indicative
3. Emphatic
4. Autistic

Illustrative gestures are "pantomimic" in that they communicate specific information ("the box was about this high and this wide").

The indicative gesture points ("It's right over there").

The emphatic gesture provides subjective rather than objective information, relating how we *felt* about something (as we say, "Now listen here!" we pound our fist on the table or jab our finger into our opponent's face).

The autistic gesture (meaning literally "to the self") is not intended for social communication, but is rather a way in which we communicate privately to ourselves. Suppose that as I listen to you I have hostile feelings, which for some reason I must conceal from you. With my arms crossed over my chest, I am viciously clutching the flesh under one of my armpits. I am secretly strangling you, the flesh of my armpit substituting for your neck. While such gestures are meant to be hidden, they are often "unconsciously" perceived and recognized by the people around us.

### Exercise 22:
### Physical Gesture Scene

Select a simple and highly physical action. Perform it four times, each time utilizing a different kind of gesture. For example, if your action is to lift a heavy box and move it across the room, you would do the following:

1. Illustrate lifting it, as if you were telling us about how you would lift it without actually doing it. In this case, you may use words together with physical gestures.

2. Indicate lifting it. ("I'll pick it up from over there and carry it over here.")
3. Use emphatic gestures that are symbolic (rather than illustrative) as you show and tell us how it felt to lift the heavy box. Notice how your voice is affected.
4. Finally, perform the action symbolically and secretly using autistic gestures (for example, hitching up your belt as a substitute for lifting the box).

Compare your experiences of each category. Do you see why indirect and symbolic gesture is often more effective and interesting than obvious pantomime or indication?

## GESTURES IN THE TEXT

When performing scripted material, the playwright will have provided your "verbal gestures" in the words of the dialogue. Your contribution as an actor will consist mainly of the many nonverbal aspects of your performance—the physical gestures, postures, vocal inflections, facial expressions, and so on. In doing this, you will again be guided by the script: either by stage directions or by implications in the highly physical language that is the mark of a good playwright. As you gain experience, you will begin to recognize and expand on these implications.

**Exercise 23:**
**Implied Gestures in the Text**

A. With a partner, read aloud some of the scene from *The Glass Menagerie* in Appendix A, *including the stage directions that pertain to your character*. Act out the behavior Williams describes. Do you begin to feel the inner states that the behavior expresses?

B. The following speech from Shakespeare's *King Lear* (Act IV, Scene vi) suggests gestures of all four types; read it aloud and feel the strong, specific impulses to gesture it gives you. Try performing it emphasizing the different categories of gesture.

*When I do stare, see how the subject quakes.*
*I pardon that man's life. What was thy cause?*
*Adultery?*
*Thou shalt not die: die for adultery! No:*
*The wren goes to 't, and the small gilded fly*

*Does lecher in my sight.*
*Let copulation thrive; for Gloucester's bastard son*
*Was kinder to his father than my daughters*
*Got 'tween the lawful sheets.*
*To 't luxury, pell-mell! for I lack soldiers.*
*Behold yond simpering dame,*
*Whose face between her forks presages snow,*
*That minces virtue, and does shake the head*
*To hear of pleasure's name;*
*The fitchew, nor the soiled horse, goes to 't*
*With a more riotous appetite.*
*Down from the waist they are Centaurs,*
*Though women all above:*
*But to the girdle do the gods inherit,*
*Beneath is all the fiend's;*
*There's hell, there's darkness, there is the sulfurous pit;*

*Burning, scalding, stench, consumption; fie, fie, fie! pah, pah! Give me an ounce of civet, good apothecary, to sweeten my imagination: there's money for thee.*

C. Now perform an "animalization" of the speech; see how far you can go, allowing the impulses for gesture to return to their deepest animal origins in biting, hitting, spitting, vomiting, embracing, and so on. Allow the words themselves to "regress" into the sounds of these activities.

## SUMMARY OF LESSON FIVE

Any external sign of a feeling or thought may be called a gesture. When you have a feeling or idea, it is natural to express it, to "move it outward" through gesture and speech. This is an automatic part of your thought process and goes on even when you are alone. Words can best say *what we mean* and gestures can best tell *how we feel* about what we mean.

Raymond Birdwhistle defines kinesics as "the study of body motion as related to the nonverbal aspects of interpersonal communication." He believes that body gestures are socially learned, that no gesture carries meaning by itself; and that the "logic of the body" has provided some gestures with conventionalized meanings.

Body gestures sometimes express feelings that run *counter* to the surface meaning of the words being spoken. In acting terms, these nonverbal gestures are conveying a *subtext*.

Though most of us read "body language" on an almost unconscious level all the time, the actor needs to heighten this skill through observation and analysis. Attempts to categorize physical gestures for the performer were made in the past, and even a few modern systems of acting locate "emotional centers" in the body, an idea borrowed from Oriental acting and medicine.

Some gestures derive their meaning from the structure of the body itself. Others are vestiges of animal behavior; when we see a person bare clenched teeth, curl the lip, narrow the eyes, deepen the breathing, and so on, we know that these are the signs of attack in our ancestors which have become for us *social symbols expressive of an emotional state* known as *anger*.

We can divide the language of gestures into four broad functional categories: illustrative, indicative, emphatic, and autistic.

When performing scripted material, the playwright will have provided your "verbal gestures" in the words of the dialogue. Your contribution as an actor will consist mainly of the many nonverbal aspects of your performance—the physical gestures, postures, vocal inflections, facial expressions, and so on. In this, you will again be guided by the script: either by stage directions or by implications in the highly physical language that is the mark of a good playwright.

# Lesson Six

## Vocal Gesture

The emphasis our culture places on words as a way of communicating information sometimes makes us forget that the voice, apart from the speaking of words, is a major element in our expressive behavior. While articulated speech is a learned ability, vocal gesture is instinctive. Perhaps for this reason, vocal sounds are universal in appeal. As Margaret Schlauch puts it in *The Gift of Language*:

> A cry, a tonal inflection, a gesture, are means of communication far more universal than language as we understand it. They are, in fact, universal enough to be conveyed to animals as well as other human beings.[1]

In this lesson, you will begin to explore the wide range of vocal behavior that surrounds and supports the speaking of words. Some theorists believe that these nonverbal sounds are, in fact, the source from which our spoken language evolved: In any case, they are still used to express those deep feelings that are "beyond speaking of."

### THE VOICE AND EMOTION

Your voice, by its physiological genesis, is integrally connected with your most basic bodily functions. As linguist Edward Sapir points out, "There are properly speaking no organs of speech. There are only organs that are incidentally useful in the production of speech sounds."[2] For this reason, your voice is called an "overlaid function," a sort of double duty performed by organs and muscles that evolved originally for other, more basic activities: the diaphragm and lungs for breathing; the larynx for swallowing; the tongue, the teeth, and the lips for chewing; the palate and tongue for tasting. In fact, the network of muscles that produce the voice is so complex and far reaching that it ultimately involves the entire body.

We said in the last lesson that your natural impulse is to externalize your feelings and that these externalizations are part and parcel of your emotions. Since the voice is produced by the deep muscles that are the seat of emotion, your voice is completely integrated with your emotional life. As Sapir puts it:

> The sound of pain or the sound of joy does not, as such, indicate the emotion, it does not stand aloof, as it were, and announce that such and such an emotion is being felt. What it does is to serve as a more or less automatic overflow of the emotional energy: in a sense, it is part and parcel of the emotion itself.[3]

There are two important ideas here: first, that the vocal sounds can be an emotional "overflow," a sort of safety-valve action when our inner dynamic becomes so high that we can no longer "contain ourselves"; second, that such vocalizations of our inner feelings are an automatic and integral part of the feelings themselves.

### Exercise 24:
### Vocal Overflow

This is an exercise in experiencing the "overflow" of vocal and physical gesture. Repeat Exercise 22: Read the speech from *King Lear* aloud, but force yourself to remain perfectly expressionless and still, suppressing all impulses for vocal and physical gesture. Do this several times until you feel the demand for physical and vocal gesture growing so strong that you can no longer "contain yourself" and are finally forced to move.

## THE VOICE AND YOUR INNER DYNAMIC

There is an old story about a highly mannered, flamboyant actor who gestured so indiscriminately that her movements ceased to have any organic relationship to the scene she was performing. Her director tied her hands together with a string. "When your impulse to move is so strong that you must break the string," he said, "then you may move."

The director was forcing her, through the string, to hold her responses in (to suppress them); a psychologist would say he was "raising her threshold of response" so that only the strongest (and therefore the most dramatically important) responses would flow over her threshold; the less deeply felt impulses would be filtered out.

I once saw a short film showing the great cinema director Jean Renoir working with an actor in preparation for a highly emotional close-up. He sits her before the camera with the script and instructs her to read the words of her speech without emotion. She goes over the speech several times, and each time her natural response to the highly charged material starts to take over. At the slightest sign of emotion, however, Renoir sternly says, "No, no, just the words!" You can literally see the emotional pressure rising in her as the suppressed responses struggle harder and harder to break free. Finally, when she is about to explode, Renoir calls "Action!" and the camera captures a splendid performance.

The repeated suppression of the impulses tended not only to filter out the weaker, less deeply felt ones, but it also strengthened those that remained by building their "inner pressure," or *inner dynamic*. This is why we often say that "less is more," and why Stanislavski encouraged actors over the course of a rehearsal process to "cut 80 percent" of the activity they began with: With less external activity to release it, internal energy has a chance to build.

Here is an exercise that will enable you to experience this inner dynamic and to hear its profound effect on the voice.

### Exercise 25:
### Running on the Inside

You are to stand and run in place, counting every other step aloud from one to fifty, but when you reach thirty, stop running "outside" but continue to run "inside"; hear the effect this has on your voice.

Inner dynamic is essential to the sense of drama, because it arouses suspense. People with a lot of energy "inside" but without much being released "outside" are dramatically interesting; they command our attention and make us wonder "What are they going to do?" This inner dynamic produces the quality of excitement or even danger we sense from an actor like Robert DeNiro.

The voice automatically carries much of this "hidden" energy out into the world, even when we are trying to suppress it. For instance, it is extremely moving to hear newscasters reporting a great tragedy, like the assassination of President John F. Kennedy, because they are trying to remain "objective," yet despite their disciplined efforts the emotion is forcing itself through.

This is why what you *don't* do on stage is often much more important than what you *do*. What happens *inside* enriches your performance without any conscious effort, and this is especially true of your voice.

## THE VOICE AND SUBTEXT

In life, the words we speak carry the information we wish to impart, while our attitude about that information is usually carried by our tone of voice. The most obvious example is sarcasm. If, during an argument, I say to you, "Well, you certainly are an expert on the subject," it is my tone of voice that lets you know that I really mean you don't know what you're talking about.

There are also *unconscious* ways in which the voice communicates attitudes that the situation forces us to hide. At such time we will—consciously or not—express ourselves indirectly, saying or doing one thing when we really mean another. You already recognize such "hidden" meanings as *subtext*.

If, for example, I am attempting to convince you that I feel strongly about what I am saying, I may increase the volume of my voice, elevate my pitch slightly, and enunciate sharply by hitting the hard consonants as a sort of vocal "pounding-on-the table"; but when I interrupt my speech to take a breath, the breath turns out to be a sigh that is very close to a yawn. I have unwittingly revealed that I am actually bored with what I am saying (and probably with you as well).

In such instances, it will be the quality of my voice which will communicate my true meaning and, as with physical gestures, it is because these sounds have their source in the common construction of our bodies and in our evolutionary background that they are so powerfully communicative. You will remember Charles Darwin's explanation of physical gesture as a vestige of animal behavior; he also believed that many vocal gestures were symbolic of general bodily functions, as explained here by Robert Breen:

> Darwin pointed to the primitive practice of children who expressed their dislike for someone or something by sticking out their tongues and making a sound something like a bleating sheep. Sticking out the tongue was for Darwin a primitive reflex of vomiting or rejecting something distasteful; so, too, was the sound, which got its peculiar

vocal quality from the extremely open throat through which it came. The open throat was, of course, a feature of the regurgitation, or vomiting, reflex. It is interesting that the civilized adult will show his contempt or distaste in much the same fashion, though much repressed. We are all familiar with the tone of voice which we recognize as "superior" or "contemptuous" because it has that "open throat" quality.[4]

Think back to the hostess/guest scene in the previous lesson; as the hostess greeted the overdue guest, she "*smiled a close-toothed smile.*" The quality of voice that would go with this gesture has the sound of biting, and although she is saying, "Oh! We were afraid you weren't coming; but good," her gesture and tone of voice is expressing the subtext "I'm so furious with you for being late I wish I could bite you!"

## USING YOUR OWN VOICE

We see in all this that the voice is a tremendously personal thing. In fact, the word *personality* comes from the root *per sona*, meaning "through sound." Your voice travels from your deepest center on its way toward the outer world, and it carries with it the qualities of your "inner world." The act of speaking literally *turns you inside out.*

This is true when your voice is allowed to function in its normal, undistorted way. But sometimes actors choose to adopt an artificialized voice for the sake of "creating a character" or "playing age" or—especially with Shakespeare—"being poetic." If you do this, your voice will no longer be authentically personal. In a very real sense, because your voice is not really present, you are not really there.

Remember, your aim is to put yourself into the place of the character, and you make that journey first and most actively by saying what the character says. If you do not say it with your own voice—if *you are not there*—you will be cut off from this fundamental point of entry into the character. While it is true that your voice may undergo some degree of transformation in the course of working on a role, this transformation must be the result of other, deeper changes that cannot be replaced by vocal fakery.

### Exercise 26:
### Using Your Own Voice

Select a speech from a play by a character who is quite "different" from you, or whose way of speaking is quite different from your own.

Standing before the group, read this speech in your own voice;

become aware of any urge to alter your voice in order to "perform" and simply release any such impulse. Don't try to do anything; simply *allow* yourself to speak the character's words in your own voice.

Of course, if you intend to act professionally you will need to expand the range and responsiveness of your vocal instrument, but no matter how much you may work on your voice you will always do so with an aim to perfecting its own natural qualities. You will do this by becoming aware of good vocal technique and relearning any bad habits you have developed. It is a slow and gentle process that must be pursued with the guidance of a qualified teacher.

## SPEECH

Humankind was once described as "the animal who talks." Speech is an amazing capacity: It is based on the ability to *symbolize* and to agree with others that a certain sound has a certain meaning even in the absence of any tangible thing to which the sound refers. (Nowadays we are examining the possibility that animals such as whales, dolphins, and chimpanzees are also capable of symbolic thought.)

Philosopher Ernst Cassirer, when theorizing about how the capacity for speech develops in us, observed that at first the sounds we make are part of feelings like hunger, pain, or joy, not in the sense that we are trying to express these feelings to others, but rather that the sounds are part of the feelings themselves:

> When we seek to follow language back to its earliest beginnings, it seems to be not merely a representative sign for ideas, but also an emotional sign for sensuous drives and stimuli. The ancients knew this derivation of language from emotion from the pathos of sensation, pleasure, and pain...it is to this final source which is common to man and beast and hence truly "natural" that we must return, in order to understand the origin of language.[5]

Speech, then, begins with our most fundamental experience of pleasure and pain, though at this stage it is only nonverbal sound, a kind of vocal gesture. In this earliest stage of development, the baby explores the world by grabbing it and literally "taking it in," usually into its mouth. Later, the baby notices that making a certain sound makes Mommy appear, or causes food to be given. It is at this point that the baby notices that *the voice can reach farther than the hand;* it realizes that it can affect the world by producing certain sounds, and speech is born.

Viewed in this way, speech is *a special kind of doing*; it is the most specific way in which we send our energies into the world in our effort to satisfy our needs.

This is a particularly useful view of speech for the actor. In creating a play, the writer develops the vision of a dramatic action involving a total human situation, then channels the full force of this vision into the relatively few words of the dialogue. Unlike the more descriptive and narrative functions of prose, the primary function of good dramatic language is *to transmit action*. Remember: Dramatic speech is *a form of doing*.

## THE PROCESS OF VERBALIZATION

In our technological world, speech has become primarily a means for the communication of information. But for the actor, speech must retain the emotive and active qualities we have been describing. Think of speech as *a physical process whereby feelings, needs, and thoughts find their expression in muscular activity that produces articulated sound*. As such, speech is a special type of active gesture intended to produce a real effect on the world.

As you form your thoughts into the physical activity called speech, you make a great many choices that are expressive of your feelings, needs, values, background, and personality. In this way, your process of verbalization expresses the kind of person you are (character) and the way in which you try to cope with your world (action).

Your character's speech begins in some felt need or reaction; as the words are chosen and are shaped into phrases and sentences, the character is constantly making conscious and—more often—unconscious choices about emphasis, word choice, and so on. These choices reflect what is really important to them and how they feel about it.

It is this living quality of speech *coming to be for the first time* that you must relive in order to enter fully into your character. If you deliver your lines merely as memorized words, you deprive yourself of the transformational power of participating actively in your character's thought processes.

Doing this does not require halting speech, long pauses, or muttering and mumbling that are too often used as easy substitutes for an honest participation in the character's thought processes. Your primary responsibility toward speech on the stage is to re-create your character's living process of verbalization in a way consistent with the life and function of your character and the style of the play. The script is both your starting point and your final judge; it is a finished verbal product that you take apart in rehearsal in order to rediscover the process of its creation; then, by embodying this process in your performance, you arrive once again at a living expression of the text.

### Exercise 27:
### The Process of Verbalization

Choose a short speech (perhaps only a few lines) and, after memorizing it thoroughly, go through it so as to experience the process of verbalization.

A. Begin with movement and sound rooted in the needs and feelings that lie beneath the words, but without the words themselves.

B. Next, allow the words of the speech to evolve gradually out of your movement, like a picture coming into focus. Do this with each phrase or sentence, working from the germinal thought and letting the words come from the need to communicate the idea.

Does a sense of character begin to emerge as you understand the choices that are being made during the process of verbalization? The playwright's choice of the words your character speaks reflects both the psychology and physiology of that character. Your ability to revitalize the process of word choice is crucial to your understanding and creation of the character. This is why some schools of acting encourage you to "just say the words," since "saying the words" in the most complete sense involves a total expression of the mind and body of the speaker.

To sum up, we can say that playwrights write not for the eye but for the human voice; the human voice is deeply involved in the body's musculature; the body's musculature is deeply involved in emotional life and thought. Through this psychophysical network, the playwright's words and implied actions provide a direct route to a fully living, vivid, and appropriate stage experience that will fill your performance with the richness of life.

### SUMMARY OF LESSON SIX

Vocal gesture is instinctive and universal in appeal. Nonverbal sounds may be the source from which our spoken language evolved.

Your voice is an "overlaid function," a sort of double duty performed by organs and muscles that evolved originally for other, more basic activities: The network of muscles that produce the voice is so far reaching that it involves the entire body.

In life, the words we speak carry the information we wish to impart, while our attitude about that information is usually carried by our tone of voice. There are also *unconscious* ways in which the voice communicates attitudes which the situation forces us to hide. You already recognize such "hidden" meanings as *subtext*.

The word *personality* comes from the root *per sona*, meaning "through sound." The act of speaking literally *turns you inside out*.

You make the journey into the character's mind first and most actively by saying what the character says. If you do not say it with your own voice, you will be cut off from this fundamental point of entry into the character.

Speech begins when the baby notices that *the voice can reach farther than the hand*. Viewed in this way, speech is *a special kind of doing*; it is the most specific way in which we send our energies into the world in our effort to satisfy our needs. On stage, especially, speech is *a form of doing*.

Think of speech as *a physical process* whereby feelings, needs, and thoughts find their expression in muscular activity that produces articulated sound.

Speech begins in some felt need or reaction; as the words are chosen and are shaped into phrases and sentences, the character is constantly making conscious and—more often—unconscious choices that reflect what is really important to the character and how he or she feels about it.

The playwright's choice of the words your character speaks reflects both the psychology and physiology of that character. Your ability to revitalize the process of word choice is crucial to your understanding and creation of the character.

To sum up, we can say that playwrights write not for the eye but for the human voice; the human voice is deeply involved in the body's musculature; the body's musculature is deeply involved in emotional life and thought.

# Lesson Seven

## Working with Others

All drama involves the interaction of people with one another, so it can be properly performed only by a team of actors working together. During training, your personal skills will receive most of your attention, and indeed a team depends on the individual strength of every member; but no matter how strong your individual technique becomes, you must also develop the skill of working effectively within the creative ensemble.

The foundation of this collaborative skill is the realization that you are, by your very nature, connected to your world and all who inhabit it. Your sense of a separate "I" bounded by the physical body is a limited understanding of your participation in the realm of nature. Your ideas of an "inner" and an "outer" world are only different modes of perception, different attitudes toward experience; the world is one world, which we merely experience as "inner" and "outer." As in so much of your work so far, your breath will be the starting point in developing this realization. As Mary Caroline Richards points out in her book *Centering*:

> The innerness of the so-called outer world is nowhere so evident as in the life of our body. The air we breathe one moment will be breathed by someone else the next and has been breathed by someone else before. We exist as respiring, pulsating organisms within a sea of life-serving beings. As we become able to hold this more and more steadily in our consciousness, we experience relatedness at an elemental

level. We see that it is not a matter of trying to be related, but rather of living consciously into the actuality of being related. As we yield ourselves to the living presence of this relatedness, we find that life begins to possess an ease and a freedom and a naturalness that fill our hearts with joy.[1]

Take a moment to sit quietly and experience your breath in the way described here.

When you work with another actor, the two of you will literally be trading energy: You will act upon the other, the other will react and in turn act upon you, and so on. The flow of this give-and-take produces the scene as a living event. On the deepest level, this exchange of energy between you can be seen as an exchange of breath; here is an exercise to explore this relatedness.

### Exercise 28:
### Trading Breath

A. Sit facing your partner, a comfortable distance from each other. One of you begins to breathe out as the other gently begins to breathe in. The breath flows between you like warm water flowing from one vessel into another and back again.

B. As you feel energy passing with the breath you are sharing, let the breath vibrate into a tone as you exchange it, as if the two of you were sawing a log with a saw of sound.

C. When you are comfortably sharing the energy of your voices, let your vibrating breath begin to form itself into words. Speak to your partner as you give the energy of your breath. Listen as you receive your partner's breath/words; let a thought pass between you; let it be shared by you both as you share the energy of the breath. Do not be restricted to a regular rhythm; share the rhythm of your communication naturally.

You may have the experience, after some practice with this exercise, of receiving and giving energy to and from your partner on a fundamental level. Even though most dramatic scenes are based on a conflict between the characters, you and your fellow actors remain teammates working together to realize that conflict, and a deep sharing of the energy of the scene produces a more unified and rhythmic result.

In fact, when a dramatic scene is flowing as it should, there will be an unbroken cycle of shared energy passing between the actors through the chain of action and reaction that moves the scene.

Sometimes it will be expressed primarily through the words of the dialogue, sometimes as motions and gestures, sometimes as silent looking, but always the energy will flow, being given and being received. When the flow of this give-and-take, this chain of action and reaction, is broken, the scene and the characters die. As playwright August Strindberg commented a century ago:

> No form of art is as dependent as the actor's. He cannot isolate his particular contribution, show it to someone and say, "This is mine." If he does not get the support of his fellow actors, his performance will lack resonance and depth. He will be held in check and lured into wrong inflections and wrong rhythms. He won't make a good impression no matter how hard he tries. Actors must rely on each other. Occasionally one sees an exceptionally egotistic individual who "upstages" a rival, obliterates him, in order that he and he alone can be seen.
>
> That is why rapport among actors is imperative for the success of a play. I don't care whether you rank yourselves higher or lower than each other, or from side to side, or from inside out—as long as you do it together.[2]

## WEIGHT AND RELATIONSHIP

The sense of your physical center is important to your sense of relationship on stage because we tend to relate to each other from our centers. To see the truth of this, try an experiment, or imagine it in your mind's eye: Stand so that your pelvis is pointed directly at your partner; then turn your head (without turning your body) so that your face points at someone off to one side. Now, who are you "facing"? That is, with whom do you seem to have the strongest relationship, your partner or the person to one side?

Take the experiment further: Turn your face back toward your partner and speak to him or her; the person at your side interrupts by asking a question, and you turn your head to him and answer; then you turn back to the original partner and continue. Did you feel that your basic relationship with your partner was only suspended while you spoke to the person at your side, so that the side conversation was only parenthetical within the unbroken relationship with your partner?

Again, speak to your partner, but this time when the person at your side interrupts, turn your pelvis toward him or her as you speak. Do you feel that you have now established a new relationship, that the original relationship with your partner has been broken?

What we do with the actual weight of our bodies, in real life and on the stage, is the most fundamental expression of our relationships with other persons. Since the weight of the body is literally at our center, we tend to read relationships by noticing (usually unconsciously) what people are doing with their centers.

We also tend to express how we feel about someone by the way we dispose our weight either toward or away from them. Imagine yourself in the first stages of an argument that threatens to become a fight; you are confronting your opponent with your hands raised, and you appear to be ready for combat. In this situation, imagine rocking your pelvis forward, toward the opponent. Do you feel more truly ready to attack? Now rock your pelvis away from the opponent so that your center of gravity shifts backward. Do you feel on the defensive, perhaps only pretending to fight?

There is no relationship where weight is not given or taken, and there is no way for you to "fake" a relationship if you fail to involve your weight in it. Have you ever seen student actors trying to do a love scene, perhaps even an embrace, while both were actually holding their weight back? Or actors on a proscenium stage standing so "cheated out" that each is facing the audience more than they are facing each other?

Neither the actors nor the audience can have a truthful sense of the relationship if either partner fails to commit their bodily center. Observe how this is true in life as well. The commitment of the weight of the body is fundamental and may, for some of us, require practice.

### Exercise 29:
### Falling in Love

Your partner stands in a relaxed alignment, and you stand about three feet behind with one foot thrust back for stability (see Figure 13). By mutual agreement and talking to each other the whole time, your partner falls gently backward into your arms, with the body straight but not stiff or tense. You gently raise your partner back up to his or her feet.

Your partner falls only a short way at first, and then gradually farther and farther until you are catching him or her only a few feet above the floor. If your partner becomes frightened and "breaks" his or her body on the way down, or remains tense during the fall, be encouraging and reassuring.

Then reverse roles.

CAUTION: DO NOT ATTEMPT THIS EXERCISE UNLESS YOU ARE CONFIDENT OF BEING ABLE TO CATCH YOUR PARTNER: OTHERWISE SERIOUS INJURY COULD RESULT.

**FIGURE 13**   Falling.

## TEAMWORK AND COMMITMENT

The greatness of a play depends on its unity, the way all of its elements have been synthesized into a single meaningful and dramatic experience. This same unity must be a quality of a good production of that play. This can be achieved only when all the many kinds of theater artists—director, actors, designers, managers, and technicians—have aligned their efforts toward the common goal of embodying the action of the play within the performance.

When the actors, designers, and the director have worked as an ensemble in accord with the text, and the audience has likewise given of itself, there occurs one of those rare moments when true theater lives. All these human energies flow to form one energy that is greater than the sum of its parts; everyone participating in the experience receives more than each has given, and we feel ourselves truly moved beyond ourselves.

This communality is the deepest wonder of the theater, transcending the experience of film and television. It depends entirely on teamwork, and teamwork results from a sense of common purpose and respect. No member of a team needs to sacrifice individuality; rather, each member contributes to the effort of all other members because their work is flowing in the same direction toward the same goal. In this way the ensemble is not a collective in which the individual members have submerged their identity, but rather a group of *aligned* individuals in which each member finds his or her individual power enhanced by membership in the group.

Alignment of effort is achieved within the group when three conditions have been met: first, when each member is genuinely committed to the group effort; second, when each member supports the others in their particular objectives as members of the group; third, when all agree to maintain the possibility of free and open communication so that any difficulties encountered in the work can be thrashed out. Let's examine each of these points.

First, *commitment*: It is part of your responsibility as an actor to find a point of personal commitment to your own talent, to each role you play, to each play you perform, *to each ensemble of which you are a member*, and to the audience you serve through your work. Only when you have committed to your work on all these levels in a deeply personal way will you be functioning at your fullest capacity.

Second, *support for your partners*: We all have different reasons for acting, different reasons for doing particular roles; whatever our reasons, we must support each other's objectives, even if we do not share them. Remember that our *reasons* for being committed don't affect the quality of the work; it only matters that we *are* committed.

Finally, *free and open communication*: Creating theater is rarely accomplished without some tension arising between members of the ensemble. No matter how friendly and supportive we may be, we are all bound to encounter differences of opinion, conflicting needs, or problems that are simply hard to solve. All of these *problems* can become *opportunities* for creativity as long as we continue to communicate freely about them.

Commitment, support, and communication: These are the cornerstones of teamwork and are equal in importance to all your other acting skills.

### Exercise 30:
### Levitations

A. Form groups of seven or nine: One person lies flat, eyes closed, arms folded across the abdomen. The others kneel, three or four on either side, and prepare to lift the first person (see Figure 14A).

B. You all begin to breathe in unison. When your rhythm is established, *gently* and *slowly* lift the person, keeping him or her perfectly level. The sensation for the person being lifted is one of *floating* or being *levitated*.

C. Float the person up as high as the group can reach and still keep him or her level (see Figure 14B). Then turn in the direction his or her head is facing so that you can carry the person a short distance, head first, still with the sensation of floating.

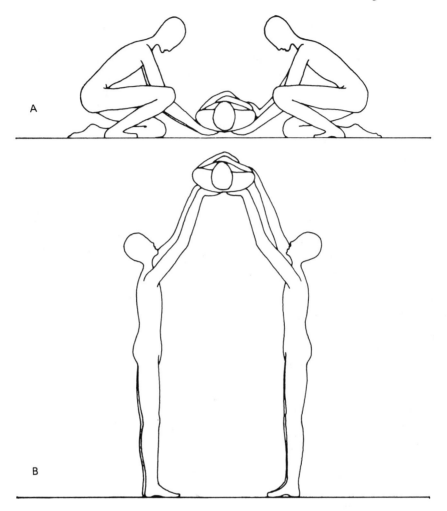

**FIGURE 14**   Levitation.

D. Slowly come to a halt and begin to float the person down, rocking him or her gently back and forth along the axis of the body, like a leaf settling to earth in a fall breeze.

E. Repeat until each member of the group has been levitated.

## TRANSACTION AND TEAMWORK

So far your sense of ensemble has been based on a general sense of trust, respect, and commitment. Of equal importance is your ability to use this foundation to enter into the give-and-take that actually produces a good scene.

It is the exchange of energy, the chain of action and reaction between the characters, that moves the play: This transacted energy flows through all the actors, and at any given moment one or another of them will be "carrying the ball." Each member of the team must be good at receiving and sending the energy of the scene, since each transaction is a link in the chain that moves the play, and a chain—as we all know—is only as strong as its weakest link. This is why Strindberg said that actors must rely on each other.

This transfer of energy from actor to actor can be described as a continual process of receiving and sending, leading and following, in which all the actors are both senders and receivers, leaders and followers simultaneously. The next three exercises will give you the experience of this simultaneous leading and following.

### Exercise 31:
### Leading and Following

A. *Blind Leading.* You and your partner lightly interlace fingertips up to the first joint. Your partner closes his or her eyes, and you silently lead him or her around the room. As you gain confidence and control, begin to move faster and extend the range of your travels. Soon you can run. If your situation permits, you can even take a trip to some distant destination.

Reverse roles and repeat for the trip back.

B. *Sound Leading.* Begin as above, but when you are well under way, break physical contact and begin to lead your partner by repeating a single word that he or she follows by sound alone. Again, extend your range and speed. Run!

CAUTION: BE PREPARED TO GRAB YOUR PARTNER TO PREVENT A COLLISION.

Check yourself: As follower, did you truly commit your weight to your movement, or were you only "pretending" to move while still holding your weight cautiously back? As leader, did you truly help the blind partner to follow?

Let's continue with another exercise to explore simultaneous leading and following.

### Exercise 32:
### Mirrors

A. You and a partner decide who is "A" and who is "B." Stand facing each other; A makes slow "underwater" movements that B can mirror completely; try to keep the partnership moving in unison. The movements flow organically in a continually changing stream; avoid repeated patterns. Notice that bigger, more complete and more continual movements are easier to follow.

B. At a signal from the leader, the roles are instantly reversed without a break in the action. B is now the leader; A is the follower. Continue moving from the deep centers of your bodies; feel yourselves beginning to share a common center through your shared movement; with it comes a common breath. Vocalize the breath and continue to share this common sound, which arises organically from your movement.

C. The roles are reversed a few more times; each time the leadership role changes, the movement and sound continue without interruption.

D. At last, there is no leader; neither A nor B leads, but both follow and the partnership continues to move and make sound together. At another signal, both close their eyes for a few moments while continuing to move, then open them again. How well did you stay together?

Watch other partnerships at work: Do you see how intense and connected to each other they seem? Our listening and seeing of each other on stage should always have this kind of literal intensity; you will be leading and following each other during a scene just as much as you are in these exercises.

### Exercise 33:
### The Cookie Search

A. All stand together in a clump at the center of your space and close your eyes. Then all spin about a few times until you are disoriented.

B. Without opening your eyes, move slowly in whatever direction you are facing until you reach a wall or other obstacle. Avoid touching anyone else; feel your way with all of your nonvisual senses.

C. When you all have gone as far as you can (and still have not opened your eyes), begin to search for your partner using only the word "cookie." You must identify every person you touch before moving on, until at last you and your partner find each other.

D. When you are together, open your eyes and wait in silence for all to finish. Feel the drama of the exercise.

In this exercise you were not led, but had to find your own way toward your partner's sound. Did you feel lonely while searching for your partner and relieved when you found him or her? Don't be the kind of actor who makes his or her partners feel lonely during performance.

As you have experienced in these exercises, connectedness depends on how well you see, hear, and feel your partner. As simple as this may seem, such significant seeing and hearing are fairly rare on the stage. Some actors are only superficially aware of their teammates; they are aware instead only of what they themselves are doing, and reacting only to their premeditated picture of what they would like their partner to be doing. While such premeditated and false reactions can sometimes fool an audience, the ensemble effort and therefore the play as a whole will inevitably suffer.

Now let's put our collaborative skills to work to create a real scene.

### Exercise 34:
### Tug of War

A. Each member of the group creates a piece of pantomimic rope.

B. Standing in a single long line, each of you "attaches" your rope to those on either side, so the group creates one long rope.

C. Now separate at the center and slide down the rope until two teams are formed.

D. Have a tug of war. At no time can the rope stretch or break. Continue until one team wins.

This exercise is a splendid example of stage reality: The rope ceases to be real if *any* member of the group fails to make his or her part real and connected to the whole; more importantly, every individual actor must believe in the *whole* rope, and we must all be creating the *same* rope. That is why we say, "There are no small parts, only small actors."

We'll conclude this sequence on working together with another group exercise that is one of my favorites.

### Exercise 35:
### Group Levitation

A. Stand in one large, perfectly round circle, facing inward. Each person puts his or her arms around the waist of the person on either side, as shown in Figure 15.

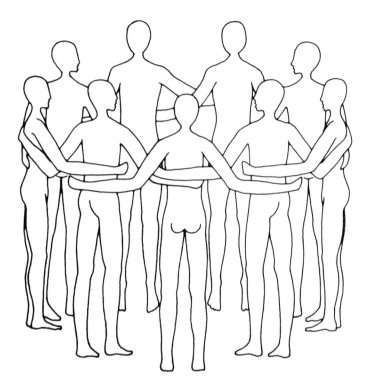

**FIGURE 15**   Group Levitation.

B. Start to breathe in unison, feeling the breath moving the rib cages of the people you are holding.

C. When a shared rhythm has been established, bend your knees slightly when exhaling; then lift the person on either side as you breathe in.

DO NOT LIFT YOURSELF; LIFT THOSE YOU ARE HOLDING AND ALLOW YOURSELF TO BE LIFTED BY THEM.

D. As you breathe out, say the word "higher," and try to lift those you are holding higher and higher. Allow the rhythm of the group to accelerate naturally until you all leave the ground.

Do you see how this exercise symbolize the way we work together? When the energy of every member of the group is aligned on the common goal, the result is greater than the sum of its parts: Everybody gets more energy back than they give.

And remember that the audience is part of the team.

## SUMMARY OF LESSON SEVEN

All drama involves the interaction of people with one another, so it can be properly performed only by a team of actors working together. You must therefore develop the skill of working effectively within the creative ensemble. The foundation of this collaborative skill is the realization that you are, by your very nature, connected to your world and all who inhabit it.

When a dramatic scene is flowing as it should, there will be an unbroken cycle of shared energy passing between the actors. When the flow of this chain of action and reaction is broken, the scene and the characters die.

What we do with the actual weight of our bodies is the most fundamental expression of our relationships with other persons. There is no relationship where weight is not given or taken.

The greatness of a play depends on its unity, and our production must have the same unity. Our energies must flow together to form one energy. This communality is the deepest wonder of the theater, transcending the experience of film and television.

The ensemble is not a collective in which the individual members have submerged their identity, but rather a group of *aligned individuals*. Alignment is achieved when three conditions have been met: first, when each member is genuinely committed to the group effort; second, when each member supports the others in their objectives; third, when there is free and open communication.

Each member of the team must be good at receiving and sending the energy of the scene, since each transaction is a link in the chain that moves the play, and a chain is only as strong as its weakest link.

When the energy of every member of the group is aligned on the common goal, the result is greater than the sum of its parts: everyone gets more energy back than they give.

And remember that the audience is part of the team.

# Lesson Eight

## The Performance Space

You have experienced how, in everyday life, you are constantly interacting with your world and are inseparable from it; you can have no meaningful sense of yourself without a heightened awareness of the environment in which you live. This environment has physical, psychological, and social aspects that profoundly influence your behavior and experience. Your sense of wholeness depends not only on internal integration of your body and mind, but also on your sense of oneness with your environment.

Unfortunately, most of us go through life largely unaware of the space we inhabit, and sometimes even feel isolated from it; this sense of physical isolation inside our "bags of skin" reflects a sense of psychological and spiritual isolation from the world in which we live that is all too common in our culture. Philosopher Alan Watts expressed it this way:

> We suffer from a hallucination, from a false and distorted sense of our own existence as living organisms. Most of us have the sensation that "I myself" is a separate center of feeling and action, living inside and bounded by the physical body—a center which "confronts" an "external" world of people and things, making contact through the senses with a universe both alien and strange. Everyday figures of speech reflect this illusion. "I came into this world," "You must face reality," "The conquest of nature." This feeling of being lonely and very temporary visitors in the universe is in flat contradiction to everything

known about man (and all other living organisms) in the sciences. We do not "come into" this world; we come out of it, as leaves from a tree. As the ocean "waves," the universe "peoples." Every individual is an expression of the whole realm of nature, a unique action of the total universe.[1]

As an actor, you have a special relationship to the environment in which you work: Your audience sees your performance in relationship to the stage space, and the nature of that space colors the experience so powerfully that it literally becomes one of the characters; it is one of your partners in creation just like your fellow actors. Your ability to share space with your fellow actors helps to create a sense of ensemble.

You will begin developing an open and responsive relationship to your world with an exploration of the physical space that you inhabit (and that inhabits you).

### Exercise 36:
### Swimming in Space

A. As a group, move freely through the space of the room. Be aware of the fluidity of your movement, of the eddies and currents in space that you are making as you move. Uncover as much of your skin as possible, and feel the resistance of the air as you move, swimming in the ocean of air.

B. Now become aware that every breath you take actually takes in space; you are not only swimming through space, but space is swimming through you; the space of the room is also in every joint and cavity of your body. Swim until you feel at one with your space, moving through it, it moving through you, and being carried along by it.

C. As you move, notice that you carry along a certain amount of space; awareness of this will help you to move smoothly, so as not to violate the momentum of your "envelope" of space.

D. Now become aware of the total space of the room and everything it contains; see how every movement of your own and every movement of every other person in the space influences the total space and everything in it.

There are certain spaces that our culture has reserved for special kinds of experience. Churches, cemeteries, operating rooms, athletic fields, and stages are a few examples. Even when empty these places have a special quality, as if we could feel the potential of the events that are to happen there.

A theater has a magic, almost "holy" quality, since it is a place where people come to believe in something together. The stage is like the "altar" of this temple, and as someone privileged to work there you should have a sense of reverence for it. In the traditional Kabuki theater of Japan, for instance, the performers spend some time each day on their knees, oiling the floor of the stage, using a bowing motion that is clearly one of devotion.

Let's take some time to explore this magic space. For the following exercises, it is important that you work on a real stage if at all possible.

### Exercise 37:
### Exploring the Stage

A. As a group, move at random throughout the stage space; attempt to influence one another's space as you move continually through the stage area. See what effect you have on others by sweeping by them, pushing space at them, and so on; notice also what effect they have on you.

B. Each of you closes your eyes and, keeping them closed, each moves very slowly throughout the stage space, trying not to touch any physical object or person, as in Figure 16. Search with your skin, hearing, and smelling for open space; crawl, stretch on tiptoe—whatever is necessary to find the most uninhabited space, but keep moving. See how, through practice, you can move with fewer and fewer collisions. Move more and more freely. Any object or person touched must be identified aloud before you move on.

## TYPES OF STAGES

The famine in ancient Thebes, a child trying to leave home, humankind confronting nothingness; anything can happen on a stage. You can make a stage seem like any place and any time; but before it becomes the world of the character, it must first of all be your world as an actor. You work in the here and now; the stage is the "here." Being fully in touch with your space provides a point of contact that anchors your work. What you create is made more real by its derivation from your physical actuality on stage.

What exactly is a stage? It is *any* space in which actors create for their audience the patterned experience called drama. Stages come

**FIGURE 16**  Exploring the Stage.

in many sizes, shapes, and types: from a circle scratched in the dirt, to a rug spread in a marketplace, to the back of a truck in a field, all the way to an elaborate building filled with high-tech machinery. Never before has such a wide variety of stage types confronted the actor.

A stage is defined by its relationship to the audience, and there are four basic types of theater configurations: *proscenium, thrust, arena,* and *environmental* (see Figure 17). Let's consider each of the basic types.

*Proscenium*   The traditional proscenium stage features an arch through which the audience sees the action. This "picture frame" evolved as a way of establishing a point of reference for settings painted in perspective (hence the word *pro-scenium,* which means "in front of the scene").

The actor on the proscenium stage must realize that the audience is limited to one side of the playing area. Standing behind the sofa during a crucial scene may not be a good idea, nor is moving

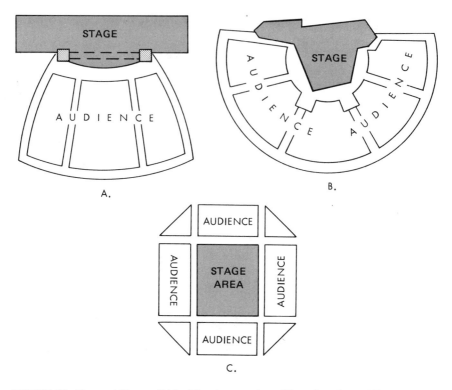

**FIGURE 17**   Types of Stages: (A) traditional proscenium; (B) modern thrust; (C) arena.

upstage so that the other actors have to turn their backs on the audience in order to speak to you (hence the dreaded charge of "upstaging"). But the possibilities of good proscenium movement are greater than you might think, and it is certainly not necessary to "cheat out" (to turn your body partly out toward the audience). This makes you look as if you are more interested in speaking to the audience than to the person on stage with you.

And don't underestimate how much acting you can do with your back; Strindberg said it was beyond his "wildest expectation" that he should ever see an actor's back during an important scene. Thus, while you may make some adjustments because of the audience's location, you must do so without destroying the internal logic of the character's environment.

***Thrust***   In the 1950s the thrust stage (so called because it "thrusts" into the midst of the audience) became very popular. It features the same stage/audience relationship as the classical and Elizabethan theaters and places the actor into close proximity with the audience, but also limits the use of scenery. For this reason, it is very much an "actor's" theater and highly "theatrical" plays, like the classics, sometimes seem more at home here than do realistic plays.

Locations on a thrust can be described in the same way as on a proscenium stage, though here you are freer to form three-dimensional patterns. There is some added responsibility to keep *open* to audience view, or at least to distribute your presence equally to all sections of the house, but the increased sense of audience contact inherent in the thrust stage makes such accommodation easy and natural.

*Arena*   The arena and other types of full-round stages stand at the opposite extreme from proscenium stages. Here the actor enters through the audience area, either down the aisles or from openings cut into the sloped audience area (called "vomitoria"). The actor's problem of keeping open to all sections of the audience is more acute here than even on a thrust stage; you always have your back to someone. In both thrust and arena, it is important to stand far enough from each other to avoid closing each other off from audience view.

The full-round offers a sense of intimacy unlike any other type of stage, and such theaters are usually quite small. For this reason, audiences tend to expect a more detailed and subtle performance here, something closer to what is required for the camera.

*Environmental*   While most stages are of the three basic types described above, we see increasingly the creation of special environments for specific productions, some of which may abandon entirely the separation of stage and audience. Here, of course, the proximity of the audience demands total commitment and attention to detail, as for film acting. For example, my production of Kafka's *The Trial* was mounted as an enormous fun house; audience groups of twelve people moved from room to room, each accompanied by an actor performing the role of the hero, Joseph K., and in each of the fifteen rooms a scene from the novel was played out. Conversations between actor and audience arose spontaneously as the groups moved through the environment. A similar environment was created for the play *Tamara*, only here the audience was free to move at will throughout a re-creation of an Italian villa in which a number of scenes were performed simultaneously, interweaving several story lines.

Whichever of these stage environments you may find yourself in, remember that the stage is only an artificially separated area within the larger theater. Your adaptation to the positioning of the audience and to the vocal demands of the shape and size of the house is essential. It is the total theatrical space that is your true working area, not the stage alone.

## DIRECTIONS ON STAGE

You will need to be able to find your way around on stage according to the traditional terms used by directors and play scripts. Though there are many different kinds of stages today, we generally use the nomenclature developed for the proscenium.

*Vertical Directions*   As we mentioned above, the proscenium stage developed as a kind of "picture frame" to establish the forced perspective of the Renaissance stage setting. To enhance this forced perspective, the stage floor was sometimes sloped or "raked" upward away from the audience. For this reason we still speak of "*down*stage" as being toward the audience and "*up*stage" as being away from the audience, since the stage floor was once actually sloped in this way. To stand "level" with another actor is for both of you to stand perpendicular (in profile) to the audience.

*Lateral Directions*   Lateral directions are determined by the actor's right as they face the audience. Thus, *stage right* is the same as the audience's left; *downstage right* means toward the audience and to the actor's right (see Figure 18).

*Turns*   Turns are described as being either *in* (toward the center of the stage, whichever side of the stage you are on) or *out* (again, *away* from center).

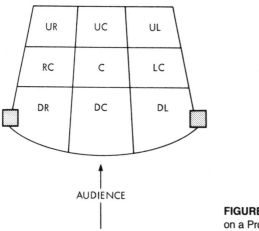

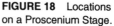

**FIGURE 18**   Locations on a Proscenium Stage.

*Crossing*   Crossing (that is, moving from one point to another) is usually not in a straight line, but in a slight arc, so that you end the cross facing more profile to the audience than you would if the cross were a straight line. A cross with an exaggerated arc is called a "circle cross" (or sometimes called a "banana").

*Positions as You Pivot*   Positions as you pivot relative to the audience are called "one-quarter," "half," and "three-quarters" depending on how far you turn from one side to the other. Thus, a director may tell you to "cheat out one-quarter," which means to pivot forty-five degrees away from center.

This system of directions must become second nature to you. Here is an exercise to help you to master it.

### Exercise 38:
### Directions on Stage

Have your partner stand in the center of the stage and stand beside him or her on the stage right side; your partner will "play director" by giving you the following directions. Keep at it until you are able to respond to each term without much conscious thought; then reverse positions.

*Go down right. / Turn out and go up right. / Turn and cheat down one-half. / Take a long cross down left, going upstage of me. / Turn in and do a circle cross up, passing on the downstage side of me and ending level with me on the right. / Cheat out one-quarter. / Now turn in one-quarter. / Go straight down and hold center. / Circle up to the right around me and exit left center.*

## BLOCKING

The patterned use of space in a stage performance is called *blocking*. Good stage blocking is much more than the creation of pleasing spatial arrangements; it must also reflect the nature of the characters, the character relationships, and most of all the underlying action of the scene. Who is dominant at this moment in the scene? What space does the character control? Who is on whose side? Who is on the attack? Who is retreating? When do they counterattack? These are the kinds of things that determine good blocking.

Blocking evolves in the course of rehearsal in a variety of ways, depending on the approach of the director (or, in the absence of a director, the actors). Some directors will plan the blocking in detail and lay it out for the actors at an early stage of rehearsal (this may be especially necessary in shows with large casts or with highly stylized material). Most directors, however, prefer the actors to provide the basic movement impulses that generate the blocking, with the director then editing the pattern as needed. Some directors do no blocking at all, waiting for the actors to find the spatial patterns that best express the action of the scene as it unfolds during the rehearsal process.

No matter how the director works, it is the actor's responsiveness to stage movement that makes the blocking truly expressive and not merely "dead" motion. Even without a director's help, you should be able to utilize your stage environment to create spatially logical patterns that express the action of your scene and your relationship to other characters.

Blocking for film and television is an even more critical matter. Here your movements are expressed not in feet but in inches. Once a shot has been established by the director and cameraperson, strips of colored tape are placed on the floor to mark the exact position of each actor's feet; if there are movements within the shot, each interim destination is marked in the same way. As you do the scene, you must "hit your marks" exactly, without looking down. It can even matter which foot your weight is on, since the composition of the shot may require your head to be in a precise location at a precise time.

The nature of film also requires that your eye movements be "blocked"; that is, you must look in precisely the right place at the right time, since the apparent location of the other character must be exactly the right distance away from the lens. If the "eye line" isn't consistent in the various shots of a scene, it can't be edited together.

Eye movements are also one of the major factors that determine when an edit will be made, so you may have to provide "a look" to a precise point at a precise time in order to motivate a cut to another character. Usually, the other actors will stand off camera in the correct locations to provide your eye lines, but not always.

As difficult as all this sounds, even this kind of critical positioning becomes second nature after a time. As you develop your performance, be it for the camera or for the stage, the blocking will emerge and be incorporated as a natural part of your total action. By concentrating on what your character is doing, you will naturally make the correct movements to the correct locations without thinking.

Here is an exercise that will enable you to experience the power of stage positioning as an expression of relationships between people and an expression of action.

**FIGURE 19** Spatial Relationship Exercises.

### Exercise 39:
### Relationship in Space

A. With a partner, select a simple relationship (for example, mother/son, husband/wife, police officer/criminal, and so on). Select also a simple message and reply with strong emotional potential (for example, "I'm not mad anymore" and "I still hate your guts").

Begin, without further planning, to move in relationship to each other around the stage. Move until a spatial relationship emerges that matches the relationship, message, and reply. Don't restrict yourselves to realistic movement; use big movements, as in Figure 19.

B. Try the same exercise with a short scene from a play.

## SUMMARY OF LESSON EIGHT

In everyday life, you are constantly interacting with your world and are inseparable from it. Your sense of wholeness depends not only on internal integration of your body and mind, but also on your sense of oneness with your environment.

As an actor, you have a special relationship to the environment in which you work; it is one of your partners in creation just like your fellow actors. Your ability to share space with your fellow actors helps to create a sense of ensemble.

A theater has a magic, almost "holy" quality, since it is a place where people come to believe in something together. You can make a stage seem like any place and any time; but before it becomes the world of the character, it must first of all be your world as an actor.

A stage is defined by its relationship to the audience, and there are four basic types of theater configurations: proscenium, thrust, arena, and environmental.

We generally use the nomenclature developed for the proscenium: We speak of "downstage" as being toward the audience and "upstage" as being away, since the stage floor was once actually sloped in this way. Lateral directions are determined by the actor's right and left as they face the audience. Turns are described as being either "in" (toward the center of the stage) or "out." Positions as you pivot are called "one-quarter," "half," and "three-quarters" depending on how far you turn.

The patterned use of space in a stage performance is called "blocking." Good stage blocking must reflect the nature of the characters, the character relationships, and most of all the underlying action of the scene.

Most directors prefer the actors to provide the basic movement impulses that generate the blocking, with the director then editing the pattern as needed. But no matter how the director works, it is the actor's responsiveness to stage movement that makes the blocking truly expressive and not merely "dead" motion.

Blocking for film and television is an even more critical matter; once a shot has been established, strips of colored tape are placed on the floor to mark the exact position of each actor's feet; you must "hit your marks" exactly, without looking down. The camera even requires that your eye movements be blocked.

# Lesson Nine

## Using the Stage

Although the sense of spatial relationship is artistically heightened on the stage, it is based on our sense of blocking in everyday life. Some years ago, I worked at a psychiatric institute helping to analyze the videotapes of family therapy sessions. It was tremendously revealing to notice where people sat in relation to others, who they faced and who they avoided, how patterns of aggression and retreat were expressed by movements and by the shifting of weight when seated.

Spend a few days watching the "blocking" of everyday life; notice how attitude, relationship, and action are expressed in the way people place themselves in a room and in relationship to each other. Record your observations in your journal.

### JUSTIFYING THE BLOCKING

Blocking is "dead" movement until it is endowed with meaning by the way you motivate it and experience it as the character.

For example, if the director suggests that you move upstage of the davenport while you say, "I don't want to hear this," that movement may be desirable for spatial or pictorial considerations: The director may, for instance, want you to move there so that focus is thrown to a doorway through which someone is about to enter (this is called "setting up" an entrance).

At first, this movement may feel awkward and unnatural to you and probably would appear that way to an audience as well. There is a marked difference between the way we move when we are responding to the external commands of another person and when we are responding to an internal need of our own. The audience will unconsciously sense that difference when you move to the sofa; in acting terminology, you have not yet *justified* the cross.

Your task now is to *justify* the movement *as a believable action performed by your character at this particular moment in the scene out of a real need*, and then to feel that need *for yourself* within the reality of the scene. You might, in this example, find that your character needs to protect himself or herself from what the other person is saying at this moment, and so goes to "hide" behind the sofa.

By justifying your movement and your spatial relationship to the setting and the other actors in this way, your blocking comes to life as believable movement. You will also find that justified blocking is easy to remember; because it has become a natural expression of your character's action at a particular moment, you need only concentrate on what your character is doing and the blocking will "happen on its own."

By the way, everything we have said about blocking in this regard is also true of your lines; you must justify dialogue by finding the inner need and action that cause your character to say what they say. Once justified, lines become easy to remember. (One of my actors once warned me, "Be patient; I have to learn the action before I can learn the lines.")

You will also find that the *timing* of lines and crosses makes a critical difference in the process of justifying a line or a cross. Deciding whether you should say "I don't want to hear this" before, during, or after the move can change the psychological meaning of the line; it can feel right one way and quite wrong another.

All these decisions are usually made by trial and error, and that is one of the main functions of rehearsal. As you gain experience, your ability to justify movement or dialogue, or to determine the timing of a move or line, will eventually become almost intuitive and almost instantaneous. For now, here is an exercise to explore these matters.

### Exercise 40:
### A Blocking Scene

Here again is the blocking pattern you learned in Exercise 38, Directions on Stage. This time, we are adding dialogue; the blocking appears below as stage directions.

Your partner will remain at center stage throughout this scene, though he or she may turn to face you as you move.

YOU: I've had enough of this. (*Go down right*)
PARTNER: I'm really sorry.
YOU: (*Turn out and go up right as you say*) That's what you said the last time.
PARTNER: This time I really mean it.
YOU: (*Stop, turn, and cheat down one-half*) I'm not falling for it this time. (*Take a long, slow cross down left, going upstage of partner, as you say*) Every time this happens, I end up taking the blame, but not this time. (*Turn in and do a circle cross up, passing on the downstage side of partner and ending level with partner on the right.*) This time, you are going to have to take your share of the responsibility! (*Cheat out one-quarter*) And don't look at me like that. (*Turn in one-quarter*) I know you think I'll probably give in eventually. (*Go straight down and hold center and speak to audience*) And you know, I probably will. (*Circle up to the right around partner and stop at left center, turning to partner*) But at least not for a while! (*Turn away and exit*)

Justify these movements by entering into the situation: Feel what the relationship might be.

Experiment with the timing of crosses and lines: Should a particular line come before, during, or after the cross? Regardless of my suggestions, find the timing that works best for you.

## THE GROUNDPLAN AND SETTING

The performance environment has two main aspects: the *spatial*, dealing with the size, configuration and other objective properties of the set, and the *psychological*, dealing with the ways in which the setting expresses a time, place, and values that affect the behavior and thought of the characters.

The environment in which the play occurs is tremendously important, affecting the action of the play profoundly. It has been determined by the playwright as part of the given circumstances of the play (these will be studied in Part Two); these environmental properties are then realized with great care by your director and the various designers.

The shaping of the stage space and the placement of entrances are decisions made with particular care by the director and scenic designer; we call this the creation of the *groundplan*, and it establishes much that influences the blocking. When directors and designers discuss groundplan and setting, for instance, they often pay special attention to territorial considerations: To whom does the space belong? Whose taste does it reflect? Are there areas within it which belong to certain persons (like Archie Bunker's chair)? Do the entrances and exits reflect status or relationship (for example, strangers use the front door, while family and friends always come in through the kitchen)?

When the groundplan has been correctly established, you will find that your character moves within it naturally as the action unfolds; the room itself will provide the reason for moving here or there as different needs are felt. For this reason, some directors say that "the groundplan really blocks the show."

Remember the hostess/guest scene: Do you see how the prolonged encounter at the door, the guest's unwillingness to cross the threshold and enter the hostess's territory, expressed the situation? Once inside, the guest refused to surrender his coat as a symbol that he was only a temporary visitor, that he "didn't belong." How would you imagine him moving in that room? How would he sit in a chair? Where would he sit? How would he eat?

## THE GROUNDPLAN IN REHEARSAL

Usually, the scenic design has been completed before rehearsals begin. As soon as you have read the play enough to have a sense of the action, and as you are beginning to learn your lines, you will put the show "up on its feet." At this point, the groundplan will be taped out on the floor of the rehearsal hall, and a picture or model of the set will usually be shown to you.

It is important that you be able to visualize the space as it will eventually look and be able to work within it with this sense early on, so you are eventually ready to move onto the real set with a minimum of disruption. Above all, allow the choices of setting that the author, your director, and your designers have made to contribute to your creative process.

While all aspects of the physical set, costumes, and props—the period, decor, color, and so forth—are usually to be determined by the director and the various designers, only *you*, the actor, can endow the space with life by justifying every aspect of it. No amount of scenery, costuming, or lighting can compensate for your failure to "live" in the character's world. Remember: An elaborate production without skillful actors can feel like a dead museum tableau, while a skillful actor can create a whole world on an empty stage.

In Part Two you will learn to identify those aspects of the character's world, as created by the playwright, that are most influential on the action of the play; for now, notice how the psychological implications of an environment may influence the events that occur within it.

### Exercise 41:
### The Psychological Space

Repeat your blocking scene from the previous exercise. Place the scene in each of the following situations; experience how each influences the relationship and the action.

1. You are in your bedroom at 3 A.M.
2. You are in your partner's office at 10 A.M.
3. You are in a public library on a cold winter day.
4. You are in a bar on a sweltering and rowdy Saturday night.

## THE SCALE OF PERFORMANCE

The type and size of the performance space require a fundamental adaptation in the size or scale of the performance. Adjusting the scale of performance is a matter of increasing or decreasing its size without distorting the content, just as you might raise or lower the contrast or color level on a television set without changing the content of the picture.

For example, an intimate scene can be played in a large theater by making an overall increase in its size and volume, as long as the behavior and attitudes of the characters continue to conform to the demands of intimacy in all other respects. The members of your audience accept the necessity of the adjustment and by convention will reinterpret the scene in their own minds to compensate for it.

In the live theater, the problem of scale is usually a matter of this sort of enlargement. For certain intimate spaces, however, such as a small full-round stage or an environmental production, you may need to *reduce* scale in order to focus on the minute details of physical and vocal behavior.

The most extreme instance of small-scale work is acting for the camera. Because of its closeness, the camera lens tends literally *to record your thought;* it is usually "too much" for the camera if you do anything more than *think* your way through a scene and allow the rest of your behavior to remain as it would be in life; some actors actually have to suppress their real-life behavior for the camera. Many of the actors who act both on stage and for the camera report the importance of learning to "do nothing" for the camera.

Since small details of behavior are usually beyond the bounds of conscious control, the completeness of your inner work and the intensity of your concentration are at a premium before the camera or in intimate theatrical situations. In general, we can say that *as the external scale of a scene decreases, the level of inner dynamic must increase.*

Scale is determined not only by the size and the distance of the audience, but also by the style of the material being performed. Broad comedy and especially farce, for instance, depend on a size, energy, and tempo of performance that is heightened beyond the limits of everyday behavior; on the other hand, the comedic naturalism of Chekhov places behavior "under the microscope" of a nearly scientific scrutiny, and great meaning is attached to even the tiniest of details. A more filmic approach is needed here, and indeed Chekhov translates to film far more easily than does Moliere.

Your ability to adjust the scale of your performance to fit the needs of your stage and the style of the play is innate: We regularly adapt the size of our behavior to fit different contexts. This automatic and usually unconscious life process is also the way you will adjust scale in performance, except that the extremes of largeness or smallness are often far greater when acting than in everyday life.

Especially when doing larger forms of performance, it will be important that you do not judge the scale of your performance according to your everyday kinetic sense. I have sometimes videotaped performances requiring large scale (such as an outdoor Shakespeare festival), and when the actors see themselves they invariably say, "I thought I was moving more than that!" While they had increased the scale of their movement beyond that of everyday life by perhaps 25 percent, so it felt like quite a stretch, an extension of 50 percent or more was actually needed.

### Exercise 42:
### Changing Scale

Repeat again the blocking scene, playing it in each of the following situations, making the adjustment of scale required for each. It will help enormously if you can actually move into physical spaces that are roughly the right size for each.

1. You are being filmed in an extremely close two-shot, so that you move around your partner as required by the blocking pattern with your faces never more than a foot apart.
2. You are in a small full-round theater at true-to-life size.
3. You are in a large thrust theater.
4. You are in an enormous proscenium theater.

In each situation, keep the quality of the scene as unchanged as possible.


## THE AUDIENCE AS ENVIRONMENT

When you perform, you join a community dedicated to experiencing the insights and aliveness offered by the drama. You, your fellow actors, and the audience all work together to achieve this experience, and you each have your own task to perform. Sometimes as actors we forget this, and we think our sole job is to please our audience, to "play to" them, and to show them what our character is feeling and thinking. This kind of illustrative acting falsifies the character's reality: It says, "Look at me. I'll show you what my character is doing, thinking, feeling." We call this kind of acting *indicating*.

Your job is not to *show* your audience anything; it is simply to *do* what your character does as completely and accurately as you can to fulfill your character's dramatic purpose within the play as a whole.

Your audience's response is certainly important, and you shape your performance with a desire to make the performance accessible to them; but when you are actually performing, your immediate concentration is on what you, as the character, are doing, *not* on the audience's response to it. Your character's task is the foreground of your awareness, and your audience is the background against which you work.

Think of the audience's presence as part of your stage environment. Accept the presence of the audience just as you accept the presence of your fellow actors: Even though the audience is not part of your character's world, and therefore cannot be acknowledged on that level, you should have an underlying sense that the other actors and the members of the audience are all your teammates. You do not "play to" your audience any more than you "play to" your fellow actors; you play "with" the audience. Your attitude is to invite the audience to join you in creating the experience of the play; the experience cannot be complete without the audience.

## SUMMARY OF LESSON NINE

Blocking is "dead" movement until you *justify* it as a believable action performed by your character out of a real need. Justified blocking (and dialogue) is easy to remember because it has become a natural expression of your character's action.

The timing of lines and crosses makes a critical difference in the process of justification. These decisions are best made by trial and error in rehearsal.

The shape of the environment in which the play occurs is the *groundplan*. When the groundplan has been correctly established, the room itself will provide the reason for moving here or there; some directors say that "the groundplan really blocks the show."

The groundplan will be taped out on the floor of the rehearsal hall; learn to visualize the space as it will eventually look. Only you can endow the space with life by justifying it; an elaborate production without skillful actors can feel like a dead museum tableau, while a skillful actor can create a whole world on an empty stage.

The type and size of the performance space require an adaptation in the scale of the performance, increasing or decreasing its size without distorting the content. The members of your audience accept the necessity of the adjustment and by convention will reinterpret the scene in their own minds.

The most extreme instance of small-scale work is acting for the camera. Because of its closeness, the camera lens tends literally to record your thought. Many actors report the importance of learning to "do nothing" for the camera on the outside, though as the external scale of a scene decreases, the level of inner dynamic must increase.

Scale is determined not only by the size and distance of the audience, but also by the style of the material being performed; do not judge the scale of your performance according to your everyday kinetic sense.

When you perform, you join a community; you, your fellow actors, and the audience all work together. We may forget this, and think our sole job is to please our audience, to "play to" them, and to show them what our character is feeling and thinking; this is called *indicating*. Instead of acting *for* the audience, you act *with* them; your immediate concentration is on what you, as the character, are doing, *not* on the audience's response to it. Your character's task is the foreground of your awareness, and your audience is the background against which you work.

## SUMMARY OF PART ONE: TECHNIQUE

This completes our brief survey of the skills you will use as an actor. For a serious professional, the material we have covered in these lessons represents the beginnings of a life's work. Advanced training, especially in voice, speech, and movement, goes far beyond what has been suggested here and will continue to challenge and benefit you for the rest of your acting life. If you want to pursue professional life, do whatever you can to seek out such training.

Also seek out opportunities to explore related skills such as mime, singing, dancing, clowning, combat, martial arts, tumbling, and meditation. Each can contribute in its way to your arsenal of acting techniques.

Technique, as Ted Danson said in his Preface to this book, is the key. It is the means whereby you are able to embody your conception; it *empowers* you. The word "craft," remember, comes from the German word for "power."

Moreover, the study of technique is itself a form of psychological and spiritual discipline. As you build your craft, your art and your spirit expand. As playwright David Mamet put it:

> This is what can and must be passed from one generation to the next. Technique—a knowledge of how to translate inchoate desire into clean action—into action capable of communicating itself to the audience.
>
> This technique, this care, this love of precision, of cleanliness, this love of the theatre, is the best way, for it is love of the *audience*—of that which *unites* the actor and the house; a desire to share something which they know to be true.[1]

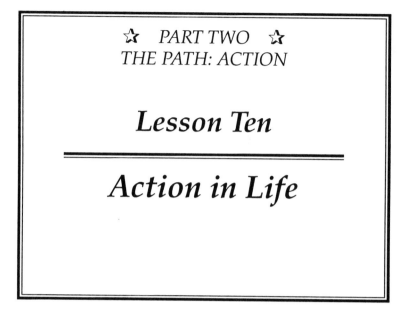

☆ PART TWO ☆
THE PATH: ACTION

Lesson Ten

Action in Life

In Part One you prepared yourself as the "ground" in which the art of acting is to grow. The seed you will sow in Part Two, the "path" that unlocks your power as an actor, is the concept and technique of *action*. First, however, we must clear up a common confusion about this term, since it is often used in at least two different ways.

Writing over two thousand years ago, the philosopher Aristotle was the first to describe how plays work. He used the term "dramatic action" to describe the underlying energy that drives a play. For instance, Aristotle might have said that the dramatic action driving Tennessee Williams's *Glass Menagerie* is the struggle between Tom's sense of obligation to his family as the "man of the house" and his need to live his own life. The events of the play are caused by this underlying conflict between these opposing forces. This action is "universal" because it involves a conflict all of us experience as we grow up and leave home.

It is this Aristotelian sense of dramatic action that we mean when we speak of "the action of the play" or "the action in this scene."

Early in this century, however, the term "action" began to be used in a different sense when referring to the acting process. The great Russian director Constantin Stanislavski was dissatisfied with the bravura acting style of his time. He felt that too often the actor's display of emotion and technique became an end in itself and overshadowed the values of the play. He created a new system of acting aimed at economy, greater psychological truthfulness, and above all respect for the ideas of the play.

He based his system on the idea that everything an actor does as the character has to be justified by the character's internal need. As Stanislavski said:

> There are no physical actions divorced from some desire, some effort in some direction, some objective....Everything that happens on the stage has a definite purpose.[1]

According to this principle, everything the actor does when in character should grow directly out of the needs of that character. As we said in the last lesson, it must be *justified*. The actor can no longer "show off" his or her skills for their own sake and is obligated to perform in an economical, purposeful way that serves the meaning of the play.

In Stanislavski's terms, the characters' needs and desires cause them to do something (which he called their *action*) in an effort to achieve a desired goal (which he called their *objective*, though some schools of acting use the terms *intention* or *task* to mean the same thing). In other words, *need* causes *action* directed toward an *objective*.

Looked at in this way, your job is to put yourself into the character's circumstances, experience the character's needs, experience the objectives the character chooses in hope of satisfying those needs, then do the things the character does in an attempt to achieve those objectives.

It is this Stanislavskian sense of action as *a purposeful doing directed toward a specific objective* that we will use throughout this book.

### Exercise 43:
### The Meaning of "Action"

A. With your fellow students, or in your journal, consider several plays you have read: How would you describe the dramatic action of these plays in the Aristotelian sense? Notice that action is deeper than plot; it is the energy causing the events of the plot to happen.

B. Pick a character from a scene in this same play. Discuss what the character wants in the scene, and how the character's behavior reflects this need. This is action in the Stanislavskian sense.

## ACTION IN LIFE

We began in the very first lesson by saying that you are already an actor. You "act" when you adapt your behavior to circumstances in order to get what you want or need. When what you need is important enough, it commands your whole attention.

We often see people in this condition of total commitment: an athlete executing a difficult play, people arguing a deeply felt issue, a student studying for a big test, lovers wooing. All these people have one thing in common: They have a *personally significant objective* and as a result they are totally focused on what they are doing. The more important the objective, the more urgent the action and complete the focus, and the more unselfconscious and committed the person becomes.

In acting terms, we say that someone who is doing something with this kind of total commitment is *in action*. Watching people in action is an invigorating experience; they seem so "alive" that we feel more alive as we watch them, even if their action is extremely simple.

For example, a Canadian mime I once saw began his performance in a striking way: The first spectators to arrive found him sitting alone on the stage, applying his white-face makeup. He worked simply and without the slightest embellishment, but his concentration and involvement were so complete that the spectators quickly became engrossed in watching him. As more spectators arrived, they too fell silent and watched in rapt attention. As the hall filled, the intensity of the experience grew, as if the spectators were adding their energy and attention to his, and indeed they were. When at last he finished, many minutes after the theater was full, there was a tremendous ovation. The bond with the audience that his simple but total action had created was unbreakable for the rest of the evening; we felt that we had come to *know* him.

Indeed, people reveal a great deal about themselves when they are in action, perhaps more than at any other time. As we say, *actions speak louder than words*. When people are in action, they are so busy *doing* that they have no energy or awareness left for deception. As a result, we judge someone who is in action as being authentic and believable.

All these are powerful reasons why being in action, *being fully focused on a personally significant objective*, is the best state for you as an actor. Through this focus, you may achieve unselfconsciousness, command of your audience's attention, and believability.

The experience of watching someone in action becomes even

more exciting when we add conditions that produce suspense, like an unresolved issue with the outcome in doubt, a deadline or some other source of urgency. These are the essential elements of drama: *a character pursuing a personally significant objective in an urgent situation with an unknown outcome.* These are the situations that we experience as being the most dramatic in life, as well as on the stage or screen.

You have been in action many times in your life; these experiences can be a foundation for developing the same kind of heightened commitment on stage, though your stage work must be artistically intensified and purified. Think back: In your life you have had experiences during which you were totally "tuned in" to something you were doing, so engrossed in your activity that you became totally unselfconscious, oblivious of passing time or of outside distractions.

### Exercise 44:
### Action in Real Life

A. For the next few days, notice which people attract your attention: What are they doing? How do they feel about it? What makes them interesting? Notice especially the people in those situations we think of as highly "dramatic": athletes at crucial moments, people in danger, people in the grip of deeply held beliefs, and so on. Record some of these in your journal; use your journal the way painters use a sketchbook to record things that may be useful in later creations.

B. Think about those times when *you* have been in action. Select one such time and relive it in your imagination. What made it possible for you to achieve this level of complete commitment and focus? Record these conditions in your journal.

## INDICATING IN LIFE AND ON STAGE

While it is true that we all "act" in everyday life, it is not true that we always act *well*: Sometimes our performance is judged to be "insincere" or "unbelievable."

How do we judge the believability of a performance? Social psychologist Erving Goffman points out that our role-playing behavior always sends two kinds of messages: the information we *give* (the impression we are trying to make) and the information we *give off* (the unconscious things we do that reveal how we really feel). In everyday life we intuitively read the information "given off" by watching for traces of unconscious behavior such as "body language" and tell-tale qualities of the voice; we then unconsciously compare this information with the message being purposely given. When the two are consistent, we judge the performance as believable; but when there are inconsistencies, we feel that the person is faking.

For example, if I am trying to convince you that I am extremely interested in what you are saying, but you catch me glancing over your shoulder at the clock, your intuitive "sincerity alarm" goes off. On the stage, I have seen actors glance at the director or audience for approval, or "break" into laughter when the character shouldn't be laughing. Such behaviors that are *inconsistent with the character's reality* make it impossible to believe in the performance.

In life and on stage, the only way to create a believable illusion is by your believing in the illusion completely, at least on one level of your consciousness (as we said, there is another level on which artistic choice continues to function). In this way, your unconscious behavior can be consistent with the conscious image you are creating. Every successful salesperson learns this; it was also the idea behind Stanislavski's system of acting.

Beside inconsistent behavior, there is another symptom of insincerity that we have all learned to recognize, and that is *overeffort*. When someone is trying too hard, being too jolly, too earnest, too lovable, we tend to judge that person as insincere. Acting students commonly do too much on stage: In addition to (or instead of) doing what their character is doing, they are also trying to *show* us how the character feels, or what kind of a character they are. Their extra effort is saying something like, "Hey, look at how angry I am" or "Look at what a victim I am."

In real life we call this "faking" or "grandstanding"; on stage we call it *indicating*. You are indicating when you are *showing* us something about your character instead of simply *doing* what the character does.

Actors indicate for various reasons: because it is a way of earning our attention (remember that sense of unworthiness we uncovered in Part One), because it is a way of maintaining control over the performance instead of surrendering to the action, or simply because it "feels" like their mistaken notion of acting.

If you can learn to recognize indicating and avoid it by committing to a specific action, you will find that your action will generate and express all the emotion and character needed. The essence of good acting is *to do what the character does completely and with the precise qualities required, but without adding anything superfluous.*

**Exercise 45:**
**A Simple Task**

Select a simple physical activity that requires great concentration, such as building a house of cards, or balancing a stick on your nose. Also give yourself a specific objective: You will build a card house three stories high, or you will walk all the way across the room balancing the stick. Find a way to endow this task with the kind of significance that the mime gave to his makeup.

As you perform your task, ask your audience to signal by making some sort of noise whenever they feel that you are indicating. Compare their feedback with your own sense of being in action: Did you know when you were indicating? How strong is your impulse to "do too much"?

## PUBLIC SOLITUDE AND DUAL CONSCIOUSNESS

As we have said, people who are in action are unselfconscious. For example, an athlete making a play in front of millions of spectators is aware only of the play and may "forget" the spectators entirely. This is a state of mind that Stanislavski called *public solitude*.

He discovered it when one of his acting teachers gave him a simple task: He was to go up onto the stage and count the floorboards while the teacher and the class went on with other business. Stanislavski, like most acting students, suffered from stage fright; he became tense and distracted on stage because he was overly aware of being watched. But while he was busy counting the floorboards, he felt at ease because no one was paying any attention to him, and soon he became totally engrossed in his task. When he finished, he discovered that at some point everyone had begun watching him but he had become so caught up in his task that *he had failed to notice*. (The class, by the way, found his "performance" engrossing, just as people had enjoyed watching the mime put on his makeup.)

Stanislavski realized that it was the first time he had ever been on stage without self-consciousness; the experience was liberating and exhilarating. He further realized that although his teacher had tricked him into thinking he was unobserved, it was his focus on his task, not his teacher's trick, that had truly allowed him to forget about being watched. He called this "public solitude."

From this experience, Stanislavski developed the concept of the character's objective as a "dramatic task" that, like the task of counting the floorboards, would provide a point of attention to help attain public solitude and reduce self-consciousness, while at the same time tying you to the life of your character and the world of the play. The more you think about what your character is trying to do, the more "in action" you are, the less self-conscious you will be.

### Exercise 46:
### The Simple Task as Drama

Repeat the simple task exercise, but this time give yourself a character and a dramatic situation. If your task was to build a three-story house of cards, perhaps you are a condemned man about to be executed, waiting for the governor to phone with your pardon. See if you can relax enough to allow yourself to "fall into" action while performing this task; can you experience something like public solitude?

Again, ask your audience to check you for indicating.

This is a difficult exercise. Trying to fall into action and to experience public solitude is a lot like trying to fall asleep or trying not to think about a pink elephant; the awareness caused by the effort itself makes the task impossible. Only relaxing and letting go of your self-critical left-brain thoughts will give your childlike right-brain self a chance to take over. This right-brain self is the part of you that played in puddles when you were little, created in them vast oceans, and didn't hear mom when she called you.

It is important that you understand one danger of the concept of public solitude. Many young actors tend to focus so much on the "solitude" that they begin to ignore the "public" part of the equation. Stanislavski would not have approved of you falling into some sort of trance in which you truly forgot that the audience was present: Doing so leads to sloppy technical work, which he hated above all.

This, then, is the question: Can you be completely engrossed in the action and world of your character while simultaneously making the artistic choices required to express that action in a public form worthy of your audience's attention?

This question is answered by your capacity for *dual consciousness*, the ability to maintain artistic choice while simultaneously becoming the character. As the young actor Kostya in Stanislavski's *Building a Character* put it:

> "I divided myself, as it were, into two personalities. One continued as an actor, the other was an observer. Strangely enough this duality not only did not impede, it actually promoted my creative work. It encouraged and lent impetus to it."[2]

Multiple consciousness is a feature of all acting: No matter how realistic a play may be, you never entirely lose a sense of your identity as separate from the character. If you lost it, you would also lose the ability to make artistic choice.

It is a natural ability. When you were a child, the rain puddle became a vast ocean, but it didn't need to stop being a puddle: You hadn't learned yet that something isn't supposed to be two different things at once and that we aren't supposed to be in two different realities at the same time. To act, you will have to rediscover this lost ability.

## SUMMARY OF LESSON TEN

Though Aristotle defined action as the energy driving a play or scene, we use this term in Stanislavski's sense of *a purposeful doing directed toward an objective*. In life, we see people doing things to accomplish important objectives: They are totally committed, unself-conscious, expressive, and believable.

The key is to remember that *need* causes *action* directed toward an objective. When you experience your character's need as if you were in the same circumstances and commit fully to your character's action with strong focus on objective, then we say you are in action.

When you can go completely into action, you achieve *public solitude*; your focus on your task is so strong that your consciousness of being in public recedes into the background. This is one reason why you always strive to be "doing" instead of "showing," which we call *indicating*.

Your ability to be in the character's world while simultaneously attending to your actor concerns is *dual consciousness* and can be easily recaptured from your childhood playfulness.

# Lesson Eleven

## Action and Character

You now understand that much of your life is spent acting, in the sense that you do certain things in order to pursue your objectives and to present yourself to others. Much of your everyday behavior can be seen as related to this process: the way you dress, the way you carry yourself, the kind of car you drive, the kind of work you do. It is a natural and largely unconscious activity.

Your personality, your "character" in real life, has developed largely through this interaction with your world. As an infant, your physical exploration of the world was the main process; as you grew up, your relationships with your parents and eventually with larger social groups shaped you, as did the customs, taboos, and value systems you inherited from your culture. Your personality emerged from this accumulation of experiences and is continually evolving under the influence of new experience. Your personality is not static; you grow and change as your circumstances and experiences change.

Nor is your personality a single, simple state. Around the turn of the century, psychologist William James described personality as a complex structure consisting of one "I" and a number of "me's." Each of us, he said, has a repertoire of roles, or "me's," that our "I" adopts in various situations. This morning, for example, I began as Loving Father as I got my children off to school; I switched to Knowledgeable Teacher during my morning class; I then became a

Good Buddy as I talked about football with my office mates; finally, I was Experienced Director at rehearsal this evening.

Your roles as daughter, son, student, employee, friend, or lover, all call upon you to modify your behavior in different situations in order to achieve your particular objectives within those situations. If you have ever been forced to perform two different social roles at once, you know how radically different some of our "me's" can be (visits by parents to their children at school often occasion such uncomfortable situations).

According to James, your "I" is your sense of the performer who plays the various "me's" and ties them together into one multifaceted personality. As Shakespeare put it, "One man in his time plays many parts." To some degree, you determine what role you will play, but you also know that your situation—especially the other people you find yourself with—has an enormous effect on your "me."

For instance, when we are in a group, we tend to "sort ourselves out" by adopting a role in relationship to the others in the group. There are a number of roles that are natural to the psychodynamics of all groups, and we may tend to fall into one or another of them, depending on our own predeliction and the others in the group. Here is an exercise to explore this kind of role-playing.

### Exercise 47:
### The Social Rep Company

Form a group of six or fewer; choose a topic to discuss or a project for the group to plan (something the group might really care about, like a political issue or planning how to start a theater).

Below are a list of six roles. Each person in the group will play one of these roles in the group discussion; every two minutes, pass your role to the person on your left; keep the flow of conversation going as the roles are passed, and keep going until everyone has played all the roles.

1. THE CHAIRPERSON, who loves to organize the group
2. THE VICTIM, who sees any group action as potentially threatening or unpleasant
3. THE PHILOSOPHER, who loves to generalize and point out the deeper meanings of things
4. THE DERAILER, who is forever trying to change the topic as a way of controlling the group
5. THE DEBATER, who loves to argue for the sake of arguing and

doesn't really care what side of the issue he or she takes
6. THE RED CROSS NURSE, who takes care of all people who seem to need help whether they want help or not

After everyone has played all the parts, share your experiences and perceptions: Why did these "characters" behave the way they did? What did they want? How did they present themselves and how did they treat others?[1]

As you played the various roles in this exercise, you probably felt how easy it was to "become" them. Some may have been more uncomfortable or unfamiliar than others, but with practice any of them could become part of your social repertoire, a new "me" to be played by your "I."

Just so, as you work on a play, your evolving character gradually becomes a new "me" to be used for the particular purpose of rehearsing and performing that play.

Notice that your dramatic character is a "me" only for acting purposes; it in no way consumes or threatens your "I" or your other "me's." In life, if we find ourselves stuck in a particular role for a long time, it can begin to consume us. If, for example, you take a job that forces you to be subservient to a tyrannical boss, you will not only *feel* like a victim, but if you stay in that job long enough you will *become* a victim; that "me" will start to take over your "I."

In fact, one way of describing mental illness would be to say that someone whose "I" has become so rigid that he or she can no longer adapt to reality is paranoid, while someone who has lost his or her "I" altogether is schizophrenic. But the actor suffers from neither of these disorders: What the actor does is a heightened and controlled use of a perfectly natural and healthy process.

## INTERNAL AND EXTERNAL ACTION

Action is not just external activity. A jeweler about to split a valuable diamond, hammer raised, is not moving at all; yet we recognize the drama, the sense of "significant doing." This is because dramatic action is felt even *before* it has manifested itself in external activity; it lives even in the *potential* for doing. At these times, the action literally lives *inside* you.

Stanislavski spoke of internal and external action, calling these the *spiritual* and the *physical* forms of action:

> The creation of the physical life is half the work on a role because, like us, a role has two natures, physical and spiritual...a role on the stage, more than action in real life, must bring together the two lives—of

external and internal action—in mutual effort to achieve a given purpose.[2]

For Stanislavksi it was the *integration* of the internal and external actions that produced a truthful stage performance, and his system was designed to bring about this integration. Best known are his early psychological techniques (fantasy, emotional recall, and so on), which were designed to work from the internal to the external, but later in the development of his method he also worked from the external toward the internal through "the Method of Physical Actions." As he said:

> The spirit cannot but respond to the actions of the body, provided of course that these are genuine, have a purpose, and are productive....[In this way] a part acquires inner content."[3]

During the first half of our century, the British acting tradition stressed the importance of externals in the acting process, working "from the outside in"; our American tradition, on the other hand, stressed the importance of internals, working "from the inside out." For the past forty years a real effort has been made in both countries to combine these approaches. Both are essential, since each is only a different aspect of the other. As Stanislavski pointed out:

> External action acquires inner meaning and warmth from inner action, while the latter finds its expression only in physical terms.[4]

In fact, don't think of "inner" action and "outer" action as being at all separate. Picture instead a single *flow* of action: Something happens to arouse you and then lives in you; when you choose to act on this need, your energy flows outward again toward an external objective. You can't truly experience one part of this flow without experiencing the whole process: If your action consists only of unmotivated external movement and speech, it will seem hollow and lifeless. If it consists only of inner intensity, without skillful outer expression, it will seem vague and self-indulgent.

### Exercise 48:
### Internal and External Action

A. Observe yourself and others to see how action lives in both internal and external forms. What do you notice about the relationship of the two? Of the two, which is more suspenseful? Record observations in your journal.

B. Here is an experiment in inner action:

1. Select some need or desire you have felt at some time in your life: loneliness, the wish to be recognized, and so on. This will be your need.
2. Imagine another person and choose something he or she could do to help you satisfy your need. This will be your objective.
3. Next create an obstacle, either internal or external, that will stand between you and your objective. For example, you want to tell someone "I love you," but you are afraid of being rejected (internal obstacle). Or you want to tell someone "I love you," but his or her current girlfriend or boyfriend is present (external obstacle).
4. Now select an irrelevant activity (it can be pantomimed) such as bowling, preparing a dinner, playing a card game, and so on.
5. Pick a partner to play the other person; don't say what your inner need is. *Stop just before you actually accomplish your objective.* Do not try to "act out" your inner need; just do the external activity.
6. Discuss the scene: Was your internal action interesting? Did you resist the temptation to "act it out"? If you didn't act it out, was it still felt by others?

## ACTION AND CHARACTER IN REHEARSAL

In this exercise you were playing yourself; in rehearsal you will be developing that other "me" of a character in the play. The personality of this character should evolve according to the same life principles and through the same ongoing process of physical exploration and social interaction that formed your own personality in life. The rehearsal process is a condensed period of evolution of the dramatic personality according to these life principles, heightened by your artistic skill.

For this reason, your primary aim in rehearsal is to open yourself to the specific experiences of your character within his or her given circumstances *as if* they were happening to you. If you can allow yourself to experience the character's situation, needs, and actions springing from those needs, a natural process of transformation will begin: A new "me" will develop and evolve in the same way that your own personality has grown in real life. Stanislavski called this process "the magic if."

Notice that *character grows out of action.* You don't become the character first and then do things "because that's what my character would do"; instead, you allow yourself to do the things your character does, for the reasons the character does them and in the way that the character does them, and see who the actions turn you into.

Every role will suggest experiences and behaviors similar to those you already know, and you will certainly want to use these established connections; but every role will also offer the possibility of reaching out into *new* modes of experience, of extending yourself into a new state of being. You possess a vast personal potential; if you can engage your own energy in your character's actions, and open yourself to their experiences and relationships within their given circumstances, you will find yourself being naturally, effortlessly transformed.

This is the most exciting aspect of the actor's creative process.

## THE ACTING PROCESS

Though we will go on to study much more about the acting process, you now understand its essential elements. We can describe the core of the process as having five steps:

1. You put yourself into the circumstances of your character.
2. You experience the needs of the character as if they were your own.
3. You allow yourself to form the same objectives the character chooses to satisfy those needs, and to care about them as urgently as the character does.
4. You allow yourself to do the things (the action) the character does in order to try to achieve those objectives.
5. If you do all this, simply and completely, you will begin to experience a natural process of transformation (the "magic if"). A new version of yourself, a new "me," will begin to develop according to the same principles by which your personality developed in life.

These five steps lay the foundation of your work as an actor. Beyond them is a sixth step: Through your acting skills, you will select, guide, heighten, and purify this evolving self. You will constantly check it against the needs of the play, since every character was created to serve a particular purpose within the play.

Finally, you will arrive at the completed characterization, which is an extension of yourself into a new state of being. It will be a marriage between who you are now, the life of the character in the play, and who you become when you begin to live that life.

Your characterization must be the result of this process; there are no shortcuts. As your acting skill develops, you will be able to work more efficiently and effectively, but no amount of posturing, false voice, or trumped-up emotion can substitute for this natural process of transformation and artistic development.

## SUMMARY OF LESSON ELEVEN

Your personality develops as you interact with your world. Since you function within various circumstances, your personality is comprised of various "me's," and you grow and change as you encounter new circumstances and experiences.

The art of acting utilizes this natural and healthy process; your dramatic character evolves in the same way as did the various "me's" that comprise your personality. When you want something in a particular situation and do certain things to get it, your own action changes who you are; character grows naturally out of action.

Action exists as a flow of energy both inside you and outside. The internal phase of action gives meaning and believability to the external, while the external gives form and expression to the internal. The two are really different aspects of the same energy, and your character can grow both from the inside out and from the outside in.

Your job as an actor, then, is to allow yourself to fully experience the totality of your character's action. You put yourself into the character's circumstances, experience the character's needs, make the choices the character makes, then do what the character does. From this, a natural process of transformation, the "magic if," will begin. Through your artistic skill you will guide and heighten this process, working to fulfill the purpose for which the author created your character.

By following this process with complete conviction you will not only create living characters of great value in themselves, you will also help to remind your audience of their own potential aliveness. As playwright David Mamet put it:

> Each time we try to subordinate all we do to the necessity of bringing to life simply and completely the intention of the play, we give the audience an experience which enlightens and frees them: the experience of witnessing their fellow human beings saying, "Nothing will sway me, nothing will divert me, nothing will dilute my intention of achieving what I have sworn to achieve": in technical terms, "My Objective"; in general terms, my "goal," my "desire," my "responsibility."
>
> If we are true to our ideals we can help to form an ideal society—a society based on an adhering to ethical first principles—not by *preaching* about it, but by *creating* it each night in front of the audience—by showing how it works. In action.[5]

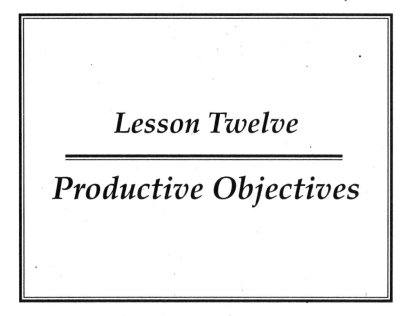

# Lesson Twelve

## Productive Objectives

Imagine a bare lightbulb burning in a room; the light it produces doesn't have much effect because it is dispersed in all directions at once. But when we put a reflector behind it and a lens in front of it, we can channel most of its light in one direction, producing a much brighter beam. We have also made the light more controllable, since the beam of our spotlight can now be colored, shaped, and focused upon a specific objective.

Like the light from the bulb, your physical and mental energies are made more effective and controllable when you find a single channel through which they may flow.

For example, a batter rehearses his stance, grip, swing, and breathing; he studies the opposing pitchers; at the plate, he takes note of the wind and the position of the fielders. As he begins to swing at a pitch, however, he ceases to be consciously aware of all this and focuses his total awareness on the ball. This single objective—to get a hit—channels all his energy into his swing, which is his action.

Having this single objective also helps the batter to synthesize all his other concerns, and all his rehearsed and intuitive skills, into a single complete action of mind and body. His swing now has *rhythm*, which unifies every aspect of his action.

For you as an actor, the "ball" is your objective, what you, as the character, want or need at any given moment (also sometimes called your intention or task). Your focus on this single objective at the moment of performance will provide your resultant action with the same kind of *rhythmic integration* achieved by the batter. It will energize your action and give it power, intensity, control, and grace.

## SPONTANEITY

Your focus on your objective will also help to keep your performance fresh and alive. What you do on stage should feel spontaneous, as if it is for the first time, no matter how many times you have done it before. To achieve this spontaneity, you must keep your awareness on your objective rather than on the mechanics of your external action, just as the batter thinks only about the ball and not about the swing. Otherwise you will just be "going through the motions," repeating the external aspects of your performance without reexperiencing the internal needs that cause the externals.

Notice that this "aliveness" does *not* mean that your performance is erratic or changeable: During the rehearsal process you gradually refine your external action until it becomes dependable, consistent, stageworthy, and *automatic*, just as the batter has rehearsed all the aspects of the swing until it can be done without thinking. Stanislavski said that "a spontaneous action is one that, through frequent repetition in rehearsal and performance, has become automatic and therefore free."[1] Because you are able to perform your action without thinking about it, your mind is free to concentrate fully on the objective and to experience what happens as if for the first time. Because you could "do it in your sleep," you are able to do it fully awake.

Notice, by the way, that a rhythmically unified action brings together both physical and mental material; it involves both body and mind. But rhythm itself lives in the muscles; thinking alone, as important as it is to give clarity, specificity, and accuracy to your work, cannot produce a living performance without the active participation of the body. For an actor, thinking and moving—mind and body—must become one.

## WANTS AND NEEDS

Your character's behavior, like your own behavior in life, is driven by both wants (desires) and needs. There are interesting—and very important—differences between wants and needs.

First, we may not always want what we need: You may *want* to become a great dancer, but you don't really *want* to spend four hours a day exercising at the barre; you do it because you *need* to.

Second, we usually think we know what we want, but we may be unconscious of our needs. In *The Glass Menagerie*, Amanda says that she *wants* her children to have independent lives, but unconsciously she *needs* them so much that she does things to keep them dependent upon her. As in this example, we usually regard needs as being stronger than wants.

In either case, characters will always feel their wants or needs as an arousal; they feel like they have to do something, even if they may not know what it is. This arousal always gives the objective an emotional aspect, whether pleasurable or painful.

So your character's behavior can be driven by a conscious want, an unconscious need, or even just a feeling of need, a vague arousal. For convenience, all three will be referred to simply as "need" from now on.

## NEEDS AND OBJECTIVES

Your character, feeling a need consciously or unconsciously, will try to do something, achieve some objective, which the character hopes will satisfy that need.

While the objective is driven by the need, it is not the same thing as the need, and the difference is important. The need is inside your character; it may have just arisen in reaction to something that has happened, or perhaps it has been there for a long time. In either case, the need will stay inside until the character consciously or unconsciously chooses to do something about it.

The longer the character waits to act upon the need, the stronger it may become. For example, Hamlet is so confused about his own wants and needs that he delays acting upon them throughout the entire play; his needs finally erupt into action in the final scene, and four people are killed in a matter of moments.

However long the need has been felt, the character cannot choose to act on it until he or she sees someone or something "out there" in the immediate circumstances that might fulfill the need. This thing in the immediate circumstance becomes the objective, and the character begins to pursue it through action.

We can sum this process up by saying that *need leads to objective, which leads to action.* You feel your character's need, you select an objective that can satisfy that need, and you do something that you think can achieve that objective.

The difference between the objective and the need driving it, then, is that the need is inside you and in the past, while your objective is outside you and in the future; your action is a kind of "bridge" that connects your inner and outer worlds, your past and future. (In Lesson Seventeen, "The Character's Mind," we will examine this process in greater detail.)

Because your need is "inside" you it is *not playable* (that is, it cannot be pursued through action). Actors sometimes make the mistake of trying to "play" a need: They try to show us how desperate Willy Loman is, or how lonely Blanche DuBois is, and the result is *indicating*, showing instead of doing. For the audience to learn something about your character in this way, by being *shown* it, is undramatic; it prevents your performance from being a living event and turns it into a lecture. We want to *experience* your character and figure out the character's needs for ourselves.

Trust that the audience will come to understand your character's inner world by observing your external doings without you needing to "show" it.

However, depending on the way your character functions in the play and on the kind of play it is, it may not be obvious from the script what your needs are; they may not even be important to the play. But they *will* be important to you in playing the part, and you will have to find out what they are and experience them *for yourself*, finding some way to feel them as strongly and as deeply as does your character. Only then can you endow the objective with dramatic significance: If the mime described earlier hadn't cared about applying his makeup, we wouldn't have either.

This is called *personalization*, and it is so important that we will devote a lesson to it later; for now here is an exercise to explore it for yourself.

### Exercise 49:
### Personalizing the Need

Pick a simple task, such as building a house of cards. Give yourself a character and situation, such as a condemned man in a cell awaiting execution. Now define a need for that character within that situation, and perform the simple task. Just allow the need to be there; do not act it out.

Find a way to enter fully into the character's need; if you find it difficult to feel the character's need for yourself, try connecting analogous personal feelings of your own to the character's situation. Again, beware of indicating.

Were you able to endow your action with the kind of significance the mime gave to his makeup while still avoiding indicating? Remember, it is not important for your audience to understand *why* the task is important, only that it *is*. Your job as an actor is to create experiences, not to explain behavior.

## DEFINING PRODUCTIVE OBJECTIVES

As you gain experience as an actor, your sense of *need leading to objective leading to action* will become a natural way of approaching a scene; it will become "intuitive," and you won't often think consciously about it. While you are learning this technique, however, it may help you to think it through by forming simple verbal descriptions of your needs, objectives, and actions, step by step through a scene.

Remember, however, that these verbal descriptions of need, objective, or action are valuable *only* insofar as they contribute to your actual experience of playing the scene. The ability to describe something (which comes from the analytical left side of the brain) is no guarantee of the ability to surrender to the playing of it (which comes from the intuitive right side of the brain), and the two often get in each other's way. This caution having been given, let's learn how to describe useful objectives.

The best objective will be important enough to compel your attention, giving you the kind of focus the batter has on the ball and helping you to be unselfconscious; it will also energize you and lead naturally to stageworthy externals that meet the demands of the play. When an objective does both these things, it is what Stanislavski called a *productive* objective.

Actors have found that objectives become more productive when they are directed toward a *single, immediate,*and *personally important goal*. Let's examine each:

1. An objective needs to be *singular* because you wish to focus your energy on one thing rather than diffuse it by trying to do two things at once. (Imagine a batter trying to hit two balls at once.) Sometimes a character in a scene may be trying to accomplish more than one thing at a time (killing two birds with one stone), or may be seeming to do one thing while actually trying to do another (subtext), but in either case your attention will be focused on one objective even though it has multiple or hidden implications.

2. An objective must be *in the immediate future*, something that can happen *right now*. The play must move forward and your energy must help propel it; *never define your character's objective in a way that*

*moves your energy into the past.* The character's needs may have come from their past, but they are aroused by the immediate circumstance and live in the present moment. Trust that the past will be carried along by your present action as you aspire to something in the immediate future. (This is why Stanislavski sometimes used the term "aspiration" when speaking of objectives.)

3. Finally, an objective must be *personally important* because it must energize you and compel your attention. Notice that it is only your attitude that determines whether an objective is important or not; you must find the importance of your character's objectives *for yourself*.

We will remember these three points as the acronym "SIP": Singular, in the Immediate future, and Personal.

Let's examine an objective from a scene to see how these principles are applied. In *Death of a Salesman*, Willy Loman wants to be a successful salesman because he has a deeper, lifelong need to be a valuable human being. But he can't be a successful salesman anymore because he's too old to drive all the way to Boston to see his clients; he keeps falling asleep at the wheel. His first boss, who was his friend, has died, and his son, Howard, has taken over the business. Willy goes to see Howard; he must get assigned to work in town.

As Willy enters, he sees Howard playing with a new recorder, and his immediate objective is *to get Howard to stop what he is doing and pay attention.* This objective is singular and in the immediate future. It is also supremely important to Willy: If he can't get Howard's attention, he won't be able to get a spot in town, he won't be able to be a successful salesman, and he won't be a valuable human being. His deepest, lifelong needs live in the present moment, giving it all the urgency of a life and death struggle. (*Please turn to Appendix A and read the scene now.*)

### Exercise 50:
### A Productive Objective

Repeat Exercise 49. This time, ask a partner to join you in a passive role: If you are the condemned man waiting for a pardon, your partner can be a guard or priest sitting with you in your cell. Form a SIP objective in your partner: perhaps you want him or her to call the governor on your behalf, since time is running out. Improvise the scene, but continue your original activity (here it was building a house of cards) as you speak to each other.

## CONNECTING WITH OTHERS

Since plays are about people doing things to each other, a good play-wright will have provided your character with needs that cause him or her to interact with the other characters. Therefore, you must understand your objectives in ways that not only energize and focus you by being SIP, but also drive your resultant action toward the other characters in the scene.

The best way to achieve this is to think of your objective as being *in* another character, to make it something you need *from that character*. The most productive kind of objective is therefore *a desired change in the other character*, a need for the character to behave or think differently.

For example, in the Willy Loman scene, your overall objective is to get a spot in town, but as you enter and find Howard busy, your immediate objective will be to get *him* to stop what he is doing and pay attention to you. Defining the objective as being "in him" helps to bring you into meaningful *transaction* with him, producing a livelier, more dramatic scene.

Here are some examples of productive objectives from other plays we have discussed, together with the need that drives them; can you identify the characters?

1. *Need*: to save the king
   *Objective*: to convince the king to hide inside the hovel
2. *Need*: to end my pain
   *Objective*: to trick Peter into picking up the knife so I can kill myself
3. *Need*: to be taken care of
   *Objective*: to make Mitch understand me so he will kiss me

Do you see how each of these conforms to the principles we have discussed?

In life, when we do something to try to change someone else's thought or behavior, we watch that person to see if what we are doing is working or not; if it's not, we try something else. This should be true on stage as well. Ask yourself, "How would I know I was achieving my objective? What changes might I see in the other character that would encourage me that my approach is working?"

This sort of *specific, observable change* is what you want to bring about in the other character. The late director Duncan Ross even encouraged his actors to think of this as "a change in the other character's eyes." In the Willy Loman scene, your first objective might be "to get Howard to stop and look at me with interest." Your full attention is on him, watching to see if your behavior is indeed producing the desired effect, or whether you might have to try a different approach.

### Exercise 51:
### Observing Objectives in Life

Watch people relating in life; see what kinds of objectives produce the most interesting interactions. Notice how people read others, and how they deal with failure and success moment by moment. Record your observations and insights in your journal.


## SUMMARY OF LESSON TWELVE

Having an objective, like the batter's focus on the ball, gives you power and control; it causes the resultant action to have rhythm and unity. While actually playing a scene, your immediate awareness will be on the objective that will trigger your well-rehearsed action, just as the batter's focus on the ball synthesizes all his rehearsed skills. By reexperiencing the objective every time you perform the action, you will keep your performance spontaneous, even though it is so well rehearsed as to be habitual.

Your character's objective is driven by his or her conscious wants, unconscious needs, or feelings of arousal. You must rediscover these needs and experience them *for yourself* as strongly as the character does.

While first learning this technique it may be useful for you to form verbal descriptions of your need, objective, and action, though eventually this process will become largely intuitive. Remember that naming something doesn't guarantee that you can play it, and sometimes gets in the way.

A productive objective energizes you and naturally generates stageworthy external action. It will also connect you to the other characters in the scene. The most productive objective is *a change we want to bring about in another character that is SIP: singular, in the immediate future, and personally important.*

# Lesson Thirteen

## Playable Actions

In the Willy Loman scene we discussed in the last lesson, you found a productive objective. As you entered you saw that the boss was busy; your single, immediate, and important task was to get his attention. It was something you wanted from him, a *change you needed to bring about in him*. The question now is, what do you *do* to achieve this objective?

This question is, of course, answered by the playwright: Willy is going to *flatter* Howard as a way of getting his attention. But you, as the actor creating Willy, must re-create this process for yourself *as if* you didn't know the answer. You must go on Willy's inner journey for yourself and find your own way to the destination provided by Arthur Miller. Only in this way can you have Willy's experience for yourself, and it is that experience that will help turn you into Willy.

Of course, although you must find the inner path for yourself, you must nonetheless arrive precisely at Miller's destination. I once directed an actor who refused to say a line that the author had given to her character. The actor claimed that "she wouldn't say that!" I responded, "Who wouldn't say that? Whoever it is, it's not the character. When you find the woman who *would* say that, *then* you'll have the character."

Your objective—what you as the character want—naturally produces an action: what you as the character *do* to try to get what you want. This is how the internal world of the character comes to be expressed in external action. A good playwright has envisioned this process, at least unconsciously, while writing. The playwright has provided external action that is *justifiable*, and it will be possible for you to "work backward" to discover an inner pathway to the given externals, which both serves you as an actor and serves the demands of the play.

## DEFINING PLAYABLE ACTIONS

We have described the qualities of productive objectives: Now we will consider how to recognize actions that flow naturally from the objective and produce stageworthy externals—what actors call *playable* actions.

Let's return to the Willy Loman scene and see how you might describe your action. You have just entered; you desperately need to get a spot in town; you see Howard playing with the recorder. At this moment, you, as Willy, want to get Howard's attention (to get him to look at you), but you want to do it in a way that will give him a positive feeling toward you. As a salesman, you instinctively appeal to something the "client" is interested in, so you flatter him by praising the recorder and the stupid recording he has made of his family (obviously, you have a strong *subtext* here).

Now let's examine three principles for describing this action, and from these principles you will understand the qualities a playable action must have.

The first principle is to include a sense of the particular *strategy* employed by the character to achieve the objective. When you choose a course of action in life, you naturally select the one that seems to offer the greatest chance for success in the given circumstances; you ask yourself, "Given what I want, what is the best way to get it in this situation, from this person? What might work?" Characters in plays do the same.

While this is usually an unconscious or "instinctive" process (what Stanislavski called an *automatic* action), we often think our strategy through (what Stanislavski called *non-automatic* action) when faced with important situations. Hamlet's famous soliloquies are all examples of this kind of conscious strategizing.

Whether your character's choice of action is conscious or unconscious, the choice will be based on what the character thinks will work within the given circumstance. We will call this aspect of action its *strategic* value, and in this sense all action is strategic.

Willy's strategic action is to *flatter* Howard; he makes this choice "automatically," out of his long experience as a salesman. In fact, what Willy is trying to do here is a classic example of "getting your foot in the door."

The second principle is to use *a simple verb phrase* in a *transitive* form—that is, a verb that involves a doing directed toward someone or something else, such as "to flatter." Avoid forms of the verb "to be," since these are intransitive verbs; they have no external object and their energy turns back upon itself, certainly not a good condition for an actor whose energies must continually flow outward into the scene. You are never interested, for example, in "being angry" or "being a victim" or "being likable"; these are not playable. Strive instead for *doing*, a transitive condition in which your energy flows toward an object that, as we have said, is usually a change in another character.

The third principle follows the second: *Include the object of the verb*, the other character, and the change you want from that character. Don't think only of the verb phrase "to flatter"; think also of the specific objective "to flatter him so he will pay attention to me."

From these principles we see that the most complete description of your action as Willy Loman at this moment is *to flatter Howard by praising the recorder (strategic action) so he will pay attention to me (objective)*.

Though you may develop this kind of complete description as part of your study of a scene, you will normally refer to only a shorthand version of it while working. The shorthand working version will usually consist only of your immediate external action, which here might be "to flatter him." Even this brief verbal description will be discarded after the scene has been developed; after that, you will have only as much awareness of all this as the character does (except for that little piece of your actor consciousness that never quite goes away).

In the last lesson we gave examples of productive objectives from several plays, with the needs that drove them; here they are with the actions added:

1. *Need*: to save the king
   *Objective*: to convince the king to hide inside the hovel
   *Action*: to go inside myself so he will follow
2. *Need*: to end my pain
   *Objective*: to trick Peter into picking up the knife so I can kill myself
   *Action*: to threaten his manhood so he will defend himself
3. *Need*: to be taken care of
   *Objective*: to make Mitch understand me so he will kiss me
   *Action*: to tell him what happened that awful night.

Do you see how each of these conforms to the principles we have discussed?

As we have said, while actually playing the scene it is useful to form a brief working version of the objective that is easy to carry in your mind. In the example actions we listed above, these working versions might be:

1. To get the king inside
2. To get Peter to pick up the knife
3. To make Mitch understand

## UNITS OF ACTION

As we do in life, a dramatic character will usually pursue an action until it either succeeds or has been deemed a failure. If the action is not working, the character will shift to a new action, *even though the objective may not change.* Or the character may abandon that objective, form a new one and find a new action for it. If, on the other hand, the action is successful and the objective is achieved, the character moves on to a new objective and forms a new action.

You see, then, that each shift, whether there is a change in objective or not, involves a change in action. Such shifts can be felt as a change in the rhythm of the scene; each creates a new *unit of action*, regardless of which character has made the change. Actors usually call these units of action *beats*. The moment in which the change of action occurs is called a *beat change*.

In the scene from *Death of a Salesman*, Willy Loman tries several ways to get a spot in town from Howard, his new boss: by flattery, by appealing for sympathy, by appealing to loyalty, by appealing to honor, by generating guilt, by demanding justice, and finally by begging. Each strategic action is abandoned as it fails and Willy grows more desperate; each shift in action is a beat change and moves the scene in a new direction.

It is Willy who is "running" the scene at first; he makes each beat change, and Howard only reacts to Willy's shifts in strategy: At the end, however, Howard takes over and makes the final beat change when he fires Willy, forcing Willy to beg. Though we will examine all this in greater detail later, please read through the scene again and see if you can feel where the beat changes occur.

Here is an exercise to explore the sense of objectives and actions. It is an exercise that can be done many times until the experience of action becomes familiar to you.

## Exercise 52:
## Simple Action Improvisation

A. Invent an objective involving someone in the room: to get him or her to go out on a date with you, to lend you money, to lie for you, and so on. Make it SIP: a single thing, something possible for them to do in the immediate future, and something important to you. Consider the need that is driving this objective.

B. Now select an initial strategy that seems likely to succeed, such as "to get Sam to promise to drive me home after class by promising him dinner." Remember to phrase your action as a transitive verb including the object and the strategy.

C. Without explaining any of this to anyone, go for it. If it's not working, try a different strategy. (Those who are on the receiving end: Accept the reality of whatever your partner brings to you; help heighten the drama of the scene by resisting through retreating or counterattacking; make it *difficult but not impossible* for him or her to earn the objective.)

In this exercise you were acting in your own person, inventing your own need, objective, and action. When working on a play, one of your early steps in rehearsal will be to explore your character's needs, and each of his or her objectives and playable actions, step-by-step through each scene. By making temporary working definitions of these needs, objectives, and actions early in the rehearsal process, you can begin to experience the logic and momentum of the scene so that it begins to "play."

It is only when you begin to experience the living scene with your partners that you begin to make your final choices of action; for it is only then that you are moved beyond yourself, taking inspiration from the energies of others and from the play itself, as the character, that new version of yourself, begins to grow.

## THE GIVEN CIRCUMSTANCES

In this exercise you were performing as yourself within the reality of your own world. As you begin to reach out to create a character different from yourself, your first step will be to enter into your character's world and do what your character does *as if you were actually in his or her circumstances.*

As we have said, your character will choose an action in relation to his or her circumstances. The playwright will have shaped those circumstances to fit the character and to give your actions special qualities such as significance or urgency.

The "givens" in any situation fall into four categories: who, where, when, and what.

*Who* refers to the relationship between your character and all the other characters who are important in the scene, whether they are physically present or not. These relationships have two aspects, the *general* relationship (for example, two sisters) and a *specific* relationship (all the special factors that make Blanche and Stella a unique pair of sisters). The general relationship provides a context; in many ways Stella and Blanche are like many other sisters in that they reminisce about the past, they enjoy going out together for a special occasion, and so on. The specific relationship between Blanche and Stella, however, is fraught with blame and guilt over the past and tension regarding the present situation. The general relationship, then, provides certain basic considerations that make a relationship similar to others of its kind, while the specific relationship reveals what is unique to this particular case.

*Where* the scene happens also has two main aspects, the *physical* and the *social*. The physical environment has a tremendous influence on the action. For example, many of Tennessee Williams's plays must take place in the hot, humid climate of the South; think what an air conditioner would do to *A Streetcar Named Desire*. Shakespeare chose to set another play of great passion, *Othello*, in the similar climate of Cyprus; on the other hand, *Hamlet* requires the cold, isolated, and bleak climate of Denmark. Move *Hamlet* to the tropical climate of Cyprus and Claudius would be dead by the third act.

Beyond the simple physical influences of climate, the social environment established by the playwright is also of great importance. The society in which Stanley Kowalski moves, for example, is an active part of Stanley's character; we mustn't forget that he was a Marine sergeant and is still the captain of his bowling team. Think over the plays you have read, and you will see how in each case the influences of the immediate locale and society have been carefully chosen and are indispensable to the specific quality of the action.

*When* a scene is happening may be equally important, both in terms of the *time of day and year* and also the *historical time*, with all its implications of manners, values, and beliefs. Imagine *The Zoo Story* at night or in the winter, or as an encounter between two Victorians. Or consider the impact of the Elizabethan view of the physical universe on *King Lear*.

Finally, *what* is happening, the specific content and structure of the action that you have already studied in some detail, is the most important element of the scene. Consider here also any *antecedent action*; things that we know have happened in the past that affect the present situation, but the playwright has not bothered to actually show us.

Here is a summary list of the givens:

1. Who
   a. General relationship
   b. Specific relationship
2. Where
   a. Physical environment
   b. Social environment
3. When
   a. Time of day and year
   b. Historical time
4. What
   a. The main event of the scene
   b. Any antecedent action that affects this scene

Each of the given circumstances must be evaluated as to its relative importance; you don't want to waste thought and energy on aspects of the character's world that do not contribute to the action. The most important givens, of course, are those that affect the choices of the characters. It is not merely the fact that *Streetcar* and *Othello* are set in hot, humid climates that is important, but the specific way these climates affect the state of mind and therefore the significant choices made by the characters.

### Exercise 53:
### The Givens Game

A. One member of the group sits quietly. The rest of you watch the person until he or she reminds you of a real person you have known.

B. Remember this person in a particular real circumstance. Recall all aspects of this real scene using the list of givens above. Keep it secret.

C. When you have a clear picture of the scene, get up and join the person on stage. Your task will be to let the person know who he or she is and what the givens are by simply relating to the person *without "telling" or "showing" him or her anything*. You can't, for example, run up and say, "Hey Dad, can I borrow the car?" Don't try to create a whole event; just be there with the person in the circumstance.

D. The other's task is to find out who and where he or she is. The person does this by simply responding to you in various ways until you are both in the same reality. The rest of the group watches and calls "foul" if they see anyone indicating.

E. When you both feel that you are in the same reality, the game is over. Discuss with each other and with the group what you thought the givens were; compare impressions and notice what produced the strongest and most dramatically satisfying impressions.

Experiencing the givens that most influence the action can be a powerful factor in rehearsing a scene. Consider even working in locations that approximate the conditions of the scene; for example, I have several times held rehearsals for Shakespeare's *A Midsummer Night's Dream* in the woods at night by lantern light, and the "sense memory" of the experience greatly enriched the stage performance.

If the givens of the play are foreign to you, some research will be required. The history, architecture, painting, music, and fashion of the time can be very useful. If you are working on *Mother Courage*, you will need to know something about the Thirty Years' War; for *The Glass Menagerie*, midwestern city life just before World War II will be important.

## SUMMARY OF LESSON THIRTEEN

Your character's objective will naturally lead to an action. Even though the resultant action is provided by the playwright, you must re-create this process for yourself so that the character's experience can lead you to transformation.

Your character will choose an action that seems to have a chance for success in the given circumstances; this is the "strategic" aspect of action. You describe an action with a transitive verb phrase that includes the object of the verb, which is the other character and the change you want from him or her.

While actually playing the scene, you will be aware of the objective that will generate the action "as if for the first time," and so you carry only a shorthand working version of it in your mind, and that only temporarily.

An action will be pursued until it either succeeds or fails. In either case, a shift is made to a new action. This shift changes the rhythm of the scene and creates a new unit of action: This is called a new "beat." The moment at which the new action is formed is called a "beat change."

You also consider the circumstances of the scene to understand how they influence your character and the action.

Armed with your understanding of need, objective and action, and the givens, you begin to play the scene. It is here, with the experience of the actual give-and-take of the living scene, that your true understanding will grow and your transformation into the character will begin.

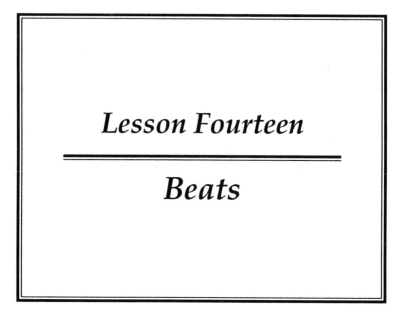

# Lesson Fourteen

## Beats

You now understand how your character's energy flows from the character's need toward an objective through his or her action. In this lesson, we will explore how your actions will join with the actions of the other characters to create the scene. Here is an exercise that will explore this process.

### Exercise 54:
### Impulse Circle

Sit in a large circle, in chairs or on the floor, about eighteen inches apart. Make the circle perfectly round.

Each person puts his or her left hand out palm up and right hand out palm down, and rests his or her right hand lightly on the left hand of the person to the right.

The leader will now initiate an impulse in the form of a light, clean slap with his or her right hand. The slap is passed on from person to person around the circle and is allowed to flow continuously.

Once the slap is moving well, try the following experiments:

A. Allow your awareness to go to the slap as it moves around the circle. Begin to experience the slap *as having a life of its own*. Notice any change in the slap's quality as the group begins to experience it as having a life of its own.

B. Now allow the slap to move as quickly as it can; see what happens when you "get out of its way."

C. Now let it slow down; see how slowly it can go *without dying*; bring it right to the brink of extinction. (Keep the external slap sharp, but slow down the impulse as it travels internally.) As it moves slowly, see what you need to do to support its life, even while it is not passing directly through you.

D. Drop your hands, and discuss the many ways in which this exercise *is like a scene on stage*. Begin by asking, "What makes it possible for the slap to flow around the group, and how is that like the way a scene moves forward?"

NOTE: Repeat this exercise on subsequent days; it is a good group "warm-up."

## ACTION AND REACTION

As you discussed this exercise, you probably agreed that the movement of the slap, like a scene on stage, depended on *cause and effect*, what a psychologist would call stimulus and response and what actors call *action and reaction*. The flow of the slap depended on the ability of every group member to receive and send (react and act).

In the exercise, you are slapped by the person on your left; you react to the slap by slapping the person on your right; that person reacts by slapping the next person, and so on. For each of you, *reaction produces an action*. In a scene, another character says or does something, to which you, as your character, react; your reaction becomes an action directed back at that character, or toward someone else; this will evoke another reaction from someone else, and so the scene will move through the action/reaction/action/reaction chain of energy being passed between the characters.

We might even say that your primary job as an actor at any given moment is to *pass the energy of the scene on in the way most useful to the next actor*. You receive energy, react, and in turn act in a way that moves the scene forward toward its ultimate destination.

More simply, we like to say that *acting is reacting*.

In order to understand what is required from your action at any given moment, then, you must consider how your individual action fits into the chain of action and reaction that moves the entire scene. This understanding will guide you in finding the precise quality of action (and therefore of need and objective leading to that action) that will best serve the scene.

## THE LIFE OF THE SCENE

During the exercise you may also have noticed that when you believed in the impulse as having a life of its own, your awareness opened, you became more relaxed, less self-conscious, your center lowered, your breath became easy, and you stopped judging what you were doing and simply *did* it. All this was because making the slap live became a productive objective, and your focus on that objective took your attention off yourself. You were, in short, *in action*.

When the group related to the slap in this way, you noticed that it began to flow more smoothly and powerfully; when you began, it was "chunky," just a sequence of individual actions as you all waited for your turns, each focused on his or her part. When all of you focused your awareness on the whole, however, all the individual parts merged into one flowing event that did indeed take on a life of its own.

At that moment, the exercise became "easier"; you were no longer *making* it happen, it was making *you* happen. You were receiving more energy from it than you were giving to it, and the whole became greater than the sum of its parts. You also felt that you were part of the whole network through which the impulse flowed all the time, not just when it was "your turn." This is the kind of continuous support and involvement required of everyone in a scene.

These are all ways in which the exercise is like an effective scene on stage. Every actor must be connected to the whole, continuously reacting and acting in order to contribute to the life of the scene. When this happens, the event begins to take on a life of its own; we say that the scene begins "to play."

## DRAMA, CONFLICT, AND CHARACTER

You may have noticed that there are several ways in which this exercise is *not* like a scene on stage: As much fun as it is, it is not particularly dramatic, though it has the *potential* for drama if it can be given certain qualities (your group might enjoy experimenting with this).

Since our sense of drama springs from an urgent situation with the outcome in doubt, and a conflict between opposing forces is the best way to produce this, our exercise would need to be given *a conflict that urgently needs to be resolved*. In many plays, this central conflict is between two characters—the hero, or *protagonist*, and the villain, or *antagonist*. In its most simple form this structure tends toward melodrama and is common in popular entertainment like episodic television.

In more complex plays, this two-person conflict can be used to ignite more profound issues: Hamlet and Claudius, Peter and Jerry, Blanche and Stanley are all examples of protagonist–antagonist conflicts, but the issues involved are far more complex than a mere contest between a "good guy" and a "bad guy."

The central conflict may also live inside the protagonist. While there is a conflict between Hamlet and Claudius, for instance, the central conflict of the play really exists within Hamlet, between his desire to follow the Ghost's command for vengeance and his moral reticence to commit murder.

A central conflict may also involve one or more characters confronting a difficult situation. In Beckett's *Waiting for Godot*, for example, there is little conflict between the characters; rather, they are in conflict with a situation that forces them to wait for someone (or something) who is unknown and who may or may not come.

Whatever its form, all plays are organized around some sort of a central conflict between opposing forces. Sensing that conflict we expect that something is about to happen, and this provides the essential ingredient of *suspense*. In fact, suspense, the feeling that something *might* happen, is more important than the event itself. This is how contemporary plays with few "events" in the traditional sense (Beckett's *Waiting for Godot*, Pinter's *The Collection*, Shepard's *Buried Child*, to name a few) can still be dramatically satisfying.

When creating a role you must find the connection between your part and the central dramatic conflict of the play, and shape your characterization to contribute to that central conflict. For example, if you were playing the next-door neighbor, Charley, in Miller's *Death of a Salesman*, you would have to see that the central conflict of the play is the choice facing Willy between his brother Ben's way of life (which is based on struggle and material success) and Charley's way of life (which is based on acceptance and spiritual success). Your main purpose in creating Charley's character would be to embody this alternative way of life that, if Willy could but choose it, would save him.

We will call this your sense of your character's *dramatic*

*function*. Here we have touched only on its structural dimension; in Part Three we will explore this essential concept in greater detail.

## THE SHAPE OF DRAMA

A central conflict is not by itself enough to provide a satisfying dramatic experience. The conflict generates a sequence of events, which we call the *plot*; in a good play, the plot is shaped to form a satisfying "two hours' traffic on the stage," as Shakespeare put it. It is this *shaping* of the play's events in a way that heightens their dramatic impact that we will now examine through another experiment.

### Exercise 55:
### A Dramatic Breath

A. Standing comfortably, try taking a single, complete breath that is as *dramatic* as you can make it. Don't think about it, do it.

B. Try another; make it even more dramatic.

C. Consider the things you did to make the breath more dramatic. Did each of these things make it truly more *dramatic* or merely more *theatrical*? If you are in a group, compare notes; was there anything that everyone did?

When trying this exercise for the first time, most people exaggerate their breath, making it louder and more visible. This, however, serves only to make the breath more "theatrical" and not necessarily more dramatic. Remember our description of drama: an urgent situation with the outcome in doubt. How would this apply to a breath? At what moment is the outcome of a breath in doubt?

The outcome is most in doubt while the breath is being held, and this is why most people who do this exercise hold their breath for a time before exhaling. They naturally feel the holding of the breath as a moment of *suspense* (which literally means "held up," as in "suspenders").

In a play, the sequence of events moves forward as the conflict intensifies and suspense builds; we begin to wonder, "How will this come out?" When the conflict is just on the verge of being resolved, suspense is at its peak. This moment of greatest suspense, just as the outcome hangs in the balance, is called a *crisis* (a "turning point"). The function of everything that happens before the crisis is to lead toward it with *rising* energy, while everything after the crisis flows naturally from it with a *falling* sense of resolution (or *denouement*, which is the French word for "unraveling").

This, then, is the fundamental shape of all dramatic events: a rising conflict, a crisis, and a resolution. (See Figure 20.) It is a shape common to all of the performing arts; symphonies and ballets have it. It is the fundamental unit of rhythm because it is the shape of a muscular contraction and relaxation. It is the fundamental shape of life itself, from birth to death. You can experience it within a single breath.

### Exercise 56:
### A Dramatic Breath Revisited

You can experience the shape of a whole play in a single breath. Start as "empty" as you can: Feel the rising energy (inhaling); prolong the crisis (holding the breath), feeling the full strength of the held-back energy; then enjoy a full resolution (exhaling). A single breath can be an exciting event.

In this exercise you heightened the "drama" of the breath in two ways: You extended its *dynamic range*, or *arc*, by stretching the low and high points of the action farther apart; you also *prolonged the crisis* to savor the period of maximum suspense. These same principles will apply to the shaping of a scene and the units of action within that scene.

Continue now to explore how this dramatic shape works in larger patterns.

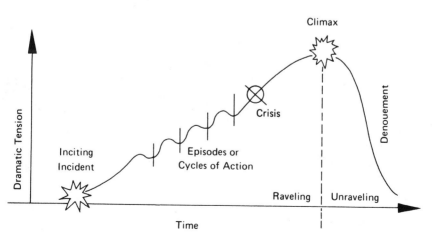

**FIGURE 20** The Shape of Drama.

**Exercise 57:**
**Shaping Action Phrases**

Perform the following sequence of actions, attempting to experience fully the dramatic potential of each. Remember to focus on the crisis in each pattern: Treat all that goes before as leading up to the crisis, and all that follows as flowing from it.

1. A single step. Where is the crisis of a step? To intensify the experience, involve your breath by inhaling during the rising action, holding the breath during the crisis, and exhaling during the release.
2. Three steps experienced as one phrase, with the crisis in the third step. The first two steps still have mini-crises of their own, but now they lead up to the main crisis in the third step. Let your breath parallel the larger pattern.
3. Three steps with the crisis in the first step, so that the mini-crises of the second and third steps will "follow through" from the first.
4. Now try a pattern composed of three units of three steps each, with the crisis of the whole pattern in the second unit of three.
5. Invent patterns of your own; add sound.

In this exercise you experienced how a number of small units of action (like breaths or steps) can be connected into a larger phrase having a shape of its own; likewise, these larger phrases can be connected into still larger patterns, which again have shapes of their own. (See Figure 21.) On all these levels, the fundamental shape of

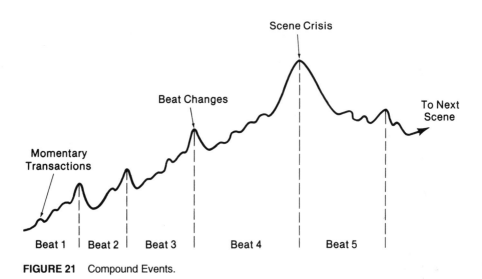

**FIGURE 21**   Compound Events.

rise, crisis, and release is the same even though the *proportion* or relationship between the parts is different.

This is how the parts of a play go together to compose the whole play. We begin with the "smallest" units, the individual transactions between characters, which we call *moments*. Moments work together to form larger units called *beats*, and the beats work together to form *scenes*; the scenes flow toward the *main event* of the play as a whole.

On each level there is one central issue. Take for example this transaction from the Willy Loman scene:

WILLY: What's that, Howard?
HOWARD: Didn't you ever see one of these? Wire recorder.
WILLY: Oh. Can we talk a minute?
HOWARD: Records things. Just got delivery yesterday....

This is a single transaction (action and reaction) or *moment* in which Willy tries to get Howard's attention but fails; it is one of several such moments that form the long first *beat* in which Willy tries to get Howard's attention through flattery; a number of beats go together to form this *scene* in which Willy is fired; this scene fits into the flow of the whole so that we see how Willy's being fired eventually leads to his suicide, which is the *main event* of the play.

Each of these levels has the same basic shape of rise and fall, and each has its own mini-crisis. As you work, you develop each part in a way that leads up to, or flows from, the crisis on that level. You explore each moment so that it will fit into its beat and create the *beat crisis*; you develop each beat so that it will link with the other beats in the scene to create the *scene crisis*; you develop each scene in order to achieve the shape of the play, leading to the *main crisis* followed by the *main event*.

Having developed your role in this way, you are free in performance to keep your focus on the most simple and immediate level, playing moment by moment, knowing that each moment will serve its beat, the beat will serve the scene, and the scene will serve the play.

## DEFINING BEATS

Some believe that the word "beat" was a misunderstanding of someone with a Russian accent saying "bits," meaning particles or units of action. As we have said, a beat is comprised of several transactions between characters; it is the smallest unit of action that has its own complete shape, with a central conflict and mini-crisis.

The conflict will come from the action of one character encountering the resistance (or even counteraction) of the other. Several transactions may occur as the conflict builds until we reach the *beat crisis* (or *beat change* as we have been calling it). Here one of the characters will shift to a new action, causing the scene to turn and flow in a new direction.

This structure is not an arbitrary choice made by the actors: It is built into the scene by the playwright. Every actor in the scene works to recognize the structure provided, and each supports the beat changes when they occur, even if they are not instigated by the character being played.

An analysis of the beat structure is called a *breakdown* of the scene (sometimes also called a *scenario*). As an example of a breakdown, let's again examine the scene from *Death of a Salesman*; follow along in the Appendix, and compare the breakdown that you did on your own in the last lesson.

> BEAT ONE: Willy, unable to go on driving as much as his job requires, goes to see his new boss, Howard. Willy enters somewhat hesitantly and finds Howard playing with a new toy, a recorder. Howard wants to avoid this unpleasant confrontation (we learn later that he has already decided to fire Willy and has been putting it off), so he goes on playing with the recorder and forces Willy to listen to inane recordings of his family. Like a good salesman, Willy listens dutifully and even flatters Howard, while trying four times to bring up the reason for his visit. The conflict in this beat is between Willy's action of getting Howard's attention by flattery, versus Howard's counterobjective of avoiding Willy by playing with the recorder. The crisis is finally reached when Howard counterattacks by asking, "Say, aren't you supposed to be in Boston?"

> BEAT TWO: In this short beat, Howard attacks by demanding to know, "What happened? What're you doing here?" Willy reacts weakly, but manages to state his case: "I've come to the decision that I'd rather not travel anymore." He reminds Howard that he had promised to find him "some spot for me here in town," but Howard responds, "Well, I couldn't think of anything for you, Willy." The main issue of the scene is now on the table: Willy *must* get off the road, but Howard refuses to help.

> BEAT THREE: This beat might be defined as three mini-beats, three quick thrusts of different strategies by Willy: appealing to sympathy ("I'm just a little tired"), appealing to loyalty ("I was with the firm when your father used to carry you in here in his arms"), and then demanding (*"with increasing anger"*); Howard parries each of these

thrusts. What unifies this beat, however, is the action of *bargaining*, as Willy steadily lowers the salary he is willing to accept in return for a spot in town.

BEAT FOUR: Willy tries to make Howard understand by telling him how he decided to become a salesman, and even lowers his price to forty dollars a week, but Howard, who is really the "kid" in this relationship, responds, "Kid, I can't take blood from a stone."

BEAT FIVE: Willy grows desperate and demands justice, reminding Howard of his thirty-four years with the firm and the promises Howard's father had made. Howard simply walks out: "You'll have to excuse me, Willy, I gotta see some people. Pull yourself together."

BEAT SIX: Willy, now alone, thinks that he sees his old boss sitting in his chair and is then frightened by accidentally turning on the recorder (which symbolizes Willy's inability to deal with the changes happening in the world). This interlude serves to prolong and heighten the sense of crisis.

BEAT SEVEN: Howard reenters, and Willy, knowing that he has made a terrible mistake, tries to put things back the way they were by saying, "I'll go to Boston." *The scene is now at its main crisis.* Howard fires Willy: "Willy, you can't go to Boston for us." *This is the main event of this scene.*

BEAT EIGHT: Willy starts to beg, but Howard refuses to take responsibility and asks, "Where are your sons? Why don't your sons give you a hand?" Of course, the last thing a proud man like Willy could do is to accept help from his sons.

A breakdown greatly simplifies the scene for you. This fairly long scene (some ten minute's playing time) can be understood as having just six beats leading to its main crisis, followed by one beat of "denouement." As you rehearse, you will begin to feel how each beat fits into this overall structure, and you will have a sense of the function of each moment and beat.

Note that within each beat each character has a single action or point of reaction. It is this fact that permits you to translate the architecture of the scene into the thoughts and actions of your character. You *as the actor* understand this structure and design the consciousness of the character to contribute to it; then, as you play the scene, you can surrender your immediate awareness *to the character's consciousness* knowing that what your character thinks, says, and does will serve the scene.

If all the actors have worked together to develop a shared understanding of the scenario, the rhythm of the scene will be strong and clear. It is as important for actors to agree on the phraseology of their shared action as it is for members of an orchestra to work together to fulfill the phraseology of a piece of music.

### Exercise 58:
### Beat Breakdown

Working with your partner, answer these questions about the scene from *The Glass Menagerie* in the Appendix, or a scene you have chosen for yourself *from a play you have read in its entirety.*

1. Decide what the main event of the scene is and how it contributes to the play as a whole.
2. Decide precisely where the crisis of the scene occurs.
3. Do a breakdown of the scene, as in the example above.
4. Select one important beat.
   a. Define its central conflict.
   b. Specify its moment of crisis.
   c. Decide who makes the choice that is the beat change.
   d. See how this beat grows out of the preceding beat and flows into the following beat.

## SUMMARY OF LESSON FOURTEEN

A scene moves through the action/reaction/action/reaction chain of energy being passed between the characters. Your primary job as an actor at any given moment is to receive energy, react, and in turn act in a way that moves the scene forward toward its ultimate destination. More simply, we like to say that *acting is reacting.*

Every actor must be connected to the whole scene, continuously reacting and acting in order to contribute to its life. When this happens, the event begins to take on a life of its own; we say that the scene begins "to play."

Our sense of drama springs from an urgent situation of conflict between opposing forces with the outcome in doubt. This central conflict may be between two characters, within the hero, or between the characters and their situation. When creating a role you must find the connection between your part and the central dramatic conflict of the play, and then shape your characterization to contribute to that central conflict.

The central conflict generates a sequence of events, which we call the *plot*; the plot moves forward as the conflict intensifies and suspense builds; suspense is at its peak just as the outcome hangs in the balance, and this is the *crisis*. Everything that happens before the

## THE HIERARCHY OF OBJECTIVES

You now understand that a play is structured on levels: Individual transactions make up beats, beats make up scenes, and the scenes form the overall shape of rising and falling action, which gives unity to the whole play.

These levels of action relate directly to the inner life of your character because you will have an objective (and therefore an action) on each level: In each individual transaction you will have an *immediate* objective; the sequence of immediate objectives leads toward your *beat objective*; the objectives of the beats in sequence lead toward your *scene objective*; and your scene objectives can be seen as springing from a deep, overall objective that is your character's "life goal" or, as it is usually called, your *superobjective*.

For example, consider again the moment from *Death of a Salesman* when Willy finds Howard engrossed in his new recorder and is told, "I'll be with you in a minute." Being a good salesman, Willy tries to get his foot in the door by engaging Howard in conversation and asks, "What's that, Howard?"

At this moment, Willy's *immediate objective* is to get Howard's attention by asking about the recorder. Once he accomplishes this, he hopes he can move on toward his *beat objective*, which is to bring up the subject of his work assignment; he would then hope to move toward his *scene objective*, which is to persuade Howard to give him a spot in town. This scene objective is connected directly to his *superobjective*: to prove himself a worthy human being by earning money and respect.

You see that Willy's objectives on each level work together in a logical way, his immediate objective leading toward his beat objective, his beat objectives being steps toward his scene objective, and the scene objective as springing directly from his superobjective.

If we were to follow each of Willy's immediate objectives through the play, we could see how he is led from objective to objective in pursuit of his superobjective. The logic of this sequence of objectives striving toward the superobjective is called the *through-line* of the character's action.

> In a play the whole stream of individual minor objectives, all the imaginative thoughts, feelings, and actions of an actor should converge to carry out this superobjective....Also this impetus toward the superobjective must be continuous throughout the whole play.[1]

Stanislavski once said that each of your character's actions fits into the through-line like vertebrae in a spine; hence, some actors call the through-line the "spine" of the role. Stanislavski elsewhere referred to "the sequence of objectives" as being *the score* of the role that the actor learns to follow automatically.

Identifying your character's through-line of action as tending toward a superobjective can help you to better understand each of your specific actions, connecting each momentary action to the character's deepest needs and desires. It can also help you to see how the sequence of objectives has a single driving force; thus, you can "play through" each moment and achieve both unity and momentum (what we call *pace*) in your performance.

## THE SUPEROBJECTIVE

Your character's superobjective may be conscious or (more commonly) unconscious. If the character is unconscious of it, you—the actor—will treat it as you treat everything you know that the character doesn't: You will take it fully into account as you work, but you will not let your actor knowledge "contaminate" your character reality. Remember the idea of dual consciousness: What you know as the actor is not the same thing as what your character knows. Lee Strasberg once said the hardest thing about acting "is not knowing what you know."

Either way, the superobjective functions as an underlying principle that affects all of your actions and establishes your attitude toward life. It is described according to the same principles as any individual objective.

Willy Loman, for example, is presented with two alternative attitudes toward life. He could, like his brother Ben, strike off on some bold venture and be the "master of his fate"; or he could, like his neighbor Charley, accept his life as it is and find inner peace. Unfortunately, Willy lacks the courage to follow his brother's example and lacks also Charley's sense of self-identity. Willy has opted instead to try to earn self-esteem through selling. In the scene with Howard, Willy describes the moment he formed this superobjective:

> ...I met a salesman in the Parker House. His name was Dave Singleman. And he was eighty-four years old, and he'd drummed merchandise in thirty-one states. And old Dave, he'd go up to his room, y'understand, put on his green velvet slippers—I'll never forget—and pick up his phone and call the buyers, and without ever leaving his room, at the age of eighty-four, he made his living. And when I saw that, I realized that selling was the greatest career a man could want.

Willy has come to confuse success as a salesman with success as a human being. Like many in our nation's work force, he "is" what he "does." We would say that his superobjective is "to prove myself worthy as a human being by earning money and respect through selling." Eventually, however, Willy is no longer able to sell either his products or himself. His last "sale" is his suicide, and the insurance money is the last paycheck he will "earn." It will give his family the financial independence he has so long sought as a measure of his worth.

What drives the entire play is Willy's constant search for the success that will prove he is a worthy person; his tragedy is that he defines his success by external measures. We can summarize Willy's superobjective as "to prove myself worthy by earning money and respect." Each scene, each beat, each moment of the role, and every aspect of Willy's psychology can be understood as reflecting this superobjective.

Because it is so important to the theme of *Death of a Salesman*, Miller was explicit about Willy's superobjective; most plays are not so specific, even in the case of the major character. In most cases you must *deduce* your character's superobjective from the character's behavior in the circumstances. Tom in *The Glass Menagerie*, for example, clearly needs to make a place for himself in the world, but he cannot do this unless he escapes his role as the "provider" for his mother and helpless sister. Tom's superobjective therefore translates into the specific need "to leave home without guilt." The through-line of his scene objectives, his beat objectives, and each of his immediate objectives can be seen as being driven by this superobjective.

It is possible for the superobjective of a character to change in the course of the play under the pressure of extraordinary circumstances. King Lear begins his play intent upon retiring from the responsibilities of kingship so that he can enjoy his last days "unburdened" and basking in the love of his family and subjects. In the course of his suffering, however, he learns that he has been ignorant of true love, and he surrenders his self-centered superobjective in favor of a desire for universal justice and the simple, personal love he feels for Cordelia at the end.

It may be difficult to find the superobjective of minor characters, since the playwright has not provided much information; here you can be inventive, so long as your understanding of the character enables you to serve your dramatic function within the play without distortion.

Even more difficult may be those plays in which the internal life of the characters is purposely mysterious, as those by Pinter,

Beckett, or Shepard. It may be useful to you as an actor to discover some sense of superobjective for such characters, but it would be disastrous if you were to try to reveal your superobjective to the audience. All great plays have some measure of mystery at their heart, and it is a mistake to "pluck it out" by exposing things that the playwright meant to remain obscure.

Though you may develop some idea about your character's superobjective before rehearsals start, it is dangerous to become too set in your thinking; these early ideas need to be tested. Ideally, the sense of superobjective will emerge gradually from your experience of the specific actions of your character. Let your sense of the superobjective be the result of your rehearsal exploration, not a substitute for it.

## FINDING AND PERSONALIZING THE SUPEROBJECTIVE

Once you have begun to identify the superobjective, you must *personalize* it; you must come to care as deeply about it as your character does. Since the superobjective of most characters is fairly "universal," this is usually not difficult; like Willy Loman, we all want to be thought of as worthy, and we can all "identify" with Willy on this basis, however much we can see that Willy's way of pursuing self-esteem is mistaken.

In some cases, however, the precise manner in which a character manifests the superobjective may be so foreign to you that it presents difficulties. Isabella in Shakespeare's *Measure for Measure*, for example, is faced with a choice between sleeping with the Duke or seeing her brother executed for a trivial crime. Isabella, who is about to become a nun, believes that losing her virginity would damn her, and she fully expects her brother to be willing to die to maintain her virtue, thus winning a place in heaven; when he begs her for his life, she angrily condemns him as a coward.

If you are playing Isabella, it may be difficult for you to identify with such strong and inflexible religious values. In such a case, you may have to find some analogous superobjective that can motivate you that strongly. In this case, you might consider what action is so loathsome to you that you would ask your brother (or someone you love) to die before you would do it; then "substitute" this in your own mind for Isabella's situation.

Such substitutions may be useful, but they carry the danger of bringing inappropriate personal material into the performance. It is better, if possible, to simply surrender yourself to your character's situation and belief system. Remember our version of Stanislavksi's "magic if": If you were in the character's situation, and if you made the same choices, who would you become? You have a vast personal potential; somewhere in you the religious fanatic, the saint, the mass murderer, the courageous hero, and the sniveling coward are all waiting to be realized.

### Exercise 60:
### The Superobjective

Working with your partner, do the following using the scene from *The Glass Menagerie* in the Appendix, or the scene you have chosen for yourself.

1. Examine your character's actions: Can you see a superobjective toward which the character is tending, whether the character is conscious of it or not?
2. Define the superobjective using a transitive verb phrase with qualifiers.
3. Look through your script: Are there any actual lines that sum up your character's superobjective?
4. Now consider ways of personalizing this superobjective so that you feel it with the same intensity as does your character.

Now rehearse your scene again and find how the superobjective is expressed in it.

## THE THROUGH-LINE OF ACTION

It is neither easy nor necessary to describe the through-line of a role in words; it is more important to *feel* the sequence and flow of the role, and the "logic" by which one action leads into another as steps tending toward scene objectives and through them to the superobjective. For this reason, the through-line will usually emerge gradually as your individual actions are explored and experienced in rehearsal.

The sense of through-line provides a background against which immediate objectives may be understood; as it becomes clear, each moment in your performance begins to "fit" with every other in a harmonious way; moments that seemed incomprehensible at first begin to fit into the flow of the whole, like steps in a single journey. When finally the whole is in place, each moment of the performance will cumulatively support every other moment, and you will be moved naturally from one to the other by a sense of necessity.

In a production of Brecht's *Mother Courage*, for example, the actor playing the role of Kattrin, the mute daughter, needed help with her last scene. In it, Kattrin climbs atop a hut and beats a drum to warn the nearby town of an impending attack. The soldiers coax and threaten her, trying to make her stop drumming, but she refuses and is shot. Obviously, her choice to sacrifice herself in order to warn the town is the most important choice she makes in the play; it is also the crisis of the entire play. It embodies the play's meaning: We have created a world in which love for your fellow human beings is suicidal.

The dramatic purpose of Kattrin's character, then, is to provide one glimmer of selflessness against which we can judge the callousness of a world in which love has been sacrificed to economic necessity. Her superobjective, which we learn in various scenes, is to have a child who she can care for; the fact that there are children in the town is crucial, because by sacrificing her life for them she is winning her superobjective in the only way that the world of the play makes possible.

Knowing all this, however, didn't help the actor with this final choice. Rehearsal after rehearsal, she tried different ways of climbing the ladder, different ways of drumming, different ways of thinking through the choice. Nothing worked, and she was in despair.

Her mistake was in thinking that the problem was in this climactic scene; her real problem was that she had not yet found the through-line that would bring her to this moment properly. She had to go back to the beginning and examine each moment of her role, each of her previous actions and reactions, to see how each contributed to this final action.

Having understood this, the actor began to go through rehearsals, moment by moment, asking herself, "What do I see going on at this moment that will eventually contribute to my beating that drum?" Each of her moments, beats, and scenes were quickly understood as contributing to this through-line, and then climaxing in her final choice. Soon, that final choice became not only easy, but unavoidable.

When your character has such a climactic action, it must be the "payoff" resulting from careful preparation. You may reap only what you have previously sown, and this cumulative effect is achieved by sensing the through-line and fitting each individual action into its proper place in the sequence.

We should note that unlike this example, a character's through-line may not be a "straight line." The character may try one thing, then another; the character may need to discover an effective course of action through trial and error. Think of the through-line as the motivational energy driving characters forward toward their super-objective; every time they have to choose what to do, they will choose the thing that seems *at that moment and in that circumstance* to move in the desired direction, even if they later discover that they were wrong.

Perhaps the greatest value in experiencing the through-line is that you will find how each moment of your performance is driven by your character's deepest energies. In *The Glass Menagerie*, Tom introduces his sister Laura to Jim, the Gentleman Caller. This simple introduction ("Jim, this is Laura; Laura, this is Jim") can be seen as part of Jim's through-line of action moving toward his superobjective:

1. *Immediate Objective*: to get Laura and Jim off to a good start
2. *Beat Objective*: to lay the seeds of a relationship between them
3. *Scene Objective*: to bring another man into the house, hopefully permanently
4. *Superobjective*: to get out of here and find my own identity (by bringing another man into the house so I can leave home without guilt, since Mother and Laura would be "looked after")

This is how the through-line of action brings unity and momentum (*pace*) to every moment of your performance. Once you have fit each moment into its place within the structure of the whole during your rehearsal preparation, you are then free in performance to give your full attention to playing each moment, secure that it will also be serving the play as a whole.

### Exercise 61:
### The Through-Line

Working with your partner, do the following using the scene from *The Glass Menagerie* in the Appendix, or the scene you have chosen for yourself.

A. Examine the sequence of your character's objectives: Do you see its logic as a reflection of an underlying movement toward a superobjective?

B. In each individual transaction, try to feel the connection of the immediate objective to the beat objective, the scene objective, and the superobjective.

C. Run the scene without stopping and feel the momentum of the sequence of objectives.

## SUMMARY OF LESSON FIFTEEN

A scene is as an arrangement of beats with its own central conflict, its own crisis, and its own main event. A scene contains *one major development in the movement of the whole play*. This development may be related to *plot* or to *theme*.

Rehearsing a scene is much like making a map of an unknown territory. You and your partners, through trial and error, find for yourselves the pathway of action that the author has hidden beneath the surface of the dialogue. Each beat change is a turning point in the journey; the destination is the scene crisis and main event. This sense of scene structure must finally live as a sort of underlying "dance" in the flow of the scene, as we feel the energy building toward the crisis and main event, then flowing naturally away from them.

Scene structure translates into the thought of your character because in each individual transaction you will have an *immediate* objective; the sequence of immediate objectives leads toward your *beat objective*; the objectives of the beats in sequence lead toward your *scene objective*; and your scene objectives can be seen as moving toward a deep, overall objective that is your character's "life goal" or, as it is usually called, your *superobjective*.

Once you have begun to identify this superobjective, you must *personalize* it; you must come to care as deeply about it as your character does.

One aim of rehearsal is to feel the "logic" by which one action leads into another as steps tending toward scene objectives and through them to the superobjective. As it becomes clear, each moment in your performance begins to "fit" with every other in a harmonious way; this is the *through-line* of your action. Stanislavski once said that each action fits into the role like vertebrae in a spine, so the through-line is sometimes called the *spine* of the role.

## SUMMARY OF PART TWO: AN ACTION/CHARACTER CHECKLIST

Here is a checklist that summarizes the material on action we have covered in Part Two. These are the questions you should be asking yourself in the earliest phases of your rehearsal process.

I. The Givens: What, Who, Where, When
    A. *What* happens in this scene?
        1. *What* is the *main event* of the scene? How does it move the plot

of the play forward? How does it contribute to the play's meaning?

    2. What *changes* in the world of the play as a result of this scene?

  B. *Who* is in this scene?

    1. What is the *general* relationship?

    2. What is the *specific* relationship?

    3. Does your relationship *change* in this scene?

    4. What is discovered about your character in this scene?

  C. *Where* is this scene?

    1. How does the *physical* environment influence what happens?

    2. How does the *social* environment influence what happens?

  D. *When* is this scene?

    1. How does the *historical* time influence the scene?

    2. How does the *season of the year* influence the scene?

    3. How does the *time of day* influence the scene?

II.  Scene Structure

  A. What is the *main conflict* of this scene? How does it relate to the overall conflict of the play?

  B. What is the *breakdown* of the scene, beat by beat? Be specific about each beat change.

  C. What is the *crisis*, the moment after which the conflict must be resolved?

  D. How does this scene grow out of preceding scenes? How does this scene lead into following scenes?

III.  Action Analysis

  A. What is your *superobjective*?

  B. What is your *scene* objective in this scene? How does it relate to your superobjective?

  C. Break down your *beat objectives* in sequence. Do you begin to feel the logic of their sequence or *through-line*?

  D. What is the sequence of your *immediate* objectives through the scene? Express each in a transitive verb as "SIP" (singular, immediate, and personally important); try to think of each as a desired change in the other character.

# Lesson Sixteen

# The Function and Elements of Character

In Part One you prepared your body, voice, and mind much in the way a gardener prepares the *ground* prior to planting a seed. In Part Two you developed a way of experiencing action that is the *seed* from which the created role will spring: As you enter into the actions of your character within the given circumstances "as if" they were your own, the transformational process begins to work and a new "me" begins to emerge. In Part Three we will explore and extend the *fruition* of this process, the character.

## THE FUNCTION OF CHARACTER

As the play unfolds, it seems as if the things that happen are "caused" by the characters; the choices they make, the way they react to one another, all seem to cause the story to proceed. In truth, however, it is the story that has "caused" the characters. By this I mean that your character was created by the playwright so that your behavior will contribute believably to the progress and meaning of the play; you were created to do a specific job, you have a purpose in relation to the whole. We will call this your *dramatic function*.

An understanding of your character's dramatic function is the single most fundamental factor influencing the success of your work. Without it, you will have no basis to judge the results of your preparation and rehearsal. As Stanislavski said, the actor's most important task is *to understand how every moment of the performance contributes to the reason why the play was written,* and we can expand this idea to add that *every aspect of characterization should contribute directly to the reason why the play was written.*

This is a powerful idea, equal in importance to the concepts of action and transformation. In fact, it is this sense of function that gives action and transformation a purpose and makes them capable of serving the play.

There are two main ways that your character may contribute to the play: by advancing the *plot* through his or her actions, and by contributing to the *meaning* of the play through the values that those actions express. Some examples: On the level of plot, your character may commit crucial actions that drive the plot forward; you may serve as a "foil" to frustrate the intentions of another character; or you may simply serve to provide some essential plot information, like the classical messenger. On the level of meaning, your character may represent values that are meant to contrast the values of other characters; you may be the spokesperson for one of several conflicting points of view; or you may serve to embody an element of a conflict within the main character (like Ben and Charley in relation to Willy Loman).

Too often actors approach their characters so personally that they begin to forget the larger purpose for which that character was created. Without a sense of function, you may create a character who is alive and believable but who doesn't fit into the play, doesn't do the job it was created to do. Even if the audience accepts or is even impressed by your performance, the play must fail, and therefore you will have failed.

### Exercise 62:
### Dramatic Function

Consider the character you have been developing over the previous exercises: What is its dramatic function within the play?

A. If your character were to be cut, what would be missing from the plot? What actions would have to be given to another character in order for the plot to proceed?

B. How would the meaning of the play suffer if your character were cut? Is there some essential value or point of view expressed by your character? Would the meaning of the other characters be as clear?

## CHARACTER TRAITS

In order for your character to serve the purpose within the play believably, the playwright will have provided the character with certain traits that make the required behavior and thought natural. Aristotle called these your character's "functional traits." Whatever other traits are suggested by the text, or whatever else you may invent in the course of rehearsal to "round out" the character, you must fulfill these functional traits first and let no other traits obscure or contradict them.

We classify all characterizational traits in four categories, as outlined here by Oscar Brockett:

> The first level of characterization is physical and is concerned only with such basic facts as sex, age, size, and color. Sometimes a dramatist does not supply all of this information, but it is present whenever the play is produced, since actors necessarily give concrete form to the characters. The physical is the simplest level of characterization, however, since it reveals external traits only, many of which may not affect the dramatic action at all.
>
> The second level is social. It includes a character's economic status, profession or trade, religion, family relationships—all those factors that place him in his environment.
>
> The third level is psychological. It reveals a character's habitual responses, attitudes, desires, motivations, likes and dislikes—the inner workings of the mind, both emotional and intellectual, which precede action. Since habits of feeling, thought, and behavior define characters more fully than do physical and social traits, and since drama most often arises from conflicting desires, the psychological is the most essential level of characterization.
>
> The fourth level is moral. Although implied in all plays, it is not always emphasized. It is most apt to be used in serious plays, especially tragedies. Although almost all human action suggests some ethical standard, in many plays the moral implications are ignored, and decisions are made on grounds of expediency. This is typical of comedy, since moral deliberations tend to make any action serious. More nearly than any other kind, moral decisions differentiate characters, since the choices they make when faced with moral crises show whether they are selfish, hypocritical, or persons of integrity. A moral decision usually causes a character to examine his own motives and values, in the process of which his true nature is revealed both to himself and to the audience.[1]

In the following lessons we will focus on several of these levels of characterization as they will develop through the rehearsal process. First, however, let's introduce each in broad outline, looking for the sort of information you might gather prior to rehearsal, during your early stages of preparation. And remember, we are looking for the *functional traits that contribute directly to the reason why the play was written.*

## PHYSICAL TRAITS

The first level is physical, and it is of primary importance to you, since the external traits of body and voice communicate all the other levels of characterization.

The playwright will have specified the essential aspects of your character's physical traits. There are four main sources of such information in any text. First, the *stage directions* or *prefaces* by the author. In his preface to *The Zoo Story*, for example, Albee specifies that Jerry is thirty-eight years old; do you see how it isn't the same play if you imagine Jerry as being only twenty-two?

Second, there are traits *described by other characters*; of course, we must evaluate such descriptions and determine if they are accurate, or perhaps distorted by the other character's prejudice. In Shakespeare's *Henry IV, Part One*, Prince Hal gives an elaborate description of the warlike Hotspur as "a popinjay," but his view is obviously clouded by the jealousy he feels for Hotspur. Aside from such distortions, however, the statements of other characters can be a valuable source of information. "Yon Cassius," in *Julius Caesar*, probably *should* have "a lean and hungry look."

Third, many traits can be deduced from the *style of the play*; a character, after all, lives in the world of the play and the style of that world is his or her reality. Someone in a Restoration comedy had better not slouch around like a Sam Shepard cowboy.

Fourth, and most important, are traits that are *implied by the action*; if you look at the most important actions that your character commits in the play, you will see that there are fundamental physical traits required in performing these actions believably. If Stanley Kowalski is going to rape Blanche, for example, he probably should have some of the "gnawing and swilling and hulking" quality that Blanche says he has, even though we can be sure that she is exaggerating.

### Exercise 63:
### Physical Traits

Examine the entire play from which your scene comes; find clues to your character's bodily and vocal traits. Check each of the following:

A. The stage directions: What does the playwright specifically tell you about your character's age, body, and so on?

B. Descriptions by other characters; What can you learn from what others say? Are their descriptions accurate, or prejudiced by their point of view?

C. What are the physical implications of the style of the play?

D. What are the physical implications of the action? Considering the most important things your character does, what physical traits do they need to believably perform these actions?


## SOCIAL TRAITS

This second level of characterization places the character in relation to the others in his or her world. This includes such factors as educational and social background, job or profession, and status. The fact that Stanley Kowalski is an ex-Marine sergeant and still dominates his peer group (he is captain of his bowling team) is important to an understanding of his personality.

The most important aspect of social characterization, of course, is the character's general and specific relationships (which we discussed as part of the given circumstances) with the other characters in the play. Just as our personality is greatly influenced by those around us in everyday life, so a dramatic character can be understood only in relationship to the other characters in the play.

As we watch characters on the stage, we get a great deal of information not only from what they do, but also from how all the other characters *relate* to them. As in life, we interpret character in relationship; if there is a disparity between the way a person wants to be perceived and the way others perceive him or her, we will always believe the others. If we are walking down the hall, for example, and I am trying to convince you that I am an important person around here, yet the people we pass are ignoring me, what will you think?

If you have ever been on stage with others who failed to relate properly to you, you will understand now why it was impossible to overcome the false impression they created of you. In fact, the common idea that your job as an actor is "to create your character" is somewhat erroneous; it would be truer to say that *you must create the other characters in the play.* If you will do that, you will find that you have inadvertently created yourself.

In *Death of a Salesman,* Willy has a relationship with each person in the play: father, husband, lover, neighbor, employee, salesman. We see Willy operating in each of these contexts, and each relationship reveals another aspect of Willy's character. Each of these relationships serves to penetrate the surface of his behavior and express the underlying truth of Willy's character, for his "I" is comprised of all of those "me's." Each of the other actors creates a part of Willy through these relationships, and so the actors must cooperate if Willy is to live fully for the audience.

In short, remember that *you create each other on stage more than you create yourself.*

### Exercise 64:
### Social Traits

A. Examine the play for information about your character's social background. If no specific information is given, make the best inferences you can. Consider each of these items:

1. Childhood environment
2. Educational background
3. Socioeconomic or class background
4. Work experiences

B. Consider your relationship to every other character in the play. How does each relationship reveal your needs, desires, and values?

C. Rehearse your scene with your partner: Your aim in this rehearsal is *to create each other.*

## PSYCHOLOGICAL TRAITS

Here we are concerned with the process of thought that is the antecedent of action. Brockett pointed out that "the psychological is the most important level of characterization" because it *justifies* and *motivates* all the others. Chekhov once said in a letter that "a playwright may invent any reality except one: the psychological." All characters in any kind of play must think before they act.

This is not to say that the psychology of character is always the most important element of the play as a whole. In plays where the external events of the plot are the dominant element, the psychological aspect of characterization may serve merely to make the action believable. On the other hand, in plays featuring interior action (like those of Chekhov and O'Neill), the psychology of the characters may be the main interest of the play while the plot is secondary.

Just as a character's body has certain qualities, so his or her mind has certain qualities. Consider the *mental processes* of the character you are developing.

1. Are they simple or complex?
2. Are they fast or slow?
3. Are they rigid or flexible?
4. Are they precise or vague?
5. Are they reasoned or intuitive?
6. Are they global or sequential?

The last two items are qualities of "right-brain" or "left-brain" dominance: Right-brained people tend to think globally, in spatial and emotional terms, while left-brained people tend to reason in a linear way, in verbal and logical terms. If you want to give someone directions to your house, for instance, you should tell a left-brained person to "go three blocks down, turn right, go to the second light, and turn left." Right-brained people will have trouble with these kinds of directions; they will do better with a map. (One of the greatest difficulties in writing this book was to translate the global and intuitive skill of acting into a linear, verbal sequence; hopefully, you are putting it back together in your mind as you read.)

Your examination of your character's action has already provided you with the basis for understanding his or her psychology, and in the following lesson we will extend this understanding in considerable detail. For now, ask these basic questions about the character you have been developing.

### Exercise 65:
### Psychological Traits

A. Consider the way your character thinks: Is his or her mind slow or fast, simple or complex, flexible or rigid, precise or vague, right-brain or left-brain dominant?

B. Select the most significant choices made by your character in the play: What does each tell you about your character's mind?

## MORAL TRAITS

This level refers to your character's values, especially the character's sense of right and wrong, sense of beauty, and religious and political beliefs. When this aspect of character is important *it will always relate directly to the thematic content of the play.* The moral choice confronting Willy Loman, for example, is an embodiment of Arthur

Miller's thesis regarding the erosion of spiritual values by our society's emphasis on material values as a measure of self-worth.

Your thinking about your character's superobjective has already brought much of the character's morality into focus; after all, the superobjective and the means used to achieve it are the active expressions of your character's values. Blanche DuBois, for instance, tries to use sex to achieve sanctuary, but we do not think of her as an immoral character, as Stanley does, because unlike Stanley we can understand the level of her desperation and we know that her affairs were hollow gestures that did not involve her essential self.

### Exercise 66:
### Moral Traits

Speaking as your character, complete the following statements:

My religious preference is...
The greatest thing one person can do for another is...
The person I admire most is...
I would define a good person as someone who...
The person I detest most in the world is...
The most evil thing I can imagine is...
The ugliest thing I ever saw was...
The most beautiful thing I ever saw was...
After I die, I want to be remembered as someone who...

## ECONOMY OF CHARACTERIZATION

We have examined each of four levels of characterization. Each works in relation to the others, and the way they are put together reflects the purpose and nature of the play. Brockett explains this:

> A playwright may emphasize one or more of these levels. Some writers pay little attention to the physical appearance of their characters, concentrating instead upon psychological and moral traits; other dramatists may describe appearance and social status in detail. In assessing the completeness of a characterization it is not enough merely to make a list of traits and levels of characterization. It is also necessary to ask how the character functions in the play. For example, the audience needs to know little about the maid who only appears to announce dinner; any detailed characterization would be superfluous and distracting. On the other hand, the principal characters need to be drawn in greater depth. The appropriateness and completeness of each characterization, therefore, may be judged only after analyzing its function in each scene and in the play as a whole.[2]

It is a common impulse of actors to try to treat the maid who answers the door as if she were Lady Macbeth. This is not to say that the maid should not be fully characterized; she should be as fully characterized *as she needs to be.* Economy of characterization is to do everything that needs to be done, but no more.

Think of great athletes whose performances you have admired. These people's "style," their grace and power, come from the complete efficiency with which every bit of their energy is focused on the job at hand. They do nothing that does not directly contribute to their purpose; this is their economy. If your purpose is to be a maid answering the door, then any energy directed toward creating qualities beyond those necessary for the fulfillment of this task is wasteful and distracting. An overly detailed performance is as disruptive as an incomplete one.

## SUMMARY OF LESSON SIXTEEN

Your character was created by the playwright so that your behavior will contribute believably to the progress and meaning of the play; you have a specific purpose in relation to the whole. This is your *dramatic function.* No matter how "alive" your characterization may be, if it does not fulfill your dramatic function, you have failed.

In order for your character to serve his or her purpose within the play believably, the playwright will have provided you with certain traits that make the required behavior and thought natural. Aristotle called these the character's "functional traits."

These traits can be classified on four levels. The first level is *physical,* and it is of primary importance to you, since the external traits of body and voice communicate all the other levels of characterization. The second level is *social* and places your character in relation to the others in their world. As in life, the character on stage is perceived mainly in relationship, so remember that you create each other more than you create yourself. The third level is the *psychological* and is the most important because it *justifies* and *motivates* all the others. The fourth is the *moral* level and refers to your character's values.

A playwright may emphasize one or more of these levels. The appropriateness and completeness of your characterization may be judged only after analyzing its function in each scene and in the play as a whole.

Here is a checklist that reviews the work of this lesson. Use it as you begin rehearsals to be sure you have all the information you need to begin work; then check again near the end of rehearsals to be sure that you have considered all the possibilities.

### Exercise 67:
### A Character Checklist

A. What are the physical traits that influence your action?

1. Those specified by the playwright
2. Those reported by other characters
3. Those that can be inferred from the action

B. What are your social traits?

1. Your background and education
2. Your socioeconomic class
3. Your attitudes and behavior toward each of the other characters

C. What are your psychological traits?

1. Are your mental processes fast or slow?
2. Are your mental processes rigid or flexible?
3. Are your mental processes complex or simple?
4. Are you intuitive and global, or analytical and verbal?

D. What moral, religious, or political values influence your choices?

# Lesson Seventeen

## The Character's Mind

In Part Two, you learned that your character's need, aroused by the immediate circumstance, drives the character to form an objective that he or she then pursues through a "strategic action." In this lesson you will examine this process in detail to see how your character's mind is reflected in it.

Your character is required to react in a certain way, moment by moment, in order to move the story forward in the proper direction and with the proper qualities of style and meaning. The playwright has created your character so that these reactions and choices are believable and natural. *The psychological aspect of characterization results when you have discovered the inner process that justifies the external activities and manner of expression required by the plot, meaning, and style of the play.*

Unlike a novelist, who can take you inside a character's mind to show you the character's thought process, a dramatist can only imply it through actions. As an actor, you will learn to understand the psychology of action so that you can re-create your character's mental processes. This will be the greatest creative and personal contribution you will make to your performance, for it will be the foundation of all the other work you do.

Let's begin to examine the psychological aspects of action by setting up a hypothetical situation: Imagine that you see a notice on the callboard that I am directing a favorite play of yours. There is a part in this play that you have been dying to play, and you want to approach me about it. Even though you fear my possible rejection, your need is strong enough that you come to see me. You begin by "buttering me up" with your admiration for my work; you express your love for this particular play; finally, you tell me why you are perfect for the part and ask me to consider casting you; to your delight, I agree.

Let's examine what happens here step by step. First, you see the notice and it arouses you: We will call this your *stimulus*. This stimulus touches your long-standing desire to play the part, and so your arousal has a particular quality that reflects this need; we will call this your *attitude*. You are already beginning to form an *objective* (to get me to give you the part) and so you begin to *consider alternatives*, various ways of satisfying your aroused need: You might consider asking a mutual friend to approach me on your behalf, or perhaps you think about merely sending a photo and resume. After surveying your alternatives, you make a *choice* to act in the way you think will work best. You will see me in person; you will flatter me and then convince me of your love for the play and rightness for the part. This choice unleashes your *action*, which takes the form of *purposeful activity* to gain your *objective*.

This whole sequence is the mental process by which action is formed: A stimulus arouses you by touching a need expressed by an attitude, which generates a strategic choice, which results in action directed toward an objective. The steps in this process can be summarized by five key words: *Stimulus/Attitude/Choice/Action/Objective*. You can see this process represented graphically in Figure 22.

In Figure 22 the large circle represents your skin, the boundary between the "outer" and "inner" worlds. The stimulus sends energy toward you that enters you through *perception* (seeing, hearing, touching). Once inside you, it arouses a response in you that touches on some need or desire; it frightens you or pleases you or angers you, and so on; this is your *attitude* toward it.

If the nature of the stimulus and situation is such that it provokes an *automatic* or reflexive action, your reaction is immediate and involuntary, bypassing conscious thought. If, on the other hand, it requires thought, you *deliberate* over alternative ways of proceeding.

At the center of the process is the *strategic choice*, which creates the *action*, which you hope will win your *objective*.

As in the impulse circle exercise, this process of action moves the scene forward: Energy coming from the scene enters you through the stimulus, just like the slap you received; it then leaves

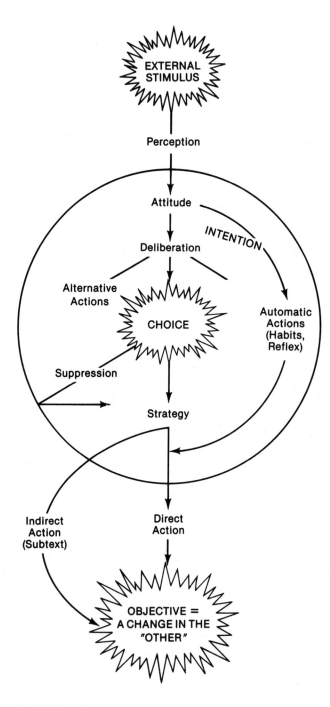

**FIGURE 22**   The Process of Action.

you through your action directed toward your objective, just like the slap you passed on. Your action becomes a stimulus for the next person, generates a reaction in them, which in turn generates another action, and so the scene moves.

Notice also that the energy leaving you as action is not the same in quality or intensity as the energy that entered you as the stimulus; it has been altered by the nature of your reaction to it.

Here is an example of the process of action from a scene in Brecht's *Mother Courage*. Anna (Mother Courage) and her mute daughter Kattrin receive word of the death of one of Anna's sons; Kattrin stares at her mother, whom she blames for her brother's death, and Anna responds by ordering her to polish some spoons. This seemingly insensitive reaction from the mother can be properly understood only by tracing Anna's inner thought process. Her "stream of consciousness" or *inner monologue* might sound like this:

1. S*timulus*: "Kattrin is looking at me with blame in her eyes."
2. *Attitude*: "I feel bad enough already; I don't need her blaming me too. Doesn't she understand that I didn't have any choice?"
3. *Alternatives*: "I could ignore her."
4. *Choice*: "No, that won't work. I'll take her mind off it by giving her something to do."
5. *Action*: "Polish the spoons!"
6. *Objective*: To stop her from looking at me and making me feel guilty.

You can see that Anna's needs, values, way of thinking, way of relating to the world—in short, her entire psychology—is involved and expressed in each step of this mental process.

## THE INSTROKE OF REACTION

In Figure 22, you see the energy coming from your external stimulus flowing inward toward your center through perception, attitude, and deliberation. At center, your choice turns the instroke of reaction into the outstroke of action toward an objective: *Choice is the point at which reaction turns into action*. It is this entire process that provides the compelling momentum of a complete action.

Actors sometimes fail to experience the instroke of reaction fully; they *do* something, but they aren't really receiving the stimulus that is *causing* them to do it. They only pretend to perceive what is said or done to them, preferring the safety of working only from their own feelings and refusing to allow the actions of others to influence them directly. When faced with this kind of actor, directors often say things like, "You didn't really hear her say that."

Don't let your fear of losing control of the performance turn you into this kind of hermetically sealed, self-stimulating actor. No matter how strong or how long-standing your character's needs are, the stimulus that triggers those needs will always be something "out there" in the scene, something someone else says or does; learn to look for stimuli that are *immediate* and *external*. Acting is not so much *doing* things as it is allowing yourself *to be made to do them*.

For example, there is a scene in *A Streetcar Named Desire* in which Blanche tells Mitch what happened years ago on the night that her young fiance killed himself (see the Appendix). Too often, actors play this scene as if the pain in Blanche is the main stimulus for the telling of the story. Played in this way, Mitch fades into the background and the story becomes a monologue instead of a scene. The actor must find the stimulus for the story not in her own need, but in Mitch and in the given circumstances; it is his capacity for understanding and the fact that they are alone on a romantic night that triggers her tremendous need to share in the hope that Mitch will take care of her.

Once the stimulus has been received, it must be interpreted; your character must evaluate it in relationship to his or her own needs. Is this a good thing? A threat? A surprise? The evaluation is expressed as an attitude toward the stimulus. Directors often help actors to be specific about attitude by asking, "How do you feel about that?" Learn to ask yourself this question as a regular part of your acting process.

You may notice that characters have a typical way of reacting to most stimuli; this can express their attitude toward the world in general. Are they optimistic or pessimistic? Does their attitude reveal any feeling that they may have about themselves? Willy Loman, for example, is quick to sense any criticism from others, and it makes him terribly defensive. This almost paranoid sensitivity reveals his fundamental insecurity and low self-esteem.

### Exercise 68:
### The Instroke of Reaction

Working with your partner, answer these questions about one of the scenes from the Appendix, or the scene you have chosen for yourself.

1. For each one of your character's actions, identify the external and the immediate stimulus.

2. Does your character respond more to some stimuli than to others? How do these sensitivities reflect his or her values and needs?
3. Consider what each stimulus means to your character; what is the character's attitude toward each? Does it trigger any needs already within the character?
4. What attitudes are typical of your character? What do they reveal about the character's attitude toward the world and the character's feelings about himself or herself?

## CHOICE

Because choice is the moment at which reaction turns into action, it is the essence of drama; the most suspenseful moments in plays occur when a character confronts a significant choice. As David Mamet points out, "The only thing we, as audience, care about in the theater is *what happens next*?"[1] From an actor's point of view, this question is really, "What is he or she going to do?"

The suspense is heightened when the choice is difficult, when the character is choosing between equally compelling (or equally unattractive) alternatives. In tragedy, these choices usually take the form of a "double bind" that involves loss no matter which alternative is chosen, as when characters must choose between their sense of truth or duty and their lives: *Antigone, A Man for All Seasons, Beckett, An Enemy of the People*, and *The Crucible* all center on such a choice. Critic Jan Kott describes it like this:

> A classic situation of tragedy is the necessity of making a choice between opposing values....The tragedy lies in the very principle of choice by which one of the values must be annihilated. The cruelty of the absolute lies in demanding such a choice and in imposing a situation that excludes the possibility of compromise.[2]

In comedy, the choices are not so serious; we might instead wonder something like, "How is he going to get away with it this time?"

Of course, not every choice your character makes is to be given the weight of the significant choices we have been discussing here, but every choice your character makes *that affects the progress of the play* must be well defined and experienced in each rehearsal or performance. These significant choices will usually be *beat changes* at which the choice forms a new action.

Choice cannot be experienced without viable *alternatives*; without real alternatives, you can only "act out" your character's choice, not relive it. If a choice is especially significant, the playwright will structure the situation so that you will know what the alternatives are; but most of the time the writer can only imply your character's view of the alternatives and you will have to supply them for yourself.

For this reason, you must consider not only what your character *does*, but also what he or she *chooses not to do*. When your character is presented with a significant choice (meaning any choice that affects the progress of the play), you must find for yourself the various alternatives and decide how the character would feel about each. The creation of these alternatives is a powerful way for you to enter into your character's mind, since they represent an inventory of the way the character sees the world.

Choice is the most revealing point in the process of action. In the making of significant choices, your character is responding to needs, to a way of seeing the world, and to relationships, beliefs, and values. If you can experience all the factors influencing your character's significant choices, you will be in touch with everything needed to create the psychological aspect of your characterization.

Following is a list of all the factors that may influence any particular choice. These may be either internal to the character or external in the character's environment.

1. Internal factors influencing choice
   a. Physiology
   b. Social background
   c. Needs and desires
   d. Psychological processes or "way of thinking"
   e. Ethical values
2. External factors influencing choice (the Givens)
   a. Relationships with, or attitudes toward, other characters
   b. The social environment
   c. The physical environment
   d. Specific immediate circumstances
3. Theatrical concerns requiring adjustment of choice
   a. The style or genre of the play
   b. The character's dramatic purpose in the play
   c. The visual and auditory demands of the performance space

While the last three are clearly "actor" concerns rather than "character" concerns, it is part of your job to justify your concerns as a performer as organic aspects of your character's inner world. In this way, the two levels of your "dual consciousness" as actor and character will work together toward the same goal and may eventually come together as a single experience.

### Exercise 69:
### Choice: The Center of the Bridge

As in Exercise 68, consider each of your actions in the scene. Focus on the choice from which each action springs.

A. Decide which are the most significant choices (there will probably be only two or three in a scene) and examine each in detail: What factors influence each? (Consider the list of factors provided above.)

B. Rehearse your scene with this awareness; take the time to experience each choice fully.

It is crucial that you truly live through your character's significant choices each time you face them, in rehearsal or performance. This means that you must keep the alternatives, the "things you don't do," alive as real possibilities. If you don't, you will simply be going through the motions. Only by reliving your character's choices within the given circumstances as if those choices were your own can you enter actively into the world and consciousness of the character; this is what triggers the transformational process, *the magic if*; if you were in the character's circumstance, and if you chose to do what the character does, who would you turn into?

Once the choice to act in a certain way has been made, your outwardly flowing action now becomes a *purposeful activity*, either a doing, a saying, or both, directed toward an objective. As you can see in Figure 22, this outstroke can take four forms: It can be an *automatic action*, which bypasses conscious choice and flows directly from perception to action; it can be a *direct action*, which goes at the objective straightforwardly; it can be an *indirect action*, which approaches the objective through some other activity; or it can be a *suppression*, a choice *not* to act. Let's examine each.

## AUTOMATIC ACTIONS

So far we have been describing a process of choice that involves conscious thought. There are obviously a great many things we do in life and on the stage that are not necessarily the result of conscious choice, however. These are called *involuntary* or *automatic actions*.

For example, when riding in a car and presented with sudden danger, you find yourself stepping on the brake, even though you are not driving. Characters on the stage have many responses of a similar kind: When the alarm bell rings, Othello reaches for his sword; when threatened, Laura runs to her menagerie or plays the phonograph. These are habitual actions that serve the needs of these characters on a deep level, and they require little or no conscious thought.

It is extremely useful when approaching a part to identify the automatic aspects of your character's behavior as soon as possible, for it is your task to re-create the character's habits in yourself for the purpose of rehearsing and performing the role. (It is neither necessary nor desirable that these habits invade your real life; we all have many habits that we "turn on and off" to suit the situation, and the habits you develop to play a role will be of this type. Remember that the aim of this personal work is not to "lose yourself" in your character, but to ensure that you don't lose the character in yourself.)

The formation of new habits is accomplished best by regular, spaced repetition over a period of time; you cannot count on rehearsals alone to do the job, nor should you waste the group's time on this sort of personal work. You must develop a program of homework that allows the formation of these habits through short, daily exercises.

When you consider how much of a character's behavior falls into the area of automatic actions, you will see what an important area of concern this is: The voice, the walk, the clothes, any special skills (like Othello's ability with the sword) or deformities (like Laura's limp)—these and more must become as natural and habitual to you as they are to your character.

Some psychologists have suggested that it takes three weeks of regular repetition to develop a new habit, so you can't wait very long to start. For instance, if your role involves swords, canes, robes, skirts, or a brace for Laura's leg, you will ask for a rehearsal substitute as soon as you can put down your script.

To sum up, follow this general rule: Whatever your character doesn't need to think about, you shouldn't need to think about; whatever your character *does* need to think about, you must think about each and every time you perform that action.

### Exercise 70:
### Automatic Actions

Again, review your scene with your partner; look for any automatic actions required of your character. Examine them to see what they tell you about your character.

What program of homework can you establish to develop these habits in yourself for this role?

## DIRECT AND INDIRECT ACTION

We have already discussed how characters will select an action that they think has the best chance for success in the given circumstances. When possible, they will probably select a direct action such as persuading, demanding, cajoling, or begging.

However, when there is an obstacle to direct action they will choose an indirect approach. Recall the Hostess/Guest scene in Part One; it showed how people in everyday life often mean one thing while saying or doing another. This is also common in drama, and we call these hidden intentions *subtext* because in such cases there is a difference between the surface activity (the text) and the submerged attitude or objective (the subtext).

The obstacle that makes the subtext necessary may be external or internal. For example, if I want to tell you that I love you, but I am afraid that you will reject me (internal obstacle), I may choose instead to talk about how lonely I am in this strange town, how dull the people I work with are, how you are the only interesting person I've met here, the only one I feel comfortable with....All this is an indirect way of expressing my love "safely." (This scene is from Chekhov's *The Three Sisters*. Chekhov explored indirect action more than any other playwright.)

Or if I want to tell a woman that I love her, but her husband is in the room with us (external obstacle), I may choose instead to talk about our pictures in the photo album, how wonderful she looked at the seashore last summer, what a wonderful time I had because she was there....Whatever I think I can say without alerting her husband. (This scene is from Ibsen's *Hedda Gabler*.)

Further, the character may be conscious of the subtext or unconscious. For instance, in *Mother Courage*, Anna's surface activity is to get Kattrin to polish the spoons, while her subtext is to stop Kattrin from making her feel guilty; this is a conscious subtext. In *The Glass Menagerie*, on the other hand, Amanda goes to great lengths to prepare Laura for her gentleman caller, but she also puts on her own party dress and hangs colored lights; we realize that Jim is also *her* gentleman caller and that she is reliving her youth through Laura; this is an unconscious subtext.

In all these cases, notice that the author has provided a surface activity through which the subtext may be expressed. You must accept this surface activity as your immediate action; it is disastrous to attempt to play the subtext. When actors make the mistake of bringing the subtext to the surface, it destroys the reality of the scene. For one thing, if the audience can see the subtext, they must wonder why the other characters can't. Iago has a continuous sub-textual objective of destroying Othello, but if we can see Iago's villainy and Othello can't, Othello will seem like a fool.

Trust the text and the audience; they will deduce from the situation what is really going on. Your job regarding subtext is to stay out of its way. Often subtext will work even if you are unaware of it. Besides, it is part of the fun for the audience to figure these things out for themselves; if you make it obvious, they don't get to play.

### Exercise 71:
### Subtext

Work through your scene with your partner; look for any indirectly expressed or hidden objectives.

1. Is the character conscious or unconscious of them?
2. Why can't they be expressed directly?
3. What surface activity has been provided through which they may be expressed?
4. Rehearse your scene with this awareness: Avoid playing the subtext.

## NOT DOING: SUPPRESSION

There is always at least one alternative available to a character in any situation, and that is the choice *not* to act, to suppress or delay action. Though we often think of "doing nothing" as a passive act, it can actually be a form of action. We call this *suppression*, which literally means "pushing down"; it often takes more effort to hold an impulse in than it would to let it out. Viewed in this way, there are no passive characters on the stage; there are only characters who are aroused but then choose *not* to act, which is itself a positive and playable action.

Repression is common in drama. Stage characters, like real people, may often be feeling and wanting much more than their overt actions indicate. The plays of Chekhov are especially rich as studies of suppression and prove that holding an impulse in can be more dramatic than its release.

Movement therapist Moshe Feldenkrais says this about the process of delaying or inhibiting impulses:

> The delay between thought process and its translation into action is long enough to make it possible to inhibit it. The possibility of creating the image of an action and then delaying its execution is the basis for imagination and for intellectual judgement....

The possibility of a pause between the creation of a thought pattern for any particular action and the execution of that action is the physical basis for self-awareness....

The possibility of delaying action, prolonging the period between the intention and its execution, enables man to know himself.[3]

The decision not to act aids in heightening dramatic tension and suspense. As you noticed in Figure 22, when characters choose to *suppress* an impulse, that unresolved energy is reflected back into them and builds up to become a source of increasing dynamic tension. There are many characters who do a lot of "not doing"; the most famous example is Hamlet, and others are Peter in *The Zoo Story* and Mitch in *A Streetcar Named Desire*.

One way to deal with suppression is to devote some rehearsal time to allowing the inhibited impulses to be released. By strengthening them in this way, you will be forced to work harder to hold them in when the scene is done in its normal form, and it is the effort to inhibit the impulse that turns the "not doing" into a "doing."

### Exercise 72:
### Not Doings

Work through your scene with your partner.

A. Considering your character in the entire play, do you see a pattern of suppression that may be affecting his or her choices in this scene? Are there any "not-doings" in this scene?

B. Rehearse allowing any suppressed material to be released, then immediately repeat the scene and hold in those same impulses.

As we said at the beginning of this lesson, re-creating your character's thought process is the most important single step toward transformation. One way to check the thoroughness of your psychological preparation is to verbalize your character's stream of consciousness. This technique is called the *inner monologue.*

Of course, the inner monologue is only an exercise and is meant to be done in private; you will *not* carry it into normal rehearsal or performance.

### Exercise 73:
### The Inner Monologue

Work through your scene with your partner; each of you softly speaks aloud the inner stream of thought that connects the external things you do and say. Go slowly and allow yourself to experience each step in the flow from stimulus to choice to objective. Your inner monologue might sound something like, "Look at that smug smile! He's not buying it at all. Maybe I could appeal to his vanity."

## SUMMARY OF LESSON SEVENTEEN

Your character is required to react in a certain way, moment by moment, in order to move the story forward with the proper qualities of style and meaning. The playwright has created your character so that these reactions and choices are believable and natural. The psychological aspect of characterization results when you have discovered the inner process that justifies the external activities and manner of expression required by the plot, meaning, and style of the play.

To re-create your character's mind you must understand the process by which action is formed: A stimulus arouses you by touching a need expressed by an attitude, which generates a strategic choice, which results in action directed toward an objective. The steps in this process can be summarized by five key words: *Stimulus/Attitude/Choice/Action/Objective.*

To keep connected to the scene, learn to look for stimuli that are immediate and external. Remember: Acting is not so much *doing* things as it is allowing yourself *to be made to do them.*

Once the stimulus has been received, it must be interpreted; your character must evaluate it in relationship to his or her own needs; this expresses the attitude toward the world in general.

Because choice is the moment at which reaction turns into action, the most suspenseful moments in plays occur when a character confronts a significant choice. Every choice your character makes that affects the progress of the play (the beat changes) must be well defined and experienced in each rehearsal or performance.

Experiencing choice requires that there be alternatives. Most of the time the writer can only imply your character's alternatives and you will have to supply them for yourself; consider not only what your character *does*, but also what he or she *chooses not to do.*

If you can experience all the factors influencing your character's significant choices, you will be in touch with everything needed to create the psychological aspect of your characterization. These factors may be either internal to the character or external in the character's environment.

Only by reliving your character's choices within the given circumstances as if they were your own can you enter actively into the world and consciousness of the character, and this is what triggers the transformational process, *the magic if.*

Once the choice to act in a certain way has been made, your outwardly flowing action becomes one of four types: It can be an *automatic action*, which bypasses conscious choice and flows directly from perception to action. It is extremely useful when approaching a part to identify the automatic aspects of your character's behavior as soon as possible; whatever your character doesn't need to think about, you shouldn't need to think about.

Your action can be *direct*, which goes at the objective straight-forwardly; or, when there is an obstacle to direct action, the character may choose an *indirect* action; we call these hidden intentions *subtext*. The obstacle that makes the subtext necessary may be external or internal, conscious or unconscious. In any case, the author has provided a surface activity through which the subtext may be expressed; it is disastrous to attempt to play the subtext.

Finally, your action can be a *suppression*, a choice *not* to act, which is itself a positive and playable action.

One way to check the thoroughness of your psychological preparation is to verbalize your character's stream of consciousness. This is a private technique called the *inner monologue* and is not intended to be used in normal rehearsal or performance.

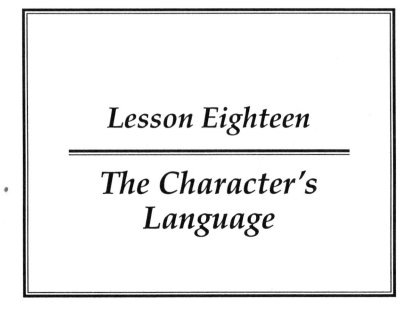

# Lesson Eighteen

## The Character's Language

In the last lesson you began to explore the character's mind. You will now continue that exploration by examining the character's speech and how it reflects thoughts and feelings as well as how it can affect you, the actor, as you recreate it in your performance.

Unlike the novelist, the playwright cannot describe the character directly (except in a limited way through stage directions or a preface). Characters must speak for themselves, and the dialogue is all that is left of the fullness of the author's conception. The words you will speak as the character, then, are the *residue* of a complete state of being; it is your job to re-create the fullness of the character by restoring body and consciousness to this residue.

This is made easier by the fact that playwrights, unlike any other writers, know that their language is going to be spoken aloud; they are writing for *you*, the actor, and only *through you* for the audience. Their first concern is the effect the language will have on you as you speak it: not only the ideas and associations it will generate in your mind, but also what the rhythm of it will do to your breathing and your body dynamic, what the sound of it will do to your articulatory muscles as you speak it, and the physical sensations its imagery can evoke in you. In a real way, the playwright is reaching deep inside your body and mind through the language of your character. As an example, read aloud this description of death from Shakespeare's *Measure for Measure, Act III*. It is spoken by a young man who has just learned that he is going to be executed in the morning. Feel the physical sensations it evokes, how the rhythm and sound of it can generate his feelings in you.

> Ay, but to die, and go we know not where;
> To lie in cold obstruction and to rot;
> This sensible warm motion to become
> A kneaded clod; and the delighted spirit
> To bathe in fiery floods, or to reside
> In thrilling regions of thick-ribbed ice;
> To be imprison'd in the viewless winds,
> And blown with restless violence round about
> The pendant world; or to be worse than worst
> Of those that lawless and in certain thought
> Imagine howling:—tis too horrible!

You don't need to be afraid of death in order to say this speech; the speech itself can terrify you.

You begin with words. A well-trained actor can find in a good text many specific clues about rhythms, inflections, emphases, and all sorts of characteristics needed to create a role. That is why performing the best writers—like Shakespeare—makes you a better actor. But a play is never like a coloring book; acting is not a matter of simply recognizing the playwright's outline and then "filling it in." The creation of a role is always a collaboration between you and the playwright, and also your director, fellow actors, and eventually your audience as well.

But the words are where you start, and at the beginning they are all you have.

## WORD CHOICE: TEXT AND SUBTEXT

You begin by understanding what the words mean, and why the playwright has chosen to have characters express themselves in precisely the way they do, not only because actors have a responsibility to communicate the meaning of their lines accurately, but also because it reveals the way their characters think and feel.

As we discussed in Lesson Six, a character's speech is the result of a process of verbalization; through a lightning-fast sequence of unconscious choices, the preverbal seed or *germ* of the idea is developed into full verbal form. This process automatically reflects the character's mind and personality, education and social background.

As you relive your character's process of verbalization you will begin to participate actively in the character's mental processes and feelings. Only when you have done this can you truly speak the words as if they were your own; until then, you are merely parroting someone else's words, learned by rote; you will sound stiff, mechanical, and false. You must *re-create* your character's words *as your own.*

In order to do this you must work backward from the residue provided by the playwright to the preverbal thought and feeling from which those words spring. For example, when Blanche DuBois arrives at her sister's apartment she looks around and says,

> ...Only Poe! Only Mr. Edgar Allan Poe!—could do it justice! Out there I suppose is the ghoul-haunted woodland of Weir!

You might begin with a germinal feeling of revulsion and disappointment: "How awful that Stella has to live here!" The awfulness of the place then gives rise to specific emotional associations with Poe, the great writer of horror stories, and the visionary painter Weir, whose imagery was fantastic and frightening.

However, this simple analysis would miss the real point. You must take the whole context of the character's speech into account. You know that Blanche has arrived here desperate; her life since the grand days on the plantation has become a series of one-night stands in cheap hotels far worse than this place (she calls one of them "The Tarantula Arms"); she lives like a prostitute (though she refuses to call it that), depending "on the kindness of strangers." She is clutching at her romantic past, still pretending to be the southern belle with her trunk of fake jewelry and furs. She must, in her heart, be jealous of Stella, who has a home, however poor, and more important a man, however crude, to take care of her. Blanche has come here as a last resort; it's the end of the streetcar line and the end of her line; the last stop before the asylum.

Understanding this context, you see that Blanche has to denigrate Stella and her home as a way of building herself up; by pretending to be repulsed by Stella's place, she is claiming to be used to much better and thereby denying her real past. She exaggerates her revulsion by comparing the place to the creations of two famous lunatics, Poe and Weir.

These artistic allusions—quite fashionable at one time—are also intended to put her above Stella as a more "refined" and "cultured" person, an attitude she probably had toward Stella even when they were young (and which may have been one cause for Stella leaving home). She is also reminding Stella that they share a sophisticated educational and social background; back home in the good old days, she is saying, Stella's present circumstances would have been considered the creation of a demented imagination.

Stella bursts Blanche's bubble with her sardonic dismissal, "No, honey, those are the L & N tracks," which really says, "I know it's not much, but it's good enough and better than what you've got," and on a deeper level, "Don't play your old games with me."

What we have done here is to *paraphrase* the character's speech, to put it into our own words in a way that expresses our understanding of both its surface meaning and its hidden meanings and attitudes, or *subtext*. This is an excellent technique for personalizing your character's speech; it forces you to return to the germinal meaning and re-create it in your own words, just as if you were translating it from some other language.

### Exercise 74:
### Paraphrase for Meaning and Subtext

Select a single speech from the scene you have been developing. Write a paraphrase on two levels:

A. First write a literal translation of the surface meaning into your own words; be sure you understand the meaning of each word and any references that the speech may make (this will inevitably sound stiff and prosaic). Blanche's speech would look like this:

*Only that drug-crazed writer of horror stories, only Mr. Edgar Allan Poe could describe this place adequately. The neighborhood looks like one of those terrible, frightening forests full of evil spirits waiting to jump at you, like the ones painted by that insane Mr. Weir.*

B. Then write a second, more personal paraphrase that expresses the subtext, if any. Again, Blanche's speech:

*This is awful! The only time I've had contact with a place like this is through the literature and painting of demented artists. How can you stand it? But then, you were always less sensitive than I am.*

C. Now perform all three: the literal paraphrase, the subtextual paraphrase, and finally the original speech. Are you beginning to feel that you "own" the words of the character, that you are speaking real words instead of memorized lines?

## RHYTHM

Rhythm is perhaps the single most powerful aspect of stage language. Rhythm functions in three primary ways: to support meaning, to express personality, and to express emotion.

Though rhythm is the most physical and least "intellectual" aspect of language, it is closely tied to and supportive of meaning. It functions not only as tempo (fast or slow), but also in the variations of tempo and force that give emphasis to certain words, sounds, images, or other elements of language.

In addition to supporting meaning through emphasis, rhythm is also highly expressive of personality. The blustery, pompous person has a rhythm much different from the thoughtful, introspective person. Even nationality and social background affect rhythm: The Irish, for example, tend to speak each thought on one long exhalation of breath, imparting an unmistakable rhythm to their speech. Good playwrights build these rhythms into the language that their characters speak so that a character's speech rhythms are appropriate to the character's personality and social background.

Emotions also have recognizable rhythmic implications. All emotion causes measurable changes in the tension of our muscles, and this has a direct effect on our speech. Take anger as an example: As anger rises in us, the body becomes tense, especially in the deep center, where the largest muscles mobilize themselves for action. Tension in the interior muscles is communicated directly to the diaphragm, limiting its movement and forcing us to take shallow breaths. Since we need to oxygenate the muscles for defense purposes, we compensate by taking more short breaths. Tension, spreading to the pharynx, causes an elevation of pitch, and coupled with the increased pressure of the breath stream, this results in a "punching" delivery and increased volume. The vestigial biting and tearing of the jaw related to anger encourage us to emphasize hard consonant sounds, so that our speech may become, in rage, similar to the snapping of an angry animal.

A skillful playwright shapes rhythm carefully, and on several levels at once: syllables, phrases, sentences, and speeches. The fundamental rhythm of a speech is established by the flow of *accented and unaccented syllables and words*. Look at the following example from Samuel Beckett's *Endgame*; you will see that Beckett has used rhythmic patterns of twos and threes; read it aloud for full rhythmic effect; let your feet move.

> One day you'll be blind, like me. You'll be sitting there, a speck in the void, in the dark, forever, like me. (pause) One day you'll say to yourself, I'm tired. I'll sit down, and you'll go and sit down. Then you'll say, I'm hungry, I'll get up and get something to eat. But you won't get up. You'll say, I shouldn't have sat down, but since I have I'll sit on a little longer, then I'll get up and get something to eat. (pause) But you won't get up and you won't get anything to eat.

The rhythmic flow of these syllables is as powerful as any formal poetry ever written.

The next level of rhythm involves *breath phrases*. The evolution of our written language was greatly influenced by the way we speak. A simple sentence can be said on a single breath. If a sentence becomes too complex for one breath, we break it up into phrases and create a compound sentence. Each of these phrases becomes a "sub-breath," a kind of "topping off" of the breath supply, within the main breath of the sentence. These sub-breath phrases are usually marked by commas, semicolons, or colons (in music, the comma is still used as a breath mark). The second sentence in the Beckett quote is a good example.

You can feel that playwrights use sentence structure to guide you into a pattern of breathing that, as you experienced in Part One, is a powerful factor in the generation of emotion. Try reading the Beckett piece above with a small breath at every comma, a full breath at each period, and a large breath at each pause. What emotional experience results?

A still larger pattern of rhythm is developed by the length of sentences, each one of which is usually one main breath. Sentence length is usually our best indicator of tempo; shorter sentences usually indicate a faster tempo, longer ones a slower tempo, though this is by no means a hard and fast rule.

Finally, sentences are grouped into *speeches*. We get a good impression of the rhythm of a scene by looking at the density of the printed script. A number of long speeches suggests a rhythm different from the back-and-forth exchange of a series of short lines. You can often see changes in a scene reflected in the speech rhythms; for example, the first character might have a number of very long speeches while the second character has only short replies, until the second "counterattacks" with a long speech, followed by a heated section in which both speak in short lines, often interrupting each other.

By responding sensitively to the rhythms and sounds the playwright has built into your character's speech, and by experiencing them fully in your own muscles, you will find them a powerful aid in entering into the consciousness of your character. As Stanislavski said:

> There is an indissoluble interdependence, interaction and bond between tempo-rhythm and feeling....The correctly established tempo-rhythm of a play or a role, can of itself, intuitively (on occasion automatically) take hold of the feelings of an actor and arouse in him a true sense of living his part.[1]

**Exercise 75:**
**Rhythm**

A. Using the same speech as in Exercise 74, mark its rhythmic units on each of the levels we have discussed; invent any system of marking that makes sense to you.

B. Read it aloud to stress each level of rhythm.

1. The flow of stressed and unstressed syllables
2. The main breath for each sentence and sub-breath for any phrases within compound sentences

C. Dance it.

D. Now examine the scene as a whole and see how the rhythm created by the give-and-take of the dialogue relates to the action and relationship. With your partner, read it aloud to experience this fully.


## MELODY

In our everyday life we have an intuitive and highly developed sense of the communicative value of sound and rhythm that together form the *melody* of speech. It is what gives our speech its color and individual flavor and helps us to catch implications, sarcasm, and other attitudes:

> Letters, syllables, words—these are the musical notes of speech, out of which to fashion measures, arias, whole symphonies. There is good reason to describe beautiful speech as musical.[2]

As Stanislavski indicates here, the actor must develop a heightened capacity for the musical aspects of speech. We do this not to produce beautiful sound, but because we must express extraordinary levels of feeling and experience. As he put it:

> Musical speech opens up endless possibilities of conveying the inner life of a role....What can we express with our ordinary register of five or six notes?...We realize how ridiculous we are when we have to express complicated emotions. It is like playing Beethoven on a balalaika.[3]

A good playwright selects and arranges words not only for meaning, but also for rhythmic and tonal values that support and enhance meaning, character, and emotion. Playwrights often say that their characters begin to "speak" to them as if they had minds and voices of their own. You can rejuvenate these inherent values of tone and rhythm: If you surrender yourself to experience them fully as muscular actions, you can bring them back to life for yourself, and through your experience for your audience as well.

Scholars have formed various theories about the relationship of sound and meaning in language. One of these was the Roback Voco-Sensory Theory. Experimental subjects were asked to assign meaning to several three-letter nonsense syllables, like *mil* and *mal*. To most people, *mal* seemed to mean something big, and *mil* something little. The theory explained this by noting that saying *mal* requires opening the mouth wide, while *mil* makes the mouth small.

The theory went on to suggest that much of language was formed by the association of the physical sensation of pronouncing certain sounds with the meaning of the sounds themselves. A word like "rough" feels rough when you say it, and "smooth" feels smooth, just as *rushing* rushes, *explode* explodes, and so on.

The voco-sensory theory can be disproved: For example, *small* is made up of "big" sounds, while *big* is "small." But the general idea is useful to you as an actor: A good playwright will have selected words that have sounds that generate appropriate sensations when pronounced. If you can let these sensations resonate in you, the physical act of pronouncing a speech will generate and support the appropriate feeling. As Stanislavski said:

> When an actor adds the vivid ornament of sound to the living content of the words, he causes me to glimpse with an inner vision the images he has fashioned out of his own creative imagination.[4]

On a larger scale, good writers will use qualities of sound to help distinguish one character from another, one mood from another, or the changing of emotional states within a role.

You might find, for example, that the sounds of Blanche's speeches are more melodious than Stella's, or that Stanley's are more animalistic (biting, guttural) than Mitch's. You might decide that the dominant sounds in one of these roles suggest a particular pitch range and inflectional pattern (regional dialect may be important here; Pinter needs his cockney as much as Williams needs the southern accent.)

To summarize, the melody and the rhythm of your stage language are very powerful sources of a true sense of character. Remember the work you did on vocal gesture in Part One and the profound relationship between sound, breath, energy, and character. As was pointed out in Part One, the word *personality* has a root meaning of *per-sona*, "through sound."

**Exercise 76:**
**Melody**

Using the same speech, read aloud:

1. What sounds are emphasized?
2. Considering the whole role, is there a pattern of sound, or any kind of sound that is dominant?
3. Are there changes in sound that reflect changes in emotion, action, or relationship?
4. Try singing the speech. What kind of music would best accompany your character?

## IMAGERY

Drama is one of the most condensed and intensified forms of literature; what a novelist needs thousands of words to do, a playwright must pack into the dialogue alone. Besides the heightened use of diction, rhythm, and melody you have already considered, the skillful playwright gets an extra measure of impact and meaning through the potential of language to evoke physical sensation. Stanislavksi reminds you: "To an actor a word is not just a sound, it is the evocation of images."[5]

In its most literal sense, an *image* is "something imagined." The painting of "word pictures" is the most common kind of imagery, but language may appeal to any of our other senses as well; hearing, smelling, touching, tasting, sense of movement and general body condition. Try speaking aloud this speech from a recent play, Peter Barnes's *Red Noses*; in it, a pope is speaking over the bodies of a troupe of friar/clowns whom he has just had killed:

> Wind blow the poppy seeds over them and us, aaaaaawwh. [*He howls softly as the lights fade down*]
> Heaven is dark and the earth a secret
> The cold snaps our bones, we shiver
> And dogs sniff round us, licking their paws
> Monsters eat our soul
> There is no way back
> Until God calls us to shadow
> So we rage at the wall and howl.
> Go down, she said, go down with me.
> World go down, dark go down,
> Universe and infinity go down,
> Go down with me, aaaaaaaawwh.
> [*The lights are out*]

Good delivery of imagery like this requires that you re-create the sights, sounds, and other sensations in yourself fully; you will then find the character's condition generated in you, and through you in the audience as well. Explore each image, re-create it in physical terms either through fantasy or memory of similar experiences, then allow this experience to remain stored in yourself as a specially created "sense memory."

One caution: Your aim is to enhance and support the meaning of the speech *as an action*. In this case, the remorse and existential horror of the pope drive the speech as a cry against nothingness. You want your delivery to remain "transparent" so that the action can be experienced *through* the language of the speech; if your audience is more aware of your delivery and language than of the ideas and sensations of the character, you will have failed.

### Exercise 77:
### Imagery

Check your speech for any physical sensations it imparts. Dwell on each, re-creating it through fantasy or memory. Then read the speech aloud, taking the time to reexperience each sensation as fully as you can.

### SUMMARY OF LESSON EIGHTEEN

The words you will speak as the character are the *residue* of a complete state of being; it is your job to re-create the fullness of the character by restoring body and consciousness to this residue.

This is made easier by the fact that the playwright's first concern is the effect the language will have on you as you speak it: In a real way, the playwright is reaching deep inside your body and mind through the language of your character.

A well-trained actor finds many specific clues about rhythms, inflections, emphases, and all sorts of characteristics needed to create a role in the language, but acting is not a matter of simply recognizing the playwright's outline and then "filling it in."

You begin by understanding what your words mean, and why the playwright has chosen to have the character express himself or herself in precisely this way, not only because you have a responsibility to the meaning of your lines, but also because the expression reveals the way your character thinks and feels.

As we discussed in Lesson Six, a character's speech is the result of a process of verbalization; as you relive your character's process of verbalization you will begin to participate actively in the character's mental processes and feelings. You must *re-create* your character's words *as your own*.

In order to do this you must work backward from the residue provided by the playwright to the preverbal thought and feeling from which those words spring, taking into account the whole context of the character's speech. One good way to do this is to *paraphrase* the character's speech, to put it into your own words in a way that expresses your understanding of both its surface meaning and its hidden meanings and attitudes, or *subtext*.

Rhythm is perhaps the single most powerful aspect of stage language. It functions in three primary ways: to support meaning, to express personality, and to express emotion.

A skillful playwright shapes rhythm carefully, and on several levels at once: syllables, phrases, sentences, and speeches. You can often see changes in a scene reflected in the speech rhythms.

Good writers will use qualities of rhythm and sound to help distinguish one character from another, one mood from another, or the changing of emotional states within a role. Remember that the word *personality* has a root meaning of *per-sona*, "through sound."

The skillful playwright gets an extra measure of impact and meaning through the potential of language to evoke physical sensation. The painting of "word pictures" is the most common kind of imagery, but language may appeal to any of our other senses as well; your job is to explore each image, re-create it in physical terms either through fantasy or memory of similar experiences, then allow it to remain stored in yourself as a specially created "sense memory."

Remember, however, that your aim is to enhance and support the meaning of the speech *as an action*. If your audience is more aware of your delivery and language than of the ideas and sensations of the character, you will have failed.

# Lesson Nineteen

## The Character's Body

In everyday life we can sense the way a person's body reflects not only mood, but also personality. We call this "body language."

The reading of "body language" has become an important skill in our culture. Singles use it to identify likely partners, lawyers to select jurors, salespeople to determine their strategy toward a customer, interviewers to help evaluate applicants, and politicians to project desirable qualities of personality. In general, we tend to trust body language as a more accurate expression of personality and attitude than spoken language, as in the Hostess/Guest scene in Part One.

The theater makes special use of this universal physical language. The image of Willy Loman walking with bent back, shuffling through the opening scene of *Death of a Salesman* communicates a vivid sense of Willy's situation to audiences in Chicago or Peking; so, in their own way, do the formal, precise gestures of the Kabuki actor as he employs the conventions of his theater to express real action and emotion.

### PERSONALITY IN THE BODY

Many aspects of personality come to be carried within the body. This is reflected not only in posture and gesture, but also in actual structure. These expressive structural patterns are caused by the cumulative effect of repeated behavioral patterns, especially those behavioral patterns in which we suppress or "hold in" certain impulses and reactions.

As Alexander Lowen, a psychoanalyst who works in the field he calls bioenergetics, puts it:

> The muscles can hold back movements as well as execute them....Consider the case of an individual who is charged with rage and yet must hold back the impulse to strike. His fists are clenched, his arms are tense and his shoulders are drawn and held back to restrain the impulse.[1]

If rage is suppressed in this way often enough, the muscular tension in the hands, arms, and upper back becomes chronic. Because of this long-term tension, the muscles and other tissues in these areas eventually harden, losing their flexibility and sensitivity. The rigidity of these areas will eventually affect the person's posture and movement, and a trained observer can diagnose the precise psychological pattern captured in this musculature.

Even without special training most of us can form fairly accurate impressions of people who "harbor a lot of resentment" or who are "sitting on a lot of grief" or who "are afraid of their own sexuality," to name a few examples.

The suppression of emotion is not the only way this kind of structure can be created. The influence of heredity, the infant's mimicry of the parents' bodily motions, and patterns of social response (like the teenager's slouching) can all become "built in" to the body.

Perhaps in your adolescence you were motivated to develop a "tough" image; you achieved this by thrusting out your chest, pelvis, or jaw. Years later, even though this social motivation has ceased, these earlier muscular patterns are still operating, literally "built in" to your body by habit; the shoulders are still pulled back, the pelvis is tilted to one side, the chin is thrust forward. These muscular patterns may have become expressive of your personality and will continue to influence the way you confront life, and people you meet may initially think, "Boy, does this person have something to prove!"

Such a long-term pattern eventually alters the muscles and connective tissues so that the pattern becomes part of the body's structure. Affected areas can become rigid, hard, overdeveloped, and cold (due to poor blood circulation) or, conversely, collapsed and weak through disuse. Some therapists call such semipermanent alterations in the body's structure a *character structure* or *armor*.

## THE CHARACTER'S CENTER

You experienced your own bodily center in Part One. Though it may move in various emotional states (we can be "up" one day and "down" the next) each of us has a normal center. The location of your energy center, and the quality of the energy it contains, can be a profound expression of your attitude toward life; likewise, in your creation of a dramatic character you will work to discover a physiovocal center that is consistent with the character's attitudes and behavior.

We can suggest five primary character centers that by bodily logic and cultural tradition are each associated with a different sort of person: head, chest, stomach, genitals, and anus. (See Figure 23.) Let's look briefly at each.

The *head*-centered person may be thought of as cerebral, "other worldly," flighty, scattered, or off-balance. These people always seem "ahead of themselves." Their energy seems to come out through their eyes or their mouth; if they're passive, they may do a lot of watching; if they're active, they may do a lot of talking or be very aware of oral activity of all sorts, which may be their way of sublimating their sexual energy ("Chew, chew, chew," Amanda tells Tom in *The Glass Menagerie.*)

The *chest*-centered person might have a lot of "heart" and be either quite sentimental or proud and "militaristic."

The *stomach* person is usually carrying the badge of self-indulgence. Stomach-centered people are usually good-natured, easygo-

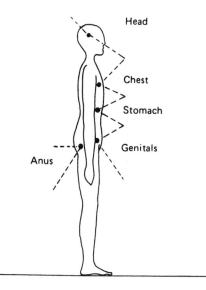

**FIGURE 23** Primary Body Centers.

ing, and nurturing people, and also usually make good parents.

The *genitally* centered person might be sexy, either in a libidinous way, or contrarily in a naive way like the "farmer's daughter."

The *anal* person seems severe, sexually withdrawn, often stingy ("constipated"), dogmatic, and rigid in behavior.

We have all known people who tend to relate to the world from one of these centers; observe some of your acquaintances from this point of view. Think also of some specific dramatic characters and imagine how this idea of centers would apply to each. What center might Amanda have in *The Glass Menagerie*? Blanche in *A Streetcar Named Desire*? Peter in *The Zoo Story*?

When we sense that someone is operating from one or another of these bodily centers, we tend to expect one of the behavior patterns described above, so the placement of the character's center is a powerful tool of characterization. Moreover, if a character undergoes a radical change in the course of the play, it is possible that the center will shift. Think of King Lear; he could be played as a man who is driven out of his mind and into his heart.

More important than its influence on an audience is the power of the bodily center to affect you as you work on the role, moving you toward a transformational experience of character. You will find that the bodily movement of your character is a powerful force in the development of characterization. Bringing your own center into conformity with your character's center is perhaps the most fundamental physical characterizational choice.

### Exercise 78:
### The Character Center

A. Examine Figure 23: "Put on" some of these character centers. Experience your energy as initiating in them; move about and enter into improvised relationships. See what attitudes are evoked in you.

B. Consider various characters from plays you have read; which center seems right for each? Which center might be right for Jerry in *The Zoo Story*? For Peter? For Charley in *Death of a Salesman*? For Amanda in *The Glass Menagerie*? Do any of these characters undergo changes that might result in a shift of their center?

## THE FLOW OF BODILY ENERGY

As we have said, the body takes on the physical qualities we associate with various kinds of characters through the repetition of certain responses to life. We will now trace the bodily path taken by this process of stimulus and response.

As you are reading this, recall a moment from the scene you have been rehearsing when you committed some strong physical action. Take a moment to recall the experience as vividly as you can, so that it feels almost as if you were doing it again right now.

Feel the energy that is in your center; what is your level of arousal? Is it a high charge or a low charge? We call this its *dynamic*.

Next, follow this energy as it flows away from your center; is it moving predominantly upward or downward or equally in both directions away from your center?

Notice that the musculature of your body offers two energy pathways running up and down the body. One pathway runs along the back of your body, another along the front. Because the muscles of the back are large and strong, the rear pathway usually carries your aggressive and sexual energies; the muscles and tissues in the front of your body are softer and more accessible or vulnerable, so that the front pathway usually carries our "tender" feelings. Which pathway are you using now?

Consider whether the energy is impeded or even blocked from flowing through certain areas of your body. Some of the most common points of blockage are the jaw, nape of the neck, small of the back, across the chest, or between the shoulder blades. You can perhaps feel such blockages of this energy within your own body; are the blocks, if any, habitual to you, or did you intuitively create them as part of the character? Finally, become aware of how the energy leaves your body: Is there an area or part of the body through which it tends to exit?

You now have traced the pathway by which any motion or sound must begin in a deep center and move through the various energy pathways of the musculature until it erupts into the outer world. When it does, it carries with it the tone, color, and shape of the interior world through which it has passed. Through this process, our physical and vocal expressions become a means by which we "turn ourselves inside out" and make a public expression of our private world.

We have all learned to read these signs, and our everyday language reflects this process: We speak of the happy person as "light-hearted" or "on cloud nine," while the depressed person is a "drag" or a "downer."

Consider the tremendous expressiveness of a person's walk. Insecure people with a weak sense of self-identity tend to be cautious, to "walk on eggshells." We speak of such people as "pushovers," people who "won't stand on their own two feet." In the opposite extreme are the "pushy" people who carry their weight on the balls of their feet and whose energy flows up the back into the aggressive stance of a fighter, and who walk as if they were punishing the floor and expecting everything to get out of their way. It is not surprising that Sir Alec Guiness has said that he knows he has found the essential ingredients of a character when he has found his walk.


## PHYSIQUE AND PERSONALITY

As we said earlier, repeated patterns of behavior may begin to alter the very structure of the body. We come to hold our energy in a way that affects the contours of our body, so that the body soon comes to announce the nature of the energy that inhabits it. The Elizabethan idea of reading character in the body (for example, "This is the forehead of a murderer") was crude but entirely accurate in principle.

When we meet someone, we tend to form a distinct impression of his or her personality and mood from his or her overall bodily condition: this fact is especially important on stage, where audiences are encouraged to read the whole body more acutely than we do in real life. We will consider, then, how the contours of the body may communicate specific impressions of personality.

We must first, however, distinguish between the way the body is held, which is called *alignment*, and the basic structure of the body itself, which is called *physique*. Certain physiques carry particular associations within our culture: The large-abdomened *endomorph*, for example, is thought of as jolly, easygoing, and a good family type; the thin, wiry *ectomorph*, on the other hand, is expected to be nervous and compulsive, while the muscular *mesomorph* is expected to be a lot like Stanley Kowalski.

These body types are of limited importance in the theater. To be sure, it might be unreasonable to cast an endomorphic actor as the mesomorphic Stanley, but within such broad limits it is possible for almost any physique to capture the psychophysical essence of a role on the stage. Though Lee J. Cobb and Dustin Hoffman have very different physiques, they were each successful in the role of Willy Loman.

The camera, on the other hand, has no tolerance for fundamental adjustments of physique that, despite the most skillful makeup and costuming, usually seem false. Insofar as this is true, film and television must be "type cast," at least as far as physique is concerned. Serious film actors sometimes go to extreme lengths in this regard, as did Robert DeNiro when he gained sixty pounds to capture the degradation of his character in *Raging Bull*.

## BODY ALIGNMENT AND CHARACTER

Bodily alignment, as opposed to physique, can be successfully adjusted both on stage and for the camera. Let's look at the specific qualities that are commonly associated with various bodily alignments. Examine Figure 24 and consider the qualities that each body suggests.

The first body, which features rounded shoulders and back, can have two very different qualities. When it is based on a low energy level, it is called the *oral* body. The chest is collapsed; the arms express yearning. The legs are weak, making the body unstable and poorly grounded. Aggressive energies at the rear are blocked, and a great deal of grief is held in the pit of the stomach.

On the other hand, when this structure is based upon a high energy level, it is called *masochistic*. The shoulders are rounded because of the overdevelopment of the muscles in the upper body, giving a gorilla-like hulking aspect. The bound-in aggressions of this type are turned inward upon the self; notice that the energy pathway along the back begins to approach a circle.

The second body is sometimes called the "militaristic character" because it resembles the stance of a soldier at attention. It is the

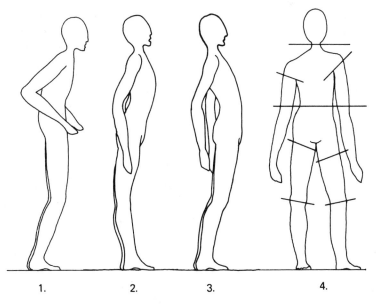

1.                2.                3.                4.

**FIGURE 24**   Basic Character Alignments.

most hostile of all alignments. The shoulders are thrown back and an enormous amount of anger is stored in the rigid area between the shoulder blades, the result of a long pattern of inhibited striking. This body is firmly rooted but so rigid in response that it is awkward, even mechanical. Aggressive energies stored in the back dominate, and the tender areas in the front of the body (chest and gut) are made hard. Small wonder that we train soldiers to stand this way and to not think for themselves.

The third body is clearly belly-centered. This "heavy" character responds with great equanimity and could be called the "aw shucks" body. We usually think of such characters as unaggressive (the sway back blocks the aggressive energies of the rear body) but jolly and sentimental (as the preponderance of the frontal energies would indicate).

The last body is called *schizoid*. Here the parts of the body at all the major joints are disassociated so that the person is literally "in pieces" and, as we say, "the right hand doesn't know what the left hand is doing." The head is often cocked in a birdlike way. This body is very unstable and poorly grounded; it lacks grace in movement.

### Exercise 79:
### Body Alignment

A. Try on each of the body alignments described in Figure 24. Focus your awareness not on how the body looks from the outside, but on how it feels from the inside. How does energy flow through it? How does it move? Where is it sensitive, where dead?

B. Do any of these alignments seem right for the character you have been developing? Try rehearsing your scene in this alignment.

## CHANGES IN BODILY ALIGNMENT

Although a bodily configuration may be deeply embedded in someone, it is still liable to surprisingly rapid change. I have seen extraordinary and permanent changes occur in people's body's almost instantaneously as a result of powerful life experiences or through therapy. Likewise, the bodies of dramatic characters who undergo radical changes in the course of their plays would believably change. The Willy Loman we see at the beginning of his play should not be the same Willy we see in his better days during the flashbacks, nor at the end when he is about to kill himself. Likewise, imagine the robust King Lear at the beginning of his play, and again after his ordeal in the storm when his daughter has to help him to walk. Do you see how such changes express not just the character's physical condition but psychological and even spiritual changes?

Remember that the theater is a bodily place. All its meanings, philosophical or psychological insights, emotions, and all that may be communicated by a play reach the spectator through the physical sensations that you, the actor, will generate. The "instrument" that creates the experience, your organism, is identical to the "instrument" that receives the experience, the spectator's organism, and there is an automatic and unconscious process by which your physical condition is mirrored in the deep muscles of your audience; whatever your physical condition is doing to you, it will also do to them. It is a real power: Use it well.

Following is an exercise that will review all the material we have covered in this lesson. It will help you to apply these principles to the physical life of the character you have been developing. It is important that these physical choices be made *after* you have experienced the character's givens, choices, and actions; you must have this foundation to ensure the rightness of your physical work, or it may become mere posturing.

### Exercise 80:
### A Journey into a Character Structure

In this exercise you will create the experience of "living inside" the body of the character you have been developing in the previous exercises. You will do this by making a series of simple choices as outlined below.

Allow at least one hour for this exercise and do it all in one session. The exercise has three ground rules:

1. Use the full range of everyday movements (walking, sitting, getting up and down) throughout the exercise; do not remain still for too long. Use the voice throughout as well; count, say the alphabet, say your lines or whatever comes to mind.
2. In each item, make your choices on the basis of what "feels" right; explore the whole range of choice before you settle on what seems to fit your subject. Remember: the basis for the choice is how the energy flow *feels* inside the body, not what "looks" right or what "ought" to be right. Allow your mind to just settle back and witness.
3. The choices are cumulative; stick to the sequence given. After you have made a choice, move on to the next and trust the body to retain the first.

Here are the choices in sequence:

1. *Attitude toward Gravity:* As in Exercise 16, experiment with your character's "root." Alternate from "plowing" to "floating" to "flying," and the stages between; select the attitude toward gravity that feels right.
2. *Center:* Review your choice of your character's center from the previous exercise; make it more specific.
3. *Dynamic:* Experience the energy flowing from center as a low charge or a high charge and the stages between; listen to the changes in the voice.
4. *Energy Pathways:* Determine the way energy flows within this body.
   a. Is it deep in the core or near the surface?
   b. Is it upward or downward from center?
   c. Is it mostly along the front or the back of the body?
5. *Blockages:* Are there places in this body where energy is blocked? Try blocking each of these locations and see if it feels right; if it does, allow the block to remain.
   a. Eyes
   b. Jaw
   c. Head/neck
   d. Space between the shoulder blades
   e. Space between the breasts
   f. Pit of the stomach
   g. Small of the back
   h. Genitals
6. *Bodily Alignment:* Try on each of the four alignments discussed.
   a. Oral
   b. Masochistic
   c. Militaristic
   d. "Aw shucks"
   e. Schizoid

Now, allowing the body to hold whatever it retains of these choices, stand with your partner or, better, in groups of four or five. Take turns speaking each of the following phrases, and allow a new spontaneous ending to erupt each time you repeat the phrase as you pass it around the group. If a spontaneous ending does not arise, simply say "pass."

When I wake up in the morning...
Ever since I was a child...
When I look in the mirror...

I can remember...
The child in me...
I need...
I hate...
Strength to me means...
Weakness to me means...
Right now I am aware...
Sometimes I want to cry out to people...
Pain to me is...
I love...
If I could be free to do what I want to do...
My body...
If you could hear the music in me...[2]

At the conclusion of the exercise, watch yourself for a time in a mirror, if possible. Then use the phasic relaxation exercise (Exercise 5) to "erase" the character structure you have created.

Share your experiences of this exercise. What did you learn about your character that you never knew before? What did your body teach you? Learn to treat the body as a source of discovery; there is much about acting that can be found only in physical experience.

### SUMMARY OF LESSON NINETEEN

Many aspects of personality come to be carried within the body. These expressive structural patterns are caused by the cumulative effect of repeated behavioral patterns, as well as heredity, the infant's mimicry of the parents, and patterns of social response. Some therapists call such semipermanent alterations in the body's structure *character structure* or *armor*.

Bringing your own center into conformity with your character's center is perhaps the most fundamental physical characterizational choice. There are five primary character centers that by bodily logic and cultural tradition are associated with different sorts of people: the *head*-centered person may be thought of as cerebral; the *chest*-centered person might have a lot of "heart," or the reverse and be "militaristic"; the *stomach* person is usually good-natured and easygoing; the *genital* person is either libidinous or naive; the *anal* person seems severe and rigid.

We must distinguish between the way the body is held, which is called *alignment*, and the basic structure of the body itself, which is called *physique*. Certain physiques carry particular associations within our culture: The large-abdomened *endomorph* is jolly, while the wiry *ectomorph* is nervous and compulsive, and the muscular *mesomorph* is a lot like Stanley Kowalski.

Within broad limits it is possible for almost any physique to capture the psychophysical essence of a role on the stage. The camera, on the other hand, has little tolerance for fundamental adjustments of physique.

Bodily alignment, as opposed to physique, can be successfully adjusted both on stage and for the camera. The oral body has a collapsed chest; the masochistic body has a gorilla-like hulking aspect. The militaristic body resembles the stance of a soldier at attention. The "aw shucks" body is unaggressive but sentimental. The schizoid body has its parts disassociated so that it is literally "in pieces."

Although a bodily configuration may be deeply embedded, it is still liable to surprisingly rapid change; the bodies of dramatic characters who undergo radical changes in the course of their plays would believably change.

Remember that the theater is a bodily place; whatever your physical condition is doing to you, it will also do to your audience. Use this power well.

# Lesson Twenty

## The Character's Emotion

What is emotion? The root meaning of the word is *an outward movement*. It is any activity that expresses the immediate condition of our organism and is directed toward the outside world. This doesn't mean that emotional activity is always meant to be communicative; rather, it arises automatically out of our efforts to relate to life. There are times, of course, when you want to make your feelings known to others, but the feelings themselves have arisen in the course of your interaction with the world.

In everyday life emotion serves several purposes. One is as a *safety valve* that provides a release of energy, pleasant or unpleasant, when your state of arousal gets too high. In this sense, emotions are one of your basic adaptive mechanisms.

Of special interest to actors is another function of emotion, that of a *value judgment* that you pass on your actions. Specifically, when you try to attain an objective and are successful, you become happy; when you try to attain an objective and fail due to your own actions, you are sad; when you try to attain an objective and are prevented by circumstance or by someone else's actions, you become angry; when you try to attain an objective and fail, and don't know why, you become afraid.

From both of these points of view, emotion is tied inextricably to action; it arises automatically from any significant effort to interact with the world. So it is on stage: *as an actor, you do not create emotion; rather, emotion arises of its own accord out of your action.*

## FROM ACTION TO EMOTION: WORKING FROM THE OUTSIDE IN

Near the turn of the century two psychologists, Fritz Lange and William James, developed a theory of emotion of special interest to the actor (Stanislavski was familiar with it). This theory holds that what we call emotion is our recognition of a bodily condition that is itself a response to some external situation; or, put another way, that *the emotion is the physical condition*.

Let's say you are stepping off a curb when, out of the corner of your eye, you see a car rushing toward you. Immediately you leap back out of danger. You are afraid, but you did not jump because you were afraid: You didn't have time to become afraid first, you had to react directly to the signal of danger; in acting terms it was an "automatic action." Your body prepared for "flight or fight," as the psychologists say, and only then, with your heart pounding, adrenalin flowing, your breath short, did you recognize your own condition and call it "fear." *Your emotion did not cause your action, your action caused your emotion.*

In *Death of a Salesman*, Miller describes Willy's first entrance:

> From the right, Willy Loman, the Salesman, enters, carrying two large sample cases... He is past sixty years of age, dressed quietly. Even as he crosses the stage to the doorway of the house, his exhaustion is apparent. He unlocks the door, comes into the kitchen, and thankfully lets his burden down, feeling the soreness of his palms. A word-sigh escapes his lips—it might be "Oh, boy, oh, boy."

This physical pattern by itself is powerful enough to generate an emotional state in you if you perform it with full participation of body and mind. As Plato noted two thousand years ago, the actor mimicking the gestures of an angry person tends to become angry. Or as some directors say today, "Do the act, and the feeling will follow."

However, Willy's action is more than the physical pattern described in this stage direction. What we are seeing is the final phase of a larger action, in which Willy tried once again to be a successful salesman by driving to Boston to see clients, but he has failed. As he says to Linda when she comes into the kitchen:

> WILLY: I suddenly couldn't drive any more. The car kept going off onto the shoulder, y'know?
>
> LINDA, [*helpfully*]: Oh. Maybe it was the steering again. I don't think Angelo knows the Studebaker.

WILLY: No, it's me, it's me. Suddenly I realize I'm goin' sixty miles an hour and I don't remember the last five minutes. I'm—I can't seem to—keep my mind to it.

His emotion is his evaluation of his action: He has failed in his objective, and it is his own fault, so he is sad. His emotion has arisen from his action, and the physical condition in which we see him has resulted. As the James–Lange Theory suggests, the emotion *is* the physical condition.

This process also aids you in rehearsal. As you try various things—movements, line readings, business—your own emotional response to what you are doing serves to guide you in checking the correctness of your action. This is what the experienced actor means when he or she tries something and then says, "It didn't feel right." This is not a judgment about an emotional state; it is an evaluation of the action itself through its resultant emotion. When you have found the *correct* act, then the *correct* feeling will follow, and it will coincide with the implied physical conditions embodied in the rhythms, sounds, and sensations of your text.

All this is meant to persuade you that you needn't be concerned with emotional behavior as such; if you are able to pursue your character's action with full involvement, the emotion *will arise automatically* and it *will* be communicated to your audience. You are *never* concerned with playing emotion.

This view of emotion, by the way, explains how feelings are communicated from actor to audience. It begins with simple physical imitation, which is unconscious and involuntary: If I watch you entering as Willy and your back is bowed and your chest collapsed, *my* back starts to bow and my chest minutely collapses. Because my body is now similar to yours, the emotion connected with that physical state is inspired in me. In this way I share your emotion directly; I participate in your exhaustion and dejection *even if I do not yet understand it.*

A note about stage directions: Some acting teachers encourage students to disregard stage directions because they want actors to discover the external form of the performance for themselves. This might make sense when you are dealing with an "acting version" of a play in which the stage directions have been inserted by a stage manager to describe what particular actors did in a particular production. But when the stage directions come from the playwright, they should be taken into account in the same way that a musician would note the diacritical markings for tempo and volume in a musical score. You and your director may eventually choose to disregard such specifics in your particular production, but you must consider the internal state that the playwright meant for them to imply, experience it, and only then express it in some other form.

### Exercise 81:
### Working from the Outside In

Examine your scene again, paying special attention to the external actions (words, gestures, movements) and the physical condition suggested for your character. Rehearse it to involve yourself in these externals as fully as possible; surrender to the experience that they produce in you.


## FROM THOUGHT TO EMOTION: WORKING FROM THE INSIDE OUT

We began by saying that emotion arises out of your attempts to cope with the world and is your way of evaluating these attempts; in this sense, emotion arises from action. But there is another way that emotion is also generated, and that is by your thoughts, expectations, and attitudes. The school of psychotherapy called "cognitive therapy" is based on this fact:

> The first principle of cognitive therapy is that all your moods are created by your "cognitions," or thoughts. A cognition refers to the way you look at things—your perceptions, mental attitudes, and beliefs. It includes the way you interpret things—what you say about something or someone to yourself. You feel the way you do right now because of the thoughts you are thinking at this moment....
>
> ...The moment you have a certain thought and believe it, you will experience an immediate emotional response. Your thought actually creates the emotion.[1]

For example, suppose you want to become an actor and are reading this, thinking, "Hey, that sounds good; Benedetti's approach could really help me!" This positive thought will make you feel good. If, on the other hand, you are thinking, "This is too silly, I could never do it," then your feeling will be negative.

Psychologists who treat depression have noticed that depressed people are seldom less "successful" in objective terms than many who are not depressed; the difference lies more in the way they subjectively view themselves and their lives. They send themselves negative messages, and every hint of failure confirms this negative self-attitude.

Some people hold a view of themselves as being unworthy: Like Willy Loman, they can't accept praise or success that they don't

Acting, as any art, must be generous; the attention of the artist must be focused outward—not on what he is feeling, but on what he is trying to accomplish.[3]

### Exercise 83:
### Emotional Recalls and Substitutions

A. Place yourself comfortably at rest and do the phasic relaxation exercise.

B. Now go through your scene mentally; picture the entire circumstance and live through your character's actions as if you were actually doing them in those circumstances. Let your body respond freely.

C. As you live through the scene, notice the emotional associations that arise. Do you remember events from your past? Do the other characters remind you of people you have known? Avoid internal censorship; release into these memories fully.

D. Now examine the most significant of these recalls. Ask yourself the following questions about this memory:

1. Where in my body is it located?
2. What is it like? How big is it, what color is it, how much does it weigh, is it hot or cold?
3. How does it make me feel about myself? About the other people in this memory?
4. Are there ideas, attitudes, or beliefs connected with this memory?
5. Do I recall making any choices at this time, even unconsciously, which have affected me since?
6. Are there images from even earlier times contained in this memory? If so, experience these: Continue to allow such images to flood up and take you back further and further in time.

E. Review this exercise and evaluate any connections that were made; are they useful to the scene? Do they need to be specified or altered to meet the exact demands of the scene or style of the play?

F. Rehearse your scene and simply allow these associations to "be there."

## THE ROLE OF EMOTION IN PERFORMANCE

Finally, we must say something about the way in which you will experience your character's emotions in performance.

Young actors sometimes think that they must re-create the character's emotion in order to generate each performance "truthfully," but this is an exhausting and unreliable way of working. Since emotion arises from action and thought, you need only *do* what your character does and *think* the thoughts involved in their action; the performance itself will give you the emotion.

We may sometimes be tempted to admire the emotionality of the actor who loses control and is overwhelmed on stage, but the display of emotion for its own sake is never our true purpose. The great actor aspires to use emotional technique to realize the truth of the character according to the demands of the play; the ultimate test of a performance is not only its emotional power, but the completeness with which it contributes to the whole play as a work of art; emotion is a means to this end, never an end in itself.

This was the position to which Stanislavski had come by the time of his last book, *Building a Character*, in which he said:

> Our art...requires that an actor experience the agony of his role, and weep his heart out at home or in rehearsals, that he then calm himself, get rid of every sentiment alien or obstructive to his part. He then comes out on the stage to convey to the audience in clear, pregnant, deeply felt, intelligible and eloquent terms what he has been through. At this point the spectators will be more affected than the actor, and he will conserve all his forces in order to direct them where he needs them most of all: in reproducing the inner life of the character he is portraying.[4]

The important idea here is that in performance "the spectators will be more affected than the actor." This is necessary for several reasons. First, strong emotion will interfere with your craftsmanship; as Stanislavski put it, "a person in the midst of experiencing a poignant emotional drama is incapable of speaking of it coherently."[5]

Second, it is unreliable to depend on emotion to generate a performance that must be done repeatedly on schedule. Stanislavski used the example of the opera singer who, at the moment the music requires a certain note with a certain feeling, cannot say to the conductor, "I'm not feeling it yet, give me four more measures."

Finally, and most important, your aim is the creation of a *transparent* performance, one through which we get a clear view of the events, characters, and ideas of the play. If your performance calls undue attention to itself, you have failed. As an audience member I am not here to watch *you* weep; I am here to weep *myself*.

## SUMMARY OF LESSON TWENTY

An emotion is any activity that expresses the immediate condition of our organism and is directed toward the outside world. It arises automatically out of our efforts to relate to life.

In everyday life emotion serves several purposes. One is as a *safety valve* that provides a release of energy; another is as a *value judgment* that we pass on our actions. From both of these points of view, emotion arises automatically from any significant effort to interact with the world. So it is on stage: *You do not create emotion; rather, emotion arises of its own accord out of your action.*

The James–Lange theory holds that what we call emotion is our recognition of a bodily condition that is itself a response to some external situation; or, put another way, that *the emotion is the physical condition.* This physical condition is powerful enough to generate an emotional state in you if you perform it with full participation of body and mind; as some directors say, "Do the act, and the feeling will follow."

This process also aids you in rehearsal. As you try various things—movements, line readings, business—your own emotional response to what you are doing serves to guide you in checking the correctness of your action. When you have found the correct act, the correct feeling will follow, and it will coincide with the implied physical conditions embodied in the rhythms, sounds, and sensations of your text.

It follows that you needn't be concerned with emotional behavior as such; if you are able to pursue your character's action with full involvement, the emotion *will arise automatically* and it *will* be communicated to your audience. You are *never* concerned with playing emotion.

While it is true that emotion arises from action, there is also another way that emotion is generated, and that is by your thoughts, expectations, and attitudes. The first principle of the approach called cognitive therapy is that you feel the way you do right now because of the thoughts you are thinking at this moment. Your thought actually creates the emotion.

In developing the emotional life of a character, it may be useful to examine the character's self-image. A character's self-image affects his or her feelings and the choices made in "acting out" his or her life.

You see that it is possible to work either from the inside out or from the outside in. Emotion arises automatically out of your involvement in *both* the actions and thoughts of your character.

Though you may find one approach more powerful than the other, most actors work both ways simultaneously.

As emotion arises in rehearsal, it often brings with it associations or memories of past situations in your own life. Stanislavski experimented with the idea that the actor could develop a wealth of emotional memories as a resource for the acting process. There are several techniques by which stored memories may be evoked; one of the easiest is *visualization*. Another involves making a mental *substitution* of someone from your own life for one of the other characters in the scene. Recalls and substitutions needn't be rooted in real events; *fantasies* sometimes supply more powerful material.

As useful as emotional recall and substitution may sometimes be, there are dangers connected with their use. Since memories and associations arise naturally in the course of preparing a role, not much is gained by using this process in a premeditated way, and much can be lost.

Young actors sometimes think that they must re-create the character's emotion in order to generate each performance "truthfully," but since emotion arises from action and thought, you need only *do* what your character does and *think* the thoughts involved in their action; the performance itself will give you the emotion.

# Lesson Twenty-One

## The Rehearsal Process I: Finding the Content

Now at last you are truly at work. Though there are various ways in which directors may choose to structure the rehearsal process, there is a common sequence to the way the work will usually progress. This sequence can be outlined as having the following ten steps:

1. Auditions
2. Preparation and homework
3. Early readings
4. Getting up and off book
5. Exploring the action
6. Establishing the score
7. Pacing the Performance
8. Polishing the performance
9. Technical and Dress Rehearsals
10. Growth after opening

The first five steps comprise the early period of exploration in which the *content* of the performance is being developed; we will discuss those five steps in this lesson. The last five steps are devoted to establishing the *form* of the performance; these steps will be discussed in the next lesson.

## AUDITIONS

Though not usually thought of as part of the rehearsal process, auditions are in fact a time when your initial approach to a role may greatly influence your later work.

Auditions are a nerve-wracking but necessary part of the actor's life. If it is any consolation to you, directors are under even more pressure during auditions than are actors; the initial casting of a play is the most influential step in the formation of an interpretation, and yet the director must usually make this crucial decision with only minimal knowledge of the actors.

Most directors have developed their own auditioning techniques, some of which can be rather disarming, but in general we can divide auditions into types, the "general" and the "specific."

Most general auditions, sometimes called "cattle calls," are used for preliminary screening for a role, or for entry into a company. In such auditions, you may be required to present two selections of different types; usually these are monologues, though in some enlightened situations scenes may be used.

You should develop a repertoire of at least three or four carefully chosen and prepared audition pieces, including comedy and tragedy, poetic and modern styles. About two minutes is a good length for each, though some might be as short as one minute, others as long as three. Beware of going on too long; actors often go on long enough to reveal their weaknesses. It is much better to make a strong initial impression and leave them hungry for more.

Shape each speech to have a smooth, logical progression; this will require some judicious editing, and internal cutting is allowable. In monologues where another character is assumed to be present, be careful to "create" the other person by the way you relate to him or her; place the character (in your mind) somewhere just off center (not off to one side) a bit closer to you than the auditioners. Do not look directly at the auditioners unless the speech is intended by the writer as direct address, and even then use everyone in the room, not just the auditioners.

Make sure each piece has a satisfying ending, even if that is not how it would be performed in context. Show the auditioners that you have a desire to satisfy an audience.

Your repertoire of speeches should be chosen to demonstrate your abilities to the best advantage, but most important, they should be material that you love; it will be a tremendous advantage to you if your positive feelings for your material outweigh your negative feelings about auditioning.

When auditioning for specific roles, you will probably be asked to read from the play at hand. In the live theater, you will usually be able to read the entire play in advance and prepare a selection from the role. In film and television, you are often given only a single scene from the play and a short time for preparation (though it is a union rule that an entire script must be available if you ask to see it).

Don't hesitate to ask questions about the character's given circumstances, about the contribution the character is expected to make to the show, or about the approach the director intends to take.

In the limited time available, your immediate job is to find a productive objective and playable action in the material, and to make that objective important to you through some kind of personalization. Use the principles you learned in Part Two.

Some actors can give good cold readings with only a few moments' work, but theater directors are sometimes suspicious of this; many times these slick cold-readers fail to develop much beyond their initial reading. In television, however, quick results are required; here, casting is often done by producers who are even more result-oriented than are directors; they want to see exactly what you will do on the set.

Perhaps the greatest challenge in an audition is to allow yourself to really be in the here and now. Usually, you will come away from an audition with only a vague sense of what happened or who was there; you are so threatened that you retreat into the back of your mind and become rigid or manic. Take a moment at the beginning to breathe, to see where you are and who is there; don't make a big thing of it; just treat it like a social situation in which you are glad to be present.

Then, as you perform, go for it. Make the event live. Don't be tied to your script (but don't ignore it either). It will be better to be a bit rough, perhaps not word-perfect, but alive, than to be technically correct but mechanical. Most important, make contact with the person you are performing with, whether an imaginary character, a stage manager, or a casting director. As in any other acting situation, the scene can live only *between* you two. Put your objective into that person; try to affect him or her.

In film and television auditions, don't try to create a character or some special emotional state: Just let yourself say what the character says and care about it as much, with your own voice and your own body. They don't want a character; they want you.

Some otherwise competent actors are slow of study and these "late bloomers" are at a disadvantage in most audition situations. Fortunately, most directors want to know about your past experience and get some reliable references about your previous work. You must be prepared to provide this information in an organized and attractive resume.

Your 8 x 10 photo will assist the director in remembering you; it should be current and "neutral"; that is, it should look like you and not limit the impression it provides of you to one quality like "sexy," "likable," or "dangerous."

Auditions will be much more enjoyable if you approach them without a sense of competitiveness. Think of them not as a contest with other actors but as an opportunity to communicate your potential to a director. Whether or not you are cast or get the particular role you wanted, auditions challenge you to face great pressure with integrity and a willing spirit.

Above all, do not take auditions personally. It usually requires many auditions before you will land a part (in film/TV about twenty seems to be an average, in live theater it varies tremendously). You can't take every rejection as a reflection on your talent. Auditions do not test your artistry so much as they test your usefulness to a director or producer for the specific role at hand. True, you have to deliver the goods, but first you have to be in the right place at the right time.

Take the long view and remember that the opinion formed of you at an audition may be important at some future time; it is therefore important that you honestly present your best abilities and avoid falsifying yourself for the sake of the particular instance. The question young actors most often ask about an audition is, "What do they want?" A much better question would be, "How can I best show them what kind of actor I am?"

## PREPARATION AND HOMEWORK

Now that you have been cast in your role, you will do some important preparation before rehearsals begin. Analysis, private experimentation, beginning to learn the lines, and private rehearsal of special skills must be accomplished outside the rehearsal hall. Never should you waste the time of your fellow actors and director by failing to do your homework.

Remember that homework is a *preparation* for rehearsal, not a *substitute* for it. Your prerehearsal work identifies the alternatives that need to be tested and prepares you to explore them aggressively in concert with your fellow workers; it does *not* determine the form of the finished product. Unfortunately, some actors are so insecure that they prepare for rehearsal as if it were performance, creating a rigidly premeditated form; the director then must be a sort of "referee," mediating between the various actors' ideas of how to play their roles. Remember that rehearsal is a time for *mutual* exploration through trial and error.

Depending on the demands of the play, your preparation may take various forms. You might need to develop certain technical skills related to the manner of the production, such as fencing, or dancing, or tumbling, or the use of canes, fans, large skirts, or robes, and so on.

There may be technical demands on your voice or body related to the specific character; Laurence Olivier devoted a full year to his vocal preparation for *Othello*; Robert DeNiro did extensive physical preparation for his role as a prizefighter in *Raging Bull*. As we noted in Part One, many of the physical and vocal skills demanded by your role will have to be practiced almost daily throughout the rehearsal period, and it is never too early to start.

In order to understand the character's world, you will want to have some sense of the fashion of the time, the ideas of grace, beauty, and social behavior. Experiencing the music, painting, and architecture of the time is valuable; documents such as diaries, letters, and newspapers can also be helpful. Review your list of the given circumstances; be sure you have considered all the possibilities.

Besides technical preparations of vocal and physical skills related to the external behavior of the character, you will also want to prepare yourself to enter the character's mind as well. For this purpose you may need to do research into the intellectual world from which the character comes; you will be most interested in those things that established the character's psychological and moral qualities, such as the religious and philosophical beliefs of the time, the educational experiences of the character, the quality of home life, the work environment, the system of government and justice, and so on.

The social backgrounds of plays as recent as *The Glass Menagerie* and *Death of a Salesman* are different enough from our own to require you to learn about life in the Great Depression and World War II, and about the popularity of "The American Dream" through such self-help methods as the Dale Carnegie books. Our credit-card culture, for example, cannot fully relate to the importance for Willy Loman of "weathering a twenty-year mortgage," or the humiliation for Amanda Wingfield of having to ask Garfinkle's Delicatessen for credit.

Two excellent ways for you to channel your research into the character's inner and outer worlds are to write an autobiography and write a diary entry for the character.

**Exercise 84:**
**Autobiography and Diary**

A. Imagine that as your character, you have been asked to write a short autobiographical sketch of yourself; limit yourself to two pages and include only those things that were most influential in your life; title your essay, "The Things That Made Me Who I Am."

B. Imagine also that you keep a diary; select an important day within the time frame of the play and write the diary entry for that day. Check your list of given circumstances and be sure you have described each.

As valuable as it is to do this sort of personal and psychological research on your character, you must also remember that your character is a creature of the theater; it will be useful for you to understand the theatrical world in which the character was created. Reading other plays by your author and his or her contemporaries can help, and so can study of the physical and social environment of the theater of the time. For instance, the open-air, thrust quality of the Elizabethan playhouse with its pit in which the "groundlings" stood throughout the performance is important to an understanding of Shakespeare's early plays. Just so, it is revealing to learn that the Moscow Art Theatre in which Chekhov's plays were first presented sat twelve hundred persons, so that the scale of the performances must have been somewhat larger than we usually think.

Likewise, coming to understand the literary conventions that influenced the playwright may help you to understand your character. It is revealing to learn of Chekhov's passion for the writing of the French Naturalists and their "scientific" approach to personality and behavior; this is even more illuminating when we consider his training as a doctor and the fact that he wrote his four great plays knowing that he was dying of tuberculosis.

In the same way, understanding the playwright's psychological and moral values can be revealing; it is helpful to know that Bertolt Brecht was an ambulance driver in World War I and was permanently affected by the carnage and misery he experienced then.

In all, remember that good plays are written out of a deep need to communicate some important insight into the human condition, and that you must approach your work with the same sense of purpose. This requires commitment, preparation, and homework beyond the confines of the rehearsal hall.

## Exercise 85:
## The Theatrical Life of the Play

A. Imagine that you are someone attending the very first performance of the play in which your character appears. Write an account of that performance, or simply relive it in your mind. Start the morning of the performance.

B. Pretend you are the author of your play and that you have just begun to write it. Write a letter to a friend and try to explain how you feel about this new play, why you are writing it, and what you hope to achieve with it.


## EARLY READ-THROUGHS

You are meeting for the first time with your fellow cast members. Your director may greet you in a variety of ways: Some will outline their interpretation and approach to the play; some will lead a discussion about it; some may do exercises to "break the ice" and to establish a working rapport in the ensemble; many will dispense with any such preliminaries and begin at once to read the play.

These first readings are your first forays into the heart of the material as it will come to live within your ensemble. Begin to work at once on the play as a whole; listen to it in the living voices of your fellow actors and begin to discover how it will live within this particular group of people.

Above all, read *in relationship*, with a spirit of give and take, reaction and action; get your awareness and your eyes out of your book as much as you can and contact the other characters in your scenes. Begin at once to search for the action that lives only in the specific transactions between the characters.

Read also with deep muscle involvement so that you involve your whole self; you will find that a wealth of associations and ideas well up.

These early rehearsals are exploration, but never indiscriminate exploration. Any meaningful exploration has a sense of goal that prevents it from degenerating into blind groping. Although a good bit of the rehearsal process consists of clarifying the goals of the production, there is usually in the vision of a play as communicated by the director some sense of the direction in which your exploration must go.

Not all of your rehearsal discoveries will result from conscious experimentation, of course; you must have the courage to be playful, to invite the *happy accident*. Such spontaneous discovery grows only from the receptiveness and responsiveness of each cast member to one another and to the moment; do not let your work on your own role make you closed to the work of others.

In these very early stages of rehearsal, before rapport has been established within the company, it is especially important that each actor make an act of faith to work together toward the defining of goals with respect, trust, good humor, and a generous heart.

## GETTING UP AND OFF BOOK

As soon as possible, you will begin to put your book aside so that you can explore the action on your feet. This, of course, requires learning the lines. You will have to find your own best method for line memorization. Some actors like to have a friend read the other parts (cue them); some make a tape recording of their lines to listen to at night; some even write out their lines. Many find it useful to begin working in paraphrase, finding the ideas behind the lines in their own words first.

However you work, learn the *action* as well as the lines; that is, learn the words in the context of the give-and-take of the scene, paying considerable attention to what the other character is saying in addition to your own responses. This is not only an easier way of learning lines; it also makes learning them a useful first step in your exploration of the action.

The transitional rehearsal period during which you are putting the book down can be a frustrating one. During the earlier phase of rehearsal, when you were still reading your lines, the information that your eyes received from the text passed directly the short distance to the brain; now you are beginning to re-create the whole process of action, the chain of reaction/choice/action that you experienced in Part Two. This requires the formation of a longer, deeper neurological pathway of response within your body from perception to attitude to alternatives to choice to action; you are literally translating the play from a "literary" form into the complete psychophysical form of the live performance.

During this period you must not waste rehearsals by stopping the flow of the emerging action, even if you must call for lines; it is expected that you will call for lines, so don't waste time apologizing, and above all *keep the action going while you call for lines in character.*

This is the time to get your rehearsal clothing and props and start using them regularly. Pay special attention to the effect of the character's clothing on your body, and be sure to wear the correct type of shoes to rehearsal to establish the correct relationship to gravity.

## EXPLORING THE ACTION

Now that you are off book, the blocking is being done or is beginning to emerge from the action. You and your partners are beginning to shape and specify the transactions of action/reaction that will form, link by link, the chain that binds the scenes and the play together, and making choices about each connection. This is the time to do a breakdown of the scene, whether you discuss it as such or not.

The many choices that must be made during rehearsal cannot be prejudged: You must actually do a thing in order to know whether it is right. Hopefully, one of the most common expressions you will hear during rehearsal is "Let's try it." Each choice you make will reveal more about the whole play, and in turn each of these revelations of the larger pattern will help you to find the rightness of each detail.

The rightness of any action will be determined by the way it fits into the cause–effect chain of interactions between characters, which in turn moves the play. There is a great difference between *making* something happen on stage and *letting* it happen; you can let a thing happen when the energies you receive and your response to them are in perfect accord with your desired results. When this has been accomplished, you *feel* the connectedness of every moment with every other moment and your through-line begins to emerge.

The through-line of your role is part of the action/reaction chain that moves the entire play. This binds you inseparably to the other actors, and them to you. Each of you has the right to receive, and the obligation to give, what will best serve the common purpose. By serving one another, we serve the play and our own creativity.

### Exercise 86:
### Making Connections

Work through your scene with your partner; either of you may stop the rehearsal at any point when you do not feel connected to the flow of the action, when you are not being "made" to do what you do.

At each point of difficulty, examine the moments that lead up to it; what can the others supply that will correct the problem? What do you need to be getting from your partner in order to be *made* to do what you do next? Work it out between you.

NOTE: You do *not* tell your partner what to do; you only say what you need; you might say something like "I need to be more threatened by that," but you leave it entirely to your partner to determine how best to threaten you.

What you are doing, of course, is creating the breakdown of the scene as a living experience.

This exercise will help you to realize that the problems we encounter in playing a scene are often symptoms of mistakes that were actually made earlier. Don't always try to fix a problem by making an immediate adjustment; retrace and see if you can clear it up by approaching the moment differently, or establishing some other value or relationship earlier. Remember that the through-line carries you along, and this is the phase of rehearsal in which you are beginning to find and establish it.

Since you have experienced all of your character's individual actions and have an emerging sense of how they connect, you will begin to form some idea about where they are ultimately headed; this, then, is the time that your *superobjective* will start to come into focus.

## SUMMARY OF LESSON TWENTY-ONE

As nerve-wracking as they are, auditions are a time when you can form an initial approach to a role. For general auditions you should develop a repertoire of three or four prepared audition pieces chosen to demonstrate your abilities to the best advantage, preferably material that you love.

When auditioning for specific roles, your immediate job is to find a productive objective and playable action in the material, and to make the objective important to you.

The greatest challenge in an audition is to allow yourself to be in the here and now. Make the event live by making contact with the person you are performing with (even if imaginary) and try to affect that person.

Take the long view and remember that the opinion formed of you at an audition may be important at some future time. Think "how can I best show them what kind of actor I am?"

Once cast, you begin your preparation: analysis, beginning to learn the lines, and private rehearsal of special skills must be accomplished outside the rehearsal hall. Remember that homework is a *preparation* for rehearsal, not a *substitute* for it.

Good plays are written out of a deep need to communicate some important insight into the human condition, and you must approach your work with the same sense of purpose.

At first readings begin at once to search for the action that lives in the transactions between the characters; read *in relationship*, with a spirit of give-and-take.

As soon as possible, put your book aside so that you can explore the action on your feet. Don't waste rehearsal time; keep the action going while you call for lines in character. This is the time to start using your rehearsal clothing and props regularly.

The breakdown of the scene will now be emerging, whether you discuss it as such or not. The rightness of any action will be determined by the way it fits into the action/reaction chain between characters; this binds you to the other actors, and them to you. Each of you has the right to receive, and the obligation to give, what will best serve the common purpose.

# Lesson Twenty-Two

## The Rehearsal Process II: Developing the Form

Having found much of the content of your performance, you now begin to develop a form that is expressive and reliable. The basis of this form is the sequence of actions that form the chain of action and reaction as the show begins to play "under its own power." This sequence of actions is the "map" of the scene's energy that you will follow each time you take the journey; it forms what Stanislavski called the *score* of the role.

### ESTABLISHING THE SCORE

You come to understand the score partly through analysis, but mostly through trial and error in rehearsal. As the score emerges from the actual experience of action and reaction, stimulus and response between you and your partner, you will begin naturally to assimilate it until it becomes part of you, an "inner model" that will guide you through the scene.

The score eventually becomes habitual; you absorb it so totally that you can begin to experience the scene fully, moment by moment, without thinking about anything except what your character is thinking about. This is the point at which your actor's awareness begins to give way to the character's awareness; when the score is completely automatic, then you can give yourself fully to each moment with complete attention to "the here and now," confident in the knowledge that the scene will move toward its proper conclusion. In a way, you must be able to do the scene "in your sleep" in order to be able to do it fully awake.

In *Creating a Role*, Stanislavski describes the operation of the score like this:

> With time and frequent repetition, in rehearsal and performance, this score becomes habitual. An actor becomes so accustomed to all his objectives and their sequence that he cannot conceive of approaching his role otherwise than along the line of the steps fixed in the score. Habit plays a great part in creativeness: it establishes in a firm way the accomplishments of creativeness....it makes what is difficult habitual, what is habitual easy, and what is easy beautiful. Habit creates second nature, which is second reality. The score automatically stirs the actor to physical action.[1]

In *Stanislavski Directs*, he is reported as saying:

> The law of theatrical art decrees: discover the correct conception in the scenic action, in your role, and in the beats of the play; and then make the correct habitual and the habitual beautiful.[2]

At what point do you commit to a choice and allow a particular element of the score to become habitual? Some actors wait a long time before making their final choices and approach their roles warily in early rehearsals, gradually filling in the full performance. Others work at performance levels right off, though they maintain enough flexibility to avoid making final choices too soon.

You will have to determine your own best approach, in terms of the disposition of the director, your fellow actors, the nature of the play, the length of the rehearsal period, and so on. To lie back and play the waiting game is usually unfair to your co-workers, since they depend upon you for their reactions, but neither should you make final choices too soon, committing yourself to insufficiently tested actions.

## PACING THE PERFORMANCE

You have seen how a sense of through-line and superobjective can provide unity and momentum to each momentary transaction of your performance. When the actors experience how each of their individual actions contribute to the flow of the whole, the performance will take on a momentum that provides a sense of urgency, significance, and rising dramatic tension. On the other hand, a performance lacking in momentum feels "flat" and fails to compel our attention: We commonly call this a lack of *pace*. Note that "pace," meaning the *momentum* of the action, is different from "tempo," which refers only to its *speed*.

When a performance lacks pace, there is a temptation to speed up or artificially "hype" the action; this is always a mistake. Good pace results only from the natural flow of the action when each transaction of reaction and action between the characters is real and complete. Rushing or forcing the scene only blurs these connections and harms the pace. Paradoxically, poor pace is usually best corrected by "taking the time" to reestablish the connections within the scene.

The best source of pace is the underlying conflict of the play itself. Whatever form the conflict has been given, it provides momentum by driving the conflicting forces against one another as the need for a resolution grows. If you can experience the conflict in this way, it can provide momentum as part of the intrinsic reality of the play, thus avoiding an artificial heightening of energy by rushing or forcing your action.

The given circumstances may also supply a sense of urgency: There may be an *external deadline* that requires that an objective be achieved as quickly as possible, such as someone coming, or the fear of discovery. More commonly there is an *internal deadline*, such as the need to do something before you lose your nerve, to say something before breaking into tears, and so on.

In some cases, since no playwright is perfect, it may be necessary for the actors to invent some external or internal source of momentum for a scene. This might involve redefining the given circumstances to provide urgency. Another strategy is to invent some surface activity—such as sewing, smoking, drinking, eating, or card playing—that might help you to channel your energy outward and thereby move the scene forward.

On the other hand, it may be that at moments of great tension or emotion, *containment* and *stillness* will produce better pace than activity. Remember that activity "spends" energy and that you must invest your stage energy with great discrimination; it is often true that "less is more," *if* it is the right "less."

One important element of good pace is *cuing*, the way in which one character begins to speak after another has finished. In real life, if you and I are discussing something, I listen to you in order to understand the idea you are trying to express. When I have grasped that idea, I form my response and am usually ready to begin answering *before* you have actually finished your sentence. Listen to real-life conversations; do you hear how we actually overlap one another's speeches slightly, or at least are *ready* to respond before the other person has stopped talking? Remember that the real source of a scene's pace is within the reality of the scene itself, not in any external technique applied by the actors. Any action, any piece of business, any emotion, or any character trait that impedes the pace of the scene should be discarded. As Stanislavski was fond of saying, "Cut 80 percent!"

### Exercise 87:
### Pacing the Scene

Examine your scene with your partner, looking for those aspects of the situation that provide urgency or a sense of deadline and thereby contribute to the scene's momentum:

1. The physical environment: time, place, and so forth
2. The social environment: customs, the presence of others
3. The situation: internal or external factors that create urgency or tension
4. The conflict between you

Now rehearse your scene to achieve good pace, and practice your listening and responding skills to produce good cuing.

## POLISHING THE PERFORMANCE

Having laid the foundation of your score and characterization, and having set the basic form of the performance, you begin to polish it by making various final *adjustments*. An adjustment is an alteration in the form of your performance made to meet some external need, such as a blocking problem, a lighting or scenic concern, the need of a fellow actor for support in a particular moment, and so on. You will make adjustments constantly in the course of rehearsal, and even in the course of performance.

Although the adjustment is in the external form of your performance, it must be *justified* by being the result of some change in the inner phase of the action. If you alter only the external form of your activity without adjusting the process of thought from which it springs, the results will seem forced, unnatural, and incomplete. For instance, if the director yells, "Louder!" you do not merely say the line more loudly: You instantaneously review the process of inner action from which the line springs and adjust something in the perception, attitude, or choice so that the line *must* be said more loudly.

You can also make adjustments by redefining the given circumstances; if the pace of the scene is poor, you might find a source of urgency by providing a deadline or other condition that will drive your character's action within the scene.

Further, since your stimulus is almost always the action of another character, you can even make adjustments by asking your fellow actor to provide you with a stimulus that will move you more readily toward the desired goal.

**Exercise 88:**
**Justifying Adjustments**

Select a section from your scene and use it to experiment with the making of performance adjustments: Justify each of the following by adjusting some phase of your inner action, the given circumstances, or the stimulus you are getting from your partner.

1. Explore adjustments that might be demanded by style:
   a. Do the scene as if it were a Classical tragedy.
   b. Do the scene as if it were a romantic comedy.
   c. Do the scene as if it were a farce.
   d. Do the scene as if it were modern realism.
2. Explore adjustments that might be demanded by the theater:
   a. Do the scene for a huge auditorium.
   b. Do the scene for an arena stage.
   c. Do the scene for a film.
3. If possible, work with someone as director, and practice justifying changes in blocking, tempo, volume, and so on., as requested by the director.

## TECHNICAL AND DRESS REHEARSALS

The final phase of the rehearsal period is devoted to incorporating the full production elements: makeup, props, costumes, set, lights, and sound. Ideally, this is a time of completion and crystallization of your performance; many actors do not feel that their work comes fully to life until all the physical production elements are in place. Stanislavski spoke of completing a characterization only when, in full makeup and costume, he would rehearse before a mirror to be sure that his external appearance was correct.

In most American theaters, only the final week of rehearsal is devoted to the assimilation of all the completed technical elements. This can be a period of tremendous frustration and distraction for you if you have not prepared yourself for it in the earlier stages of rehearsal.

Above all, avoid the temptation to "freeze" your work during this final phase of rehearsal. Many fine performances wither on the vine before opening because the outer form becomes the focus of the actor's attention and the inner phase of action ceases to live and grow. Use the addition of the technical elements as an opportunity to extend and specify the score of your role, and to explore further the life of the character within a more complete environment.

There are two main ways in which you must be prepared: first, to have a solid score—your "energy map" or "sequence of actions"—that helps you to keep your focus on the action without being distracted by all the new elements; second, to have used good rehearsal substitutes for props and costumes.

Be sure to study the set drawing or model and be clear about how the tape marks in the rehearsal hall represent the final set; select rehearsal props and costumes with care as accurate substitutes for the real things; take full advantage of costume fittings to get the feel of your clothes, making all the movements your part may require (and to alert the costumer to any problems of motion); once the set is in place, make it part of your homework to spend some time in it, walking your part or simply getting the feel of the environment.

Once you have a good idea of what the finished product is going to look like, you can begin to *visualize* the performance as it will be under audience conditions. Visualization is an excellent form of private rehearsal; it is most effective when used during periods of relaxation when your deep muscles will actually participate. Here is an exercise in the technique called Visuo-Motor Behavior Rehearsal, which was first developed for the 1980 Winter Olympics, and used by athletes like Jean-Claude Killy with great effectiveness.

### Exercise 89:
### Visuo-Motor Behavior Rehearsal

Using the phasic relaxation, put yourself into deep muscle relaxation and mental restful alertness.

Now visualize the following: You are about to open in the play from which your scene comes; the theater is ready, you hear the buzz of the audience in the house, you are standing in your costume with your fellow actors ready to take your places.

Go into the set and take your opening positions; feel the stage lights shining on you, smell the makeup, feel your clothing, see your fellow actors and the set.

The scene begins; live through it totally; let your deep muscles respond to the experience; feel the props and all the business.

Tests have shown that this form of rehearsal can be just as effective as ordinary rehearsal, and sometimes more so.

## GROWTH AFTER OPENING

The opening of the show is never the completion of your work, but only the start of a new phase of the growth process. The audience contributes in many ways, perhaps most by providing the responses that complete the rhythmic shaping of the work. These responses take many forms, from the overt (such as laughter or sobs) to the covert (such as rapt stillness or restlessness, or just the "feeling" inside the auditorium). Whatever their form, the audience's responses are an important element in the rhythm of the scene; so far, you have been guessing what those responses will be, and your director has been substituting for them as "an ideal audience of one," but now you have the real thing and can get to work fine-tuning the shape and flow of your action accordingly. This is the business of "previews," if you are lucky enough to have them.

The audience's presence will also probably cause a shift in context, a change in the way you will experience your own work; there will likely be many discoveries for you to make from this altered point of view. Some things you thought would work well may turn out to be too personal or obscure, while other things that you hadn't really noticed turn out to be powerful or worth developing further. At last you have a sure basis for judgment.

This sure basis for judgment will naturally cause you to begin economizing. You will find after a time that you expended more energy during rehearsals than you do in performance, and that you will generally expend less and less energy as the run continues. This is not because you begin doing your part mechanically, without thought or feeling, but because you will penetrate deeper and deeper to its essence; as this happens, unessential detail begins to fall away. Your performance is made more effective by distilling it to its essentials in this way; you are doing more with less.

## SUMMARY OF LESSON TWENTY-TWO

Having developed the content of your performance, you now develop its form. The basis is the sequence of actions, which forms what Stanislavski called the *score* of the role. The score eventually becomes habitual; you must be able to do the scene "in your sleep" in order to be able to do it fully awake. This is also the time that your *superobjective* will start to come into focus.

At what point do you commit to a choice? You will have to determine your own best approach; to play the waiting game is unfair to your co-workers, since they depend upon you for their reactions, but neither should you make final choices too soon.

As you begin to polish the performance, you will make adjustments in form to meet external needs. These must be *justified* by being the result of some change in the inner phase of the action.

A performance will move with good pace naturally when the through-line of the action is strong, when the underlying conflict has been felt, and when the actors deliver their lines with good cuing.

The final phase of the rehearsal period is devoted to incorporating the full production elements: Technical rehearsals can be a period of tremendous frustration and distraction for you if you have not prepared yourself properly.

The opening of the show is never the completion of your work, but only the start of a new phase of the growth process. At last you have a sure basis for judgment and you will penetrate deeper and deeper to its essence; as this happens, unessential detail begins to fall away. Your performance is made more effective by distilling it to its essentials; you are doing more with less.

# Lesson Twenty-Three

## The Actor at Work

Underlying all the techniques and principles you have studied so far are your attitudes and values as an actor. These are reflections of the motivations that brought you to acting, your personal beliefs, your relationship to your world, and your hopes for your future as an actor. These values and hopes profoundly affect the way you work, though their influence is often unconscious. If you can develop productive attitudes as the foundation of your working process, you will be able to take charge of your own growth as an actor.

An effective work process depends on three things: good collaboration skills, a creative attitude, and a clear sense of purpose. We will end our study by exploring these fundamental attitudes.

### SUPPORTING EACH OTHER

The interactive nature of drama means that your individual creation cannot be separated from the work of all the other actors and the director. Your attitude toward your fellow workers is as important as your attitude toward your own work. Remember this observation by playwright August Strindberg quoted in Part One:

> No form of art is as dependent as the actor's. He cannot isolate his particular contribution, show it to someone and say, "This is mine." If he does not get the support of his fellow actors, his performance will

lack resonance and depth....He won't make a good impression no matter how hard he tries. Actors must rely on each other....

That is why rapport among actors is imperative for the success of a play. I don't care whether you rank yourselves higher or lower than each other, or from side to side, or from inside out—as long as you do it together.[1]

Your working relationships will be most effective when they are based upon three principles: (1) mutual commitment to the relationship and to the work itself; (2) mutual support for one another's individual objectives and methods; (3) free and open communication so that problems can be thrashed out and thereby become opportunities for creative interaction. Let's examine each.

First, you are committed to the working relationship because it will enable you to do better work as an individual. Friendship will result from most of your working relationships; there is a wonderfully warm sense of kinship among theater people; often you will meet someone for the first time and because of your mutual friends, you know at once that you are family; but commitment to the working relationship is not the same thing as being "nice." While group membership requires generosity, good humor, and a spirit of reasonable compromise, it should *not* involve either the sacrifice of self-esteem or the surrender of personal standards; the need to be "nice" should never cause you to falsify your values or discipline. Remember: A group doesn't make good work because it is a good group; it becomes a good group because it creates good work.

Second, your support for one another's objectives and methods is the basis of respect. You might not share another actor's reasons for doing what he or she does, nor might you work the same way, but you respect the motives and support someone's right to work his or her own way, just as you expect respect for your motives and methods. If your different ways of working cause a problem (as they sometimes do), negotiate compromises on both sides that, as much as possible, meet everyone's needs equally.

Finally, the possibility of free and open communication is critical. Problems arise in any creative process and they must be worked through and negotiated; only good communication will make that possible.

## FREE AND OPEN COMMUNICATION

Free and open communication does not mean that we say everything that's on our minds in the name of "honesty"; some things are best left unsaid—as Falstaff says, "Discretion is the better part of valor"—but the *possibility* of discussing problems needs to be felt by everyone. Otherwise, an atmosphere of repression will develop and tensions will mount, perhaps to a boiling point.

In addition to the group's need for good communication, you have an individual need for it. We have already discussed how actors depend on feedback more than most other artists; the notes you get from your teachers, directors, and fellow actors are tremendously important in guiding your growth. Actors therefore have a solemn responsibility to provide accurate and useful feedback to one another. The most effective feedback we can give each other is based upon a few basic principles:

Most important, say *what you see* and *how it makes you feel*. Don't say, "Why are you hiding from us," say, "I noticed that you rarely looked at your partner during this scene, and that made me feel as if you were hiding from us. What was going on?" Do you see the difference between these two statements?

In the first statement, you interpreted the reason for what you saw, then reported your interpretation as if it were true. If the other person doesn't feel that he or she was "hiding," the person will probably have to reject your input, and they will lose an opportunity for improvement. In the second statement you reported your specific observation, then reported the feeling it engendered in you. Both these statements must be true because neither involves interpretation: You saw what you saw, and it made you feel a certain way. Now you can go on to discuss the situation profitably.

Having an effective message to send, consider some effective ways of sending it:

1. Be *clear* about your message before you deliver it.
2. Be *specific*, *simple*, and *direct*; use examples.
3. Pick an *appropriate time* to communicate.
4. *Check* to see if your message was received accurately.

Here is an exercise to practice these communication skills.

### Exercise 90:
### Attractions and Reservations, Agonies and Ecstasies

A. Join with one of your fellow workers to share impressions of your own and each other's work. Take turns completing the following statements, and in each case say what you saw and how it made you feel; be specific and direct; supply examples.

My greatest agony about my own work just now is...
The greatest reservation I have about your work is...

The thing I feel best about in my own work is…
The thing that attracts me most about your work is…

B. Compare your feelings about praise and criticism. Which do you take more seriously? Did you learn equally from each?
  Are you benefiting enough from the feedback of others? Or are you *too* dependent on them?

Unfortunately, despite the nature of their work, most actors have no better communication skills than butchers or bankers. Here is an exercise that will help you to avoid the most common pitfalls in good communication.

### Exercise 91:
### Communication Disorders

With your partner, think back over your working experiences. Have either of you suffered from or been guilty of any of the following communication disorders?

1. *Fogging:* Using generalities without referring to specifics. Example: "You need to work on your voice."
2. *Mind-Raping:* Assuming you know what someone is thinking without bothering to check. Example: "Why are you hiding from us in this scene?"
3. *Defusing:* Excessive self-criticism that makes it impossible for anyone else to criticize you. Example: "I just couldn't concentrate at all today; I know the scene was terrible, but what did you think?"
4. *Dumping:* Using criticism as an emotional release or as a weapon.
5. *Gunnysacking:* Saving up grievances until an explosion becomes likely.
6. *No Trespassing:* When unstated rules exist within a group that bar criticism of certain people or certain issues.
7. *Holier-than-Thou:* Criticism of others for the purpose of avoiding criticism of self.
8. *Doomsaying:* Feedback that emphasizes only the negative without acknowledging the positive.

## YOU AND YOUR DIRECTOR

The relationship between actor and director deserves special attention. Since the director is the focus of the group's working process, your ability to work effectively together is critical. It will help if you have a clear sense of what each of your functions, rights, and responsibilities are.

The director has three main functions: to guide the development of an overall interpretation for the production, to align the efforts of all the different artists contributing to the production, and to provide feedback during rehearsals by being an ideal audience of one.

The interpretive function makes the director a "central intelligence" for the production, establishing its point of view. The director either provides this focus at the outset or guides the cast in discovering it during rehearsals.

Your performance, like every other element of the production, must be aligned toward this central interpretation. Even if your personal preference might be for a different interpretation or emphasis, once you have accepted the role it is your job to work effectively within the director's production concept.

Perhaps the most destructive attitude is that of the actor who becomes an apologist for the character, arguing from the character's point of view as if every scene belonged only to the character. Group interpretation can be ruined by actors who insist upon adopting their character's point of view at the expense of the play as an artistic whole.

On the other hand, we do a great disservice to our director, our fellow actors, and ourselves if, out of our desire to avoid conflict, we fail to express ourselves honestly. An actor who is too pliable is as destructive as one who is too rigid. Your ideas will be appreciated if they are presented in a reasoned, timely, and respectful fashion. While a show has only one director, everyone connected with it must feel responsible for the whole production and provide any ideas that may be of value.

There are many ways in which the responsibilities of director and actor can overlap and where compromise will be necessary. The actor, intimately involved with the life of the character, possesses insights into the life of that character that are denied to the director. At the same time, the director has an objective overview unavailable to the actor. In an effective working relationship, each will respect and value the insights of the other and seek to join their points of view to the best possible advantage.

Even in the best situations there are times when insoluble disagreements occur; when this happens, ties go to the director. The director has assumed public responsibility for the interpretation of the play, while you have assumed public responsibility only for the portrayal of your character within the context established by that interpretation. Once the director's interpretation has been clarified, it is your responsibility to find the best possible means of implementing it; if this proves to be impossible, the relationship must be severed for the sake of the play. Unless you have become a major star, this means that you get fired.

Besides interpretation, another important function of the director is to establish a common approach in the conduct of rehearsals. Each director has a characteristic way of working, and it is easier for the actors to adapt to the director's method than for the director to adopt an individual approach to each of the actors. It is therefore part of your job to adapt, as much as is reasonable, to the director's approach, and to help the director develop the most effective channel of communication with you.

To sum up, you and your director are co-workers, not master and slave. Though you share many responsibilities, you have essentially different functions that are interdependent and equal. The director's first responsibility is to the overall patterning of the play as a theatrical experience; your responsibility is to bring your role to life in a way that will best contribute to that pattern. Therefore, it is ultimately the director's function to evaluate *what* the actor does, and the actor's job is to find *how* best to do it.

## THE FEAR OF FAILURE

Your work process will also be profoundly influenced by your motivation as an actor. The fundamental drive for most actors, like most people, is the desire for success and its flip side, the fear of failure. Everyone has both, of course, though one may be said to be dominant over the other in many individuals. Each is a powerful source of energy, but the differences between them are important.

At the 1984 Olympics in Los Angeles, the athletes were tested to see which were driven primarily by a desire for success, and which were motivated primarily by the fear of failure; it was found that over 70 percent were driven by the desire for success, while less than 30 percent were motivated by the fear of failure. While the study was not specific about the differences between these two groups of athletes, I would suspect that those motivated by fear of failure tended to be technically precise but cautious, while the larger group would include more "inspired" athletes who were greater risk-takers; the fear of failure encourages safe and conservative choices, while the desire for success can generate energetic and sometimes risky choices.

No one has ever tested a group of actors in this way, but I suspect that a larger proportion of actors would be found to be driven by the fear of failure. There are many unsuccessful or marginal actors, perhaps 80 percent, who hang on in the business for year after undistinguished year, whose work is competent but uninspired, who deliver reliable but cautious performances, and who simply don't "go for it." Their motto seems to be "Nothing ventured, nothing lost."

The fear of failure encourages the "I must do it exactly right" attitude, producing, at best, technical skill, precision, and consistency. These are qualities that, in athletics, are rewarded for their own sake, but when you reach the top levels of competition the absence of creative inspiration is damaging; you can't win on technical points alone; you have to have the style points as well. In acting, the situation is even clearer: Technical skill, while valued, will never entirely compensate for a lack of creativity. For the actor, technical skill is only the means toward the expression of an artistic vision.

An excessive fear of failure can cause you to censor creative impulses, fearing, "I'll look foolish." When you censor an impulse, you must literally "hold it in," and this causes muscular tension. It is no accident that we tell overly cautious people to "loosen up."

Finally, and most important, the fear of failure may cause you to continually judge your own performance to see if you are "doing it right," and this judgmental attitude encourages self-consciousness. As George C. Scott once observed in an interview:

> I think you have to be schizoid three different ways to be an actor. You've got to be three different people: you have to be a human being, then you have to be the character you're playing, and on top of that, you've got to be the guy sitting out there in row 10, watching yourself and judging yourself. That's why most of us are crazy to start with or go nuts once we get into it. I mean, don't you think it's a pretty spooky way to earn a living?[2]

### Exercise 92:
### The Fear of Failure

Think back to your most recent work in an audition, rehearsal, or performance: Do you remember censoring yourself? Were you sending yourself messages like "This isn't going to work" or "This might make me look stupid"? What physical tensions resulted from "holding in" your impulses?

Next time you work, notice these moments of self-censorship as they occur: Simply release the tension, take a breath, and get back to work.

## THE DESIRE FOR SUCCESS

A working actor needs the drive, courage, and long-term tenacity that a strong desire for success can provide. Each of us must define success for ourselves: What constitutes true success for you?

There are really two ways of measuring success: in purely internal terms, like pride, sense of accomplishment, feelings of growth; and by external measurements, like reviews, grades, and the response of the audience. Obviously, all actors are, and should be, concerned with both. What we need is perspective and balance between the two.

Most actors err on the side of emphasizing external measures of success over internal. Even if they have a sense of their own work, they usually don't trust it, and they feel so dependent on the opinions of others that a negative response from anyone damages their self-esteem.

Of course, it hurts any actor when their work is not received well. But the serious actor strives to balance the healthy desire for immediate success with the equally important long-range demands of artistic development. You should approach each new role, each rehearsal, and each performance with a desire not only to please others but also a desire to *learn and grow* for yourself. When evaluating the experience, you must not only ask, "Did I do the job well?" but also "Am I now a better actor for having done it?"

Winning parts, applause, and good reviews, as important as these things are, is not enough. I know some actors, especially in film and television, who are wildly successful in commercial terms but who derive little personal satisfaction from their careers. The "business" demands that they use the same skills, play the same sort of character in the same type of material, role after role; no matter how highly developed these skills may become, they can bring only limited artistic satisfaction.

Serious actors insist on continuing to develop and extend their abilities with disciplined regularity throughout their lifetime. There is no real substitute for meeting the day-to-day demands of rehearsal and performance; this is why the actor in a repertory company, preparing a continual variety of roles, may develop much faster than the actor who works in long runs, or repeatedly plays the same kinds of roles.

Most difficult is the situation of the film/TV actors who, unless they are among the 6 percent who work regularly, work only a few weeks out of every year. Classes, workshops, and little theater roles are the only chance such actors have to maintain and extend their skills. In the waiting room at a TV audition I heard one actor tell the others this joke:

> Three actors were complaining about being out of work. "Heck," said the first actor, "I haven't had a part for four months." "That's nothing," said the second actor, "I haven't even had a decent *audition* for a year!" "I've got you both beat," the third actor said, "I haven't had a part for six years. It's gotten so bad, I'm thinking of leaving the business."

**Exercise 93:**
**Measuring Success**

Think back to your most recent performance; did you have your own independent evaluation of it? Did you trust that evaluation? How did the comments of others affect you?

Did you distinguish between the short-term measurement of your success in the role and the long-term benefits of the work to you as a developing artist?

## YOUR SENSE OF PURPOSE

Finally, your life as an actor will be most deeply influenced by your sense of purpose, and it is this that distinguishes the true professional. We use the word "professional" to describe a high level of skill, reliability, and commitment in many fields, but it means something special among actors. When actors want to pay someone a real compliment, they say the actor is "a real pro." But what is it that defines a professional?

In athletics, we distinguish between professional and amateur on the basis of money: The professional is paid, while the amateur (from the root *amat*, "to love") participates only for the love of the sport itself. But in acting, "professional" seems to mean much more than the fact that someone receives money; the term carries an implication of integrity, reliability, high standards, and most of all *commitment*.

The root of the word comes from an old French verb, *profes*, which means "to make a solemn vow," as in joining a religious order. In our culture, professionals have special knowledge or skills that give them power over other people: doctors, lawyers, members of the clergy, and others of the "professional class" are responsible for the well-being of their clients. Society has placed a special trust in them, and in return they are expected to use their special powers only for the benefit of those they serve. Thus, a professional is *someone who has taken a solemn vow of an ethical standard.* He or she has accepted personal responsibility for work that will affect the lives of others.

As an actor, you will have special power over others. We don't usually take acting as seriously as that, but it is true. With this power comes a public responsibility for the well-being of those whose lives you will affect, and this demands an enormous commitment.

This commitment operates on three levels simultaneously: First, you must be committed to *your own development as an artist.* Without this commitment to yourself, you cannot offer to others all of which you are capable.

Second, you must be committed to *your work;* if you are merely using your work to advance yourself, you will obscure its value to others.

Third, you must be committed *to the world you serve through your work.* Acceptance of this social responsibility gives you a sense of purpose to something greater than yourself, and this can lead you to extraordinary accomplishments. As the director Eugenio Barba said in a letter to one of his actors:

> Whatever hidden, personal motives led you to the theater, now that you have entered that profession you must find there a sense that goes beyond your proper person and fixes you socially in the sight of others....If the fact of being an actor means all that to you, then a new theater will be born.[3]

The philosopher Descartes said that reading good books was like conversing with the greatest minds of history, minds that had distilled their experience and wisdom in their art. We who perform good plays go a step further: We actively participate in the experience of peoples, places, and times that have been shaped and condensed by the artistic consciousness of great playwrights. Theatre is the most human of all the arts, and we can preserve and expand our humanity through our art in ways denied us by everyday life. As the American playwright David Mamet says:

> What can be preserved? What can be communicated from one generation to the next?
>
> Philosophy. Morality. Aesthetics.
>
> These can be expressed in technique, in those skills that enable the artist to respond truthfully, fully, lovingly to whatever he or she wishes to express.

This is what can and must be passed from one generation to the next. Technique—a knowledge of how to translate inchoate desire into clean action—into action capable of communicating itself to the audience.

This technique, this care, this love of precision, of cleanliness, this love of the theater, is the best way, for it is love of the *audience*—of that which *unites* the actor and the house; a desire to share something that they know to be true.[4]

The desire of which Mamet speaks, this *need to express the truth through the techniques of art*, is not merely personal. It involves a sense of service to something greater than ourselves, and as such it is the deepest and most lasting motivation of the actor. As he says:

Our workers in the theater—actors, writers, directors, teachers—are drawn to it not out of intellectual predilection, but from *necessity*. We are driven into the theater by our need to express—our need to answer the question of our lives—the questions of the time in which we live. Of this moment.[5]

This need "to answer the question of our lives" demands both the highest artistry and the deepest humanity. Again, Mamet:

Who is going to speak up? Who is going to speak for the American spirit? For the human spirit?

Who is capable of being heard? Of being accepted? Of being believed? Only that person who speaks without ulterior motives, without hope of gain, without even the desire to *change*, with only the desire to *create*: The artist. The actor. The strong, trained actor dedicated to the idea that the theater is the place we go to hear the truth, and equipped with the technical capacity to speak simply and clearly.[6]

This sentiment, expressed here by one of our leading playwrights, harkens back to the original impulses of the founders of our modern school of acting when, more than eighty years ago, Stanislavski and his partner debated the requirements for actors to be taken into the company of the Moscow Art Theatre:

"Take actor A," we would test each other. "Do you consider him talented?"

"To a high degree."

"Will you take him into the troupe?"

"No."

"Why?"

"Because he has adapted himself to his career, his talents to the demands of the public, his character to the caprices of the manager, and all of himself to theatrical cheapness. A man who is so poisoned cannot be cured."

"And what do you say about Actress B?"

"She is a good actress, but not for us."

"Why?"

"She does not love art, but herself in art."

"And actress C?"

"She won't do. She is incurably given to hokum."

"What about actor D?"

"We should bear him in mind."

"Why?"

"He has ideals for which he is fighting. He is not at peace with present conditions. He is a man of ideas."

"I am of the same opinion. With your permission I shall enter his name in the list of candidates."[7]

It is important, then, for you to consider how you may serve through acting. Traditionally, artists have announced their specific commitment through the publication of a *manifesto*; this was their way of taking the same kind of public vow that lawyers and doctors take when they are licensed. A manifesto is a brief, passionate, and personal statement of belief and purpose. It requires considerable thought and should be as simple and direct as possible.

### Exercise 94:
### Your Manifesto

Write your own manifesto for the art of acting. Make yours just two paragraphs long:

A. What you want to do for the world through your acting: How do you want to make a difference?

B. What techniques and process are necessary to achieve your purpose? What skills and capabilities must *you* develop to empower yourself to achieve your purpose?

C. When you are satisfied with it, publish it in some public forum; read it in class, or put it up on the wall.

### SUMMARY OF LESSON TWENTY-THREE

An effective work process depends on good collaboration skills, a creative attitude, and a clear sense of purpose. Likewise, your working relationships will be most effective when they are based on mutual commitment, support for one another's objectives and methods, and free and open communication.

Good communication about the work of others requires that you be specific about what you see them do and how it makes you feel. This should be expressed in a clear, specific, direct, and timely manner.

Your relationship with your director is crucial in coordinating your work with the production as a whole. The director is responsible for the interpretation of the play and unity of the production, while you are responsible for creating your role in a way that will best contribute to that interpretation and unity.

Your work process will also be influenced by your motivation as an actor. The fear of failure can lead to excessive caution and self-censorship, while the desire for success can be a source of courage and liberation. Success is measured in both external and internal ways, and these must be balanced, fulfilling the needs for acceptance and for growth and self-esteem.

Finally, it is the sense of purpose that distinguishes the true professional. This sense of purpose involves commitment to your own artistry, commitment to your work, and commitment to the world you serve through your work. It is this sense of responsibility to express the truth through the techniques of art, to stand up for the human spirit, that can best drive a lasting and satisfying career as an actor.

## SUMMARY OF PART THREE: TRANSFORMATION

Your sense of purpose grows from your respect for your own talent, your love for the specific material you are performing, and your desire to use both to serve your audience. It is this drive to be *at service* through your art that will finally overcome the self-consciousness of your ego and carry you beyond yourself, giving you a transcendent purpose from which comes dignity, fulfillment, and ongoing artistic vitality.

Stanislavsky called this ongoing artistic vitality "theatrical youthfulness." Near the end of his life he addressed a group of young actors who were entering the Moscow Art Theatre with these words:

> The first essential to retain a youthful performance is to keep the idea of the play alive. That is why the dramatist wrote it and that is why you decided to produce it. One should not be on the stage, one should not put on a play for the sake of acting or producing only. Yes, you must be excited about your profession. You must love it devotedly and passionately, but not for itself, not for its laurels, not for the plea-

sure and delight it brings to you as artists. You must love your chosen profession because it gives you the opportunity to communicate ideas that are important and necessary to your audience. Because it gives you the opportunity, through the ideas that you dramatize on the stage and through your characterizations, to educate your audience and to make them better, finer, wiser, and more useful members of society....

You must keep the idea alive and be inspired by it at each performance. This is the only way to retain youthfulness in performance and your own youthfulness as actors. The true recreation of the play's idea—I emphasize the word true—demands from the artist wide and varied knowledge, constant self-discipline, the subordination of his personal tastes and habits to the demands of the idea, and sometimes even definite sacrifices.[8]

The art of acting has always had a very special service to render, one that has become increasingly important today: It is rooted in the actor's ability to transform, to become "someone else." At a time when mass culture, big business, and bigger government make us, as individuals, feel more and more insignificant and impotent, the actor's ability to be "in charge" of personal reality can be a source of hope and inspiration to others.

The actor's ability to undergo transformation is itself a kind of potency, a kind of power over the future. While a play may teach us something about who we are, it is the actor's ability to be transformed that teaches us something about whom we may *become*. The actor's ability to redefine personal reality before our very eyes reminds us of our own spiritual capacity for self-definition, and thus the theater becomes a celebration of our vitality and of the ongoing flow of life.

Sensing the capacity of the theater to help enrich our spiritual lives at a time when we have a great need of spiritual revivification, we have begun to explore more than ever the full richness of the experience that may pass between actor and spectator, and the way in which the theatrical moment can affect our lives long after the curtain has fallen.

The actor's horizons are thus being continually broadened, and the art of acting has begun to encompass not only an expanding range of performance techniques and possibilities, but a renewed sense of ethical and spiritual purpose as well.

It is a wonderful time to be an actor.

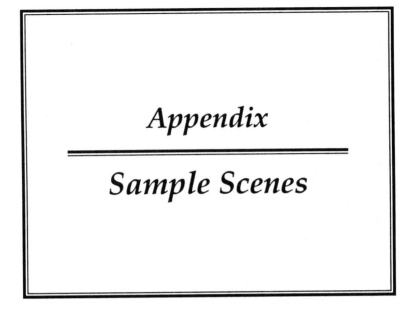

# *Appendix*

## *Sample Scenes*

## FROM *DEATH OF A SALESMAN* BY ARTHUR MILLER[1]

[*Howard Wagner, thirty-six...is intent on threading the (recording) machine and only glances over his shoulder as Willy appears*]

WILLY: Pst! Pst!

HOWARD: Hello, Willy, come in.

WILLY: Like to have a little talk with you, Howard.

HOWARD: Sorry to keep you waiting. I'll be with you in a minute.

WILLY: What's that, Howard?

HOWARD: Didn't you ever see one of these? Wire recorder.

WILLY: Oh. Can we talk a minute?

HOWARD: Records things. Just got delivery yesterday. Been driving me crazy, the most terrific machine I ever saw in my life. I was up all night with it.

WILLY: What do you do with it?

HOWARD: I bought it for dictation, but you can do anything with it. Listen to this. I had it home last night. Listen to what I picked up. The first one is my daughter. Get this. [*He flicks the switch and "Roll out the Barrel!" is heard being whistled*] Listen to that kid whistle.

WILLY: Ts, ts. Like to ask a little favor of you...

[*The whistling breaks off, and the voice of Howard's daughter is heard*]

HIS DAUGHTER: "Now you, Daddy."

HOWARD: She's crazy for me! [*Again the same song is whistled*] That's me! Ha! [*He winks*]

WILLY: You're very good!

[*The whistling breaks off again. The machine runs silent for a moment*]

HOWARD: Sh! Get this now, this is my son.

HIS SON: "The capital of Alabama is Montgomery; the capital of Arizona is Phoenix; the capital of Arkansas is Little Rock; the capital of California is Sacramento..." [ *and on, and on*]

HOWARD [*Holding up five fingers*]: Five years old, Willy!

WILLY: He'll make an announcer some day!

HIS SON [ *Continuing*]: "The capital..."

HOWARD: Get that—alphabetical order! [*The machine breaks off suddenly*] Wait a minute. The maid kicked the plug out.

WILLY: It certainly is a—

HOWARD: Sh, for God's sake!

HIS SON: "It's nine o'clock, Bulova watch time. So I have to go to sleep."

WILLY: That really is—

HOWARD: Wait a minute! The next is my wife.[*They wait*]

HOWARD'S VOICE: "Go on, say something." [*Pause*] "Well, you gonna talk?"

HIS WIFE [*shyly, beaten*]: "Hello." [*Silence*] "Oh, Howard, I can't talk into this..."

HOWARD [*snapping the machine off*] That was my wife.

WILLY: That is a wonderful machine. Can we—

HOWARD: I tell you, Willy, I'm gonna take my camera, and my bandsaw, and all my hobbies, and out they go. This is the most fascinating relaxation I ever found.

WILLY: I think I'll get one myself.

HOWARD: Sure, they're only a hundred and a half. You can't do without it. Supposing you wanna hear Jack Benny, see? But you can't be at home at that hour. So you tell the maid to turn the radio on when Jack Benny comes on, and this automatically goes on with the radio...

WILLY: And when you come home you...

HOWARD: You can come home twelve o'clock, one o'clock, any time you like, and you get yourself a Coke and sit yourself down, throw the switch, and there's Jack Benny's program in the middle of the night!

WILLY: I'm definitely going to get one. Because lots of time I'm on the road, and I think to myself, what I must be missing on the radio!

HOWARD: Don't you have a radio in the car?

WILLY: Well, yeah, but who ever thinks of turning it on?

HOWARD: Say, aren't you supposed to be in Boston?

WILLY: That's what I want to talk to you about, Howard. You got a minute? [*He draws a chair in from the wing*]

HOWARD: What happened? What're you doing here?

WILLY: Well...

HOWARD: You didn't crack up again, did you?

WILLY: Oh, no. No...

HOWARD: Geez, you had me worried there for a minute. What's the trouble?

WILLY: Well, tell you the truth, Howard. I've come to the decision that I'd rather not travel any more.

HOWARD: Not travel! Well, what'll you do?

WILLY: Remember, Christmas time, when you had the party here? You said you'd try to think of some spot for me here in town.

HOWARD: With us?

WILLY: Well, sure.

HOWARD: Oh, yeah, yeah. I remember. Well, I couldn't think of anything for you, Willy.

WILLY: I tell ya, Howard. The kids are all grown up, y'know. I don't need much any more. If I could take home—well, sixty-five dollars a week, I could swing it.

HOWARD: Yeah, but Willy, see I—

WILLY: I tell ya why, Howard. Speaking frankly and between the two of us, y'know—I'm just a little tired.

HOWARD: Oh, I could understand that, Willy. But you're a road man, Willy, and we do a road business. We've only got a half-dozen salesmen on the floor here.

WILLY: God knows, Howard, I never asked a favor of any man. But I was with the firm when your father used to carry you in here in his arms.

HOWARD: I know that, Willy, but—

WILLY: Your father came to me the day you were born and asked me what I thought of the name Howard, may he rest in peace.

HOWARD: I appreciate that, Willy, but there just is no spot here for you. If I had a spot I'd slam you right in, but I just don't have a single solitary spot.

[*He looks for his lighter. Willy has picked it up and gives it to him. Pause*]

WILLY [*With increasing anger*]: Howard, all I need to set my table is fifty dollars a week.

HOWARD: But where am I going to put you, kid?

WILLY: Look, it isn't a question of whether I can sell merchandise, is it?

HOWARD: No, but it's a business, kid, and everybody's gotta pull his own weight.

WILLY [*Desperately*]: Just let me tell you a story, Howard—

HOWARD: 'Cause you gotta admit, business is business.

WILLY [*Angrily*]: Business is definitely business, but just listen for a minute. You don't understand this. When I was a boy—eighteen, nineteen—I was already on the road. And there was a question in my mind as to whether selling had a future for me. Because in those days I had a yearning to go to Alaska. See, there were three gold strikes in one month in Alaska, and I felt like going out. Just for the ride you might say.

HOWARD [*Barely interested*]: Don't say.

WILLY: Oh, yeah, my father lived many years in Alaska. He was an adventurous man. We've got quite a little streak of self-reliance in our family. I thought I'd go out with my older brother and try to locate him, and maybe settle in the North with the old man. And I was almost decided to go, when I met a salesman in the Parker House. His name was Dave Singleman. And he was eighty-four years old, and he'd drummed merchandise in thirty-one states. And old Dave, he'd go up to his room, y'understand, put on his green velvet slippers—I'll never forget—and pick up his phone and call the buyers, and without ever leaving his room, at the age of eighty-four, he made his living. And when I saw that, I realized that selling was the greatest career a man could want. 'Cause what could be more satisfying than to be able to go, at the age of eighty-four, into twenty or thirty different cities, and pick up a phone, and be remembered and loved and helped by so many different people? Do you know? when he died— and by the way he died the death of a salesman, in his green velvet slippers in the smoker of the New York, New haven and Hartford, going into Boston—when he died, hundreds of salesmen and buyers were at his funeral. Things were sad on a lotta trains for months after that. [*He stands up. Howard has not looked at him*] In those days there was personality in it, Howard. There was respect, and comradeship, and gratitude in it. Today, it's all cut and dried, and there's no chance for bringing friendship to bear—or personality. You see what I mean? They don't know me any more.

HOWARD [*Moving away, to the right*]: That's just the thing, Willy.

WILLY: If I had forty dollars a week—that's all I'd need. Forty dollars, Howard.

HOWARD: Kid, I can't take blood from a stone, I—

WILLY [*Desperation is on him now*]: Howard, the year Al Smith was nominated, your father came to me and—

HOWARD [*Starting to go off*]: I've got to see some people, kid.

WILLY [*Stopping him*]: I'm talking about your father! There were promises made across this desk! You mustn't tell me you've got people to see—I put thirty-four years into this firm, Howard, and now I can't pay my insurance! You can't eat the orange and throw the peel away—a man is not a piece of fruit! [*After a pause*]: Now pay attention. Your father—in 1928 I had a big year. I averaged a hundred and seventy dollars a week in commissions.

HOWARD [*Impatiently*]: Now, Willy, you never averaged—

WILLY [*Banging his hand on the desk*]: I averaged a hundred and seventy dollars a week in the year of 1928! And your father came to me—or rather, I was in the office here—it was right over this desk—and he put his hand on my shoulder—

HOWARD *Getting up*]: You'll have to excuse me, Willy, I gotta see some people. Pull yourself together. [*Going out*] I'll be back in a little while.

[*On Howard's exit, the light on his chair grows very bright and strange*]

WILLY: Pull myself together! What the hell did I say to him? My God, I was yelling at him! How could I! [*Willy breaks off, staring at the light, which occupies the chair, animating it. He approaches this chair, standing across the desk from it*] Frank, Frank, don't you remember what you told me that time? How you put your hand on my shoulder, and Frank... [*He leans on the desk and as he speaks the dead man's name he accidentally switches on the recorder, and instantly*]

HOWARD'S SON: "...of New York is Albany. The capital of Ohio is Cincinnati, the capital of Rhode Island is..." [*The recitation continues*]

WILLY: [*Leaping away with fright, shouting*]: Ha! Howard! Howard! Howard!

HOWARD [*Rushing in*]: What happened?

WILLY [*Pointing at the machine, which continues nasally, childishly, with the capital cities*]: Shut it off! Shut it off!

HOWARD [*Pulling the plug out*]: Look, Willy…

WILLY [*Pressing his hands to his eyes*]: I gotta get myself some coffee. I'll get some coffee…

[*Willy starts to walk out. Howard stops him*]

HOWARD [*Rolling up the cord*]: Willy, look…

WILLY: I'll go to Boston.

HOWARD: Willy, you can't go to Boston for us.

WILLY: Why can't I go?

HOWARD: I don't want you to represent us. I've been meaning to tell you for a long time now.

WILLY: Howard, are you firing me?

HOWARD: I think you need a good long rest, Willy.

WILLY: Howard—

HOWARD: And when you feel better, come back, and we'll see if we can work something out.

WILLY: But I gotta earn some money, Howard. I'm in no position to—

HOWARD: Where are your sons? Why don't your sons give you a hand?

WILLY: They're working on a very big deal.

HOWARD: This is no time for false pride, Willy. You go to your sons and you tell them that you're tired. You've got two great boys, haven't you?

WILLY: Oh, no question, no question, but in the meantime…

HOWARD: Then that's that, heh?

WILLY: All right, I'll go to Boston tomorrow.

HOWARD: No, no.

WILLY: I can't throw myself on my sons. I'm not a cripple!

HOWARD: Look, kid, I'm busy this morning.

WILLY [*Grasping Howard's arm*]: Howard, you've got to let me go to Boston!

HOWARD [*Hard, keeping himself under control*]: I've got a line of people to see this morning. Sit down, take five minutes, and pull yourself together, and then go home, will ya? I need the office, Willy. [*He starts to go, turns, remembering the recorder, starts to push off the table holding the recorder]* Oh, yeah. Whenever you can this week, stop by and drop off the samples. You'll feel better, Willy, and then come back and we'll talk. Pull yourself together, kid, there's people outside.

## FROM *THE GLASS MENAGERIE* BY TENNESSEE WILLIAMS[2]

*[Laura is seated in the delicate ivory chair at the small claw-foot table....She is washing and polishing her collection of glass. Amanda appears on the fire-escape steps....Before entering she looks through the door. She purses her lips, opens her eyes very wide, rolls them upward and shakes her head. Then she slowly lets herself in the door. Seeing her mother's expression Laura touches her lips with a nervous gesture]*

LAURA: Hello, Mother, I was— *[She makes a nervous gesture toward the chart on the wall. Amanda leans against the shut door and stares at Laura with a martyred look]*

AMANDA: Deception? Deception? *[She slowly removes her hat and gloves, continuing the sweet suffering stare. She lets the hat and gloves fall on the floor—a bit of acting]*

LAURA *[Shakily]*: How was the D.A.R. meeting? *[Amanda slowly opens her purse and removes a dainty white handkerchief which she shakes out delicately and delicately touches to her lips and nostrils]* Didn't you go to the D.A.R. meeting, Mother?

AMANDA *[Faintly, almost inaudibly]*: —No.—No. *[then more forcibly]* I did not have the strength—to go to the D.A.R. In fact, I did not have the courage! I wanted to find a hole in the ground and hide myself in it forever! *[She crosses slowly to the wall and removes the diagram of the typewriter keyboard. She holds it in front of her for a second, staring at it sweetly and sorrowfully—then bites her lips and tears it in two pieces]*

LAURA *[Faintly]*: Why did you do that, Mother? *[Amanda repeats the same procedure with the chart of the Gregg Alphabet]* Why are you—

AMANDA: Why? Why? How old are you, Laura?

LAURA: Mother, you know my age.

AMANDA: I thought that you were an adult; it seems that I was mistaken. *[She crosses slowly to the sofa and sinks down and stares at Laura]*

LAURA: Please don't stare at me, Mother.

*[Amanda closes her eyes and lowers her head. Count ten]*

AMANDA: What are we going to do, what is going to become of us, what is the future? *[Count ten]*

LAURA: Has something happened, Mother? [*Amanda draws a long breath and takes out the handkerchief again. Dabbing process*] Mother, has—something happened?

AMANDA: I'll be all right in a minute, I'm just bewildered— [*Count five*] —by life....

LAURA: Mother, I wish that you would tell me what's happened!

AMANDA: As you know, I was supposed to be inducted into my office at the D.A.R. this afternoon. [*Screen image: A swarm of typewriters*] But I stopped off at Rubicam's Business College to speak to your teachers about your having a cold and ask them what progress they thought you were making down there.

LAURA: Oh...

AMANDA: I went to the typing instructor and introduced myself as your mother. She didn't know who you were. "Wingfield," she said. "We don't have any such student enrolled at the school!"

I assured her she did, that you had been going to classes since early in January. "I wonder," she said, "if you could be talking about that terribly shy little girl who dropped out of school after only a few days' attendance?"

"No," I said, "Laura, my daughter, has been going to school every day for the past six weeks!"

"Excuse me," she said. She took the attendance book out and there was your name, unmistakably printed, and all the dates you were absent until they decided that you had dropped out of school.

I still said, "No, there must have been some mistake! There must have been some mix-up in the records!"

And she said, "No—I remember her perfectly now. Her hands shook so that she couldn't hit the right keys! The first time we gave a speed-test, she broke down completely—was sick at the stomach and almost had to be carried into the wash-room! After that morning she never showed up any more. We phoned the house but never got any answer"—While I was working at Famous and Barr, I suppose, demonstrating those— [*She indicates a brassiere with her hands*] Oh!

I felt so weak I could barely keep on my feet! I had to sit down while they got me a glass of water!

Fifty dollars' tuition, all of our plans—my hopes and ambitions for you—just gone up the spout, just gone up the spout like that. [*Laura draws a long breath and gets awkwardly to her feet. She crosses to the Victrola and winds it up*] What are you doing?

LAURA: Oh! [*She releases the handle and returns to her seat*]

AMANDA: Laura where have you been going when you've gone out pretending that you were going to business college?

LAURA: I've just been going out walking.

AMANDA: That's not true.

LAURA: It is. I just went walking.

AMANDA: Walking? Walking? In winter? Deliberately courting pneumonia in that light coat? Where did you walk to, Laura?

LAURA: All sorts of places—mostly in the park.

AMANDA: Even after you'd started catching that cold?

LAURA: It was the lesser of two evils, Mother. [*Screen image: Winter scene in a park*] I couldn't go back there. I—threw up—on the floor!

AMANDA: From half past seven till after five every day you mean to tell me you walked around in the park, because you wanted to make me think that you were still going to Rubicam's Business College?

LAURA: It wasn't as bad as it sounds. I went inside places to get warmed up.

AMANDA: Inside where?

LAURA: I went in the art museum and the birdhouses at the Zoo. I visited the penguins every day! Sometimes I did without lunch and went to the movies. Lately I've been spending most of my afternoons in the Jewel-box, that big glass house where they raise the tropical flowers.

AMANDA: You did all this to deceive me, just for deception? [*Laura looks down*] Why?

LAURA: Mother, when you're disappointed, you get that awful suffering look on your face, like the picture of Jesus' mother in the museum!

AMANDA: Hush!

LAURA: I couldn't face it.

[*Pause. A whisper of strings*]

[*Screen legend: "The Crust of Humility"*]

AMANDA [*Hopelessly fingering the huge pocketbook*]: So what are we going to do the rest of our lives? Stay home and watch the parades go by? Amuse ourselves with the glass menagerie, darling? Eternally play those worn-out phonograph records your father left as a painful reminder of him?

We won't have a business career—we've given that up because it gave us nervous indigestion! [*She laughs wearily*] What is there left but dependency all our lives? I know so well what becomes of unmarried women who aren't prepared to occupy a position. I've seen such pitiful cases in the South—barely tolerated spinsters living upon the grudging patronage of a sister's husband or a brother's wife!—stuck away in some little mousetrap of a room—encouraged by one in-law to visit another—little birdlike women without any nest—eating the crust of humility all their life!

Is that the future that we've mapped out for ourselves?

I swear it's the only alternative I can think of!

It isn't a very pleasant alternative, is it?

Of course—some girls *do marry*.

[*Laura twists her hands nervously*]

Haven't you ever liked some boy?

LAURA: Yes. I liked one once. [*Rises*] I came across his picture a while ago.

AMANDA [*With some interest*]: He gave you his picture?

LAURA: No, it's in the year-book.

AMANDA [*disappointed*]: Oh—a high-school boy.

[*Screen image: Jim as the high school hero bearing a silver cup*]

LAURA: Yes. His name was Jim. [*Laura lifts the heavy annual from the claw-foot table*] Here he is in *The Pirates of Penzance*.

AMANDA [*Absently*]: The what?

LAURA: The operetta the senior class put on. He had a wonderful voice and we sat across the aisle from each other Mondays, Wednesdays and Fridays in the Aud. Here he is with the silver cup for debating! See his grin?

AMANDA [*Absently*]: He must have had a jolly disposition.

LAURA: He used to call me—Blue Roses.

[*Screen image: Blue roses*]

AMANDA: Why did he call you such a name as that?

LAURA: When I had that attack of pleurosis—he asked me what was the matter when I came back. I said pleurosis—he thought that I said Blue Roses! So that's what he always called me after that. Whenever he saw me, he'd holler, "Hello, Blue Roses!" I didn't care for the girl that he went out with. Emily Meisenbach. Emily was the best-dressed girl at Soldan. She never struck me, though, as being sincere...It says in the Personal Section—they're engaged. That's six years ago! They must be married by now.

AMANDA: Girls that aren't cut out for business careers usually wind up married to some nice man. [*Gets up with a spark of revival*] Sister, that's what you'll do!

[*Laura utters a startled, doubtful laugh. She reaches quickly for a piece of glass*]

LAURA: But, Mother—

AMANDA: Yes? [*Crossing to photograph*]

LAURA [*In a tone of frightened apology*]: I'm—crippled!

AMANDA: Nonsense! Laura, I've told you never, never to use that word. Why, you're not crippled, you just have a little defect—hardly noticeable, even! When people have some slight disadvantage like that, they cultivate other things to make up for it—develop charm—and vivacity—and—*charm*! That's all you have to do! [*She turns again to the photograph*] One thing your father had *plenty of*—was *charm*!

[*The scene fades out with music*]

# Bibliography

Aristotle. *The Poetics*, trans. Kenneth A. Telford. Chicago: Gateway, 1961.

Artaud, Antonin. *The Theatre and Its Double*. New York: Grove Press, 1958.

Bach, George. *Aggression Lab*. Dubuque, IA: Kendall/Hunt, 1971.

Bacon, Wallace A., and Robert S. Breen. *Literature as Experience*. New York: McGraw-Hill, 1959.

Ball, David. *Backwards and Forwards: A Technical Manual for Reading Plays*. Carbondale: Southern Illinois University Press, 1983.

Barton, John. *Playing Shakespeare*. London and New York: Metheun, 1984.

Bates, Brian. *The Way of the Actor*. Boston: Shambhala, 1987.

Beck, Julian. *The Life of the Theatre*. San Francisco: City Lights Books, 1972.

Beckerman, Bernard. *Dynamics of Drama*. New York: Drama Book Publishers, 1979.

Benedetti, Robert. *Seeming, Being, and Becoming*. New York: Drama Book Specialists, 1975.

———*The Director at Work*. Englewood Cliffs, NJ: Prentice Hall, 1984.

———"Zen in the Art of Actor Training," in *Master Teachers of Theatre*, ed. Burnet Hobgood. Carbondale: Southern Illinois University Press, 1988.

Berne, Eric. *Games People Play*. New York: Grove Press, 1964.

Birdwhistle, Raymond. *Introduction to Kinesics*. Louisville: University of Louisville Pamphlet, 1957.

Boleslavsky, Richard. *Acting: The First Six Lessons*. New York: Theatre Arts Books, 1933.

Branden, Nathaniel. *The Disowned Self*. New York: Bantam, 1973.

————*The Psychology of Self-Esteem*. New York: Bantam, 1971.

Braun, Edward, trans. and ed. *Meyerhold on Theatre*. New York: Hill & Wang, 1969.

Brockett, Oscar G. *The Theatre: An Introduction*, 4th ed. New York: Holt, Rinehart & Winston, 1979.

Brook, Peter. *The Empty Space*. New York: Atheneum, 1968.

Bullough, Edward. *Aesthetics*. Stanford, CA: Stanford University Press, 1957.

Campbell, Joseph. *The Masks of God*. New York: Viking, 1959.

Cassirer, Ernst. *The Philosophy of Symbolic Forms*, trans. Ralph Manheim. New Haven: Yale University Press, 1953.

Chaikin, Joseph. *The Presence of the Actor*. New York: Atheneum, 1972.

Chekhov, Michael. *To the Actor*. New York: Harper & Row, 1953.

Cohen, Robert. *Acting Power*. Palo Alto, CA: Mayfield, 1978.

Cole, Toby, ed. *Acting: A Handbook of the Stanislavski Method*. New York: Crown, 1971.

Cole, Toby, and Helen Chinoy, eds. *Actors on Acting*. New York: Crown, 1970.

Crawford, Jerry. *Acting in Person and in Style*, 3rd ed. Dubuque, IA: Wm. C. Brown, 1983.

Dewey, John. *Experience and Nature*. La Salle, Il.: Open Court, 1925.

Ernst, Earle. *The Kabuki Theatre*. New York: Grove Press, 1956.

Esslin, Martin. *Brecht: The Man and His Work*. New York: Doubleday, 1960.

————*The Theatre of the Absurd*. New York: Doubleday, 1961.

Feldenkrais, Moshe. *Awareness through Movement*. New York: Harper & Row, 1972.

Gielgud, John. *An Actor and His Time*. New York: Penguin, 1981.

Goffman, Erving. *The Presentation of Self in Everyday Life*. New York: Doubleday, 1959.

Gorchakov, Nikolai. *Stanislavski Directs*. New York: Funk & Wagnalls, 1954.

Green, Michael. *Downwind of Upstage*. New York: Hawthorn, 1964.

Grotowski, Jerzy. *Towards a Poor Theatre*. New York: Simon & Schuster, 1968.

Guthrie, Tyrone. *Tyrone Guthrie on Acting*. New York: Viking, 1971.

Hagen, Uta. *Respect for Acting.* New York: Macmillan, 1973.

Hall, Edward. *The Silent Language.* New York: Doubleday, 1959.

Halprin, Lawrence. *The RSVP Cycles.* New York: George Braziller, 1969.

Harrop, John, and Sabin Epstein. *Acting with Style.* Englewood Cliffs, NJ: Prentice Hall, 1982.

Herrigel, Eugen. *Zen in the Art of Archery.* New York: Vintage, 1971.

Jacobson, Edmund. *Progressive Relaxation.* Chicago: University of Chicago Press, 1938.

Johnstone, Keith. *Impro: Improvisation and the Theatre.* New York: Theatre Arts Books, 1983.

Jones, Frank Pierce. *Body Awareness in Action.* New York: Schocken Books, 1976.

Joseph, Bertram. *Acting Shakespeare.* New York: Theatre Arts Books, 1960.

Kalter, Joanmarie. *Actors on Acting.* New York: Sterling, 1978.

Kirby, E. T., ed. *Total Theatre.* New York: Dutton, 1969.

Kuritz, Paul. *Playing.* Englewood Cliffs, NJ: Prentice Hall, 1982.

Lang, R. D. *The Politics of Experience.* New York: Ballantine, 1967.

Lao Tsu. *Tao Te Ching.* trans. Gia Fu Feng and Jane English. New York: Vintage, 1972.

Lessac, Arthur. *Body Wisdom: The Use and Training of the Human Body.* New York: Drama Book Specialists, 1978.

Lewis, Robert. *Advice to Players.* New York: Harper & Row, 1980.

———*Method or Madness?* London: Heinemann, 1960.

Linklater, Kristin. *Freeing the Natural Voice.* New York: Drama Book Specialists, 1976.

Lowen, Alexander. *The Language of the Body.* New York: Collier, 1971.

Maslov, Abraham. *Motivation and Personality.* New York: Harper & Row, 1954.

May, Rollo. *The Courage to Create.* New York: Norton, 1975.

O'Connor, Gary. *Ralph Richardson: An Actor's Life.* New York: Atheneum, 1982.

Olivier, Laurence. *Confessions of an Actor.* New York: Simon & Schuster, 1982.

Otto, Walter. *Dionysus.* Bloomington: Indiana University Press, 1965.

Perls, Frederick S., Ralph F.Hefferline, and Paul Goodman. *Gestalt Therapy.* New York: Julian Press, 1951.

Ram Dass. *Be Here Now.* New Mexico: Lama Foundation, 1971.

————*The Only Dance There Is*. New York: Doubleday/Anchor, 1974.

Redgrave, Michael. *In My Mind's I*. New York: Viking, 1983.

Richards, Mary Caroline. *Centering*. Wesleyan: Wesleyan University Press, 1964.

Sainer, Arthur. *The Radical Theatre Notebook*. New York: Discus/Avon, 1975.

St. Denis, Michel. *Theatre: The Rediscovery of Style*. New York: Theatre Arts Books, 1960.

Sapir, Edward. *Language*. New York: Harcourt, Brace & World, 1949.

Schechner, Richard. *Environmental Theatre*. New York: Hawthorn, 1973.

Schlauch, Margaret. *The Gift of Language*. New York: Dover, 1955.

Shurtleff, Michael. *Audition*. New York: Walker & Co., 1978.

Spolin, Viola. *Improvisation for the Theatre*. Evanston, IL.: Northwestern University Press, 1963.

Stanislavski, Constantin. *An Actor Prepares*, trans. Elizabeth Reynolds Hapgood). New York: Theatre Arts Books, 1936.

————*Building a Character*, trans. Elizabeth Reynolds Hapgood. New York: Theatre Arts Books, 1949.

————*Creating a Role*, trans. Elizabeth Reynolds Hapgood. New York: Theatre Arts Books, 1949.

————*My Life in Art*, trans. J. J. Robbins. New York: Theatre Arts Books, 1952.

Suzuki, D.T. *Zen Buddhism*. New York: Doubleday/Anchor, 1956.

Suzuki, Shunrya. *Zen Mind, Beginner's Mind*. New York: Weatherhill, 1970.

Trungpa, Chogyam. *Cutting through Spiritual Materialism*. Berkeley: Shambhala, 1973.

Watts, Alan. *The Book:On the Taboo against Knowing Who You Are*. New York: Random House, 1972.

Wellek, Rene, and Austin Warren. *Theory of Literature*. New York: Harvest/Harcourt, Brace & Co., 1942.

Willet, John, ed. *Brecht on Theatre*. New York: Hill & Wang, 1964.

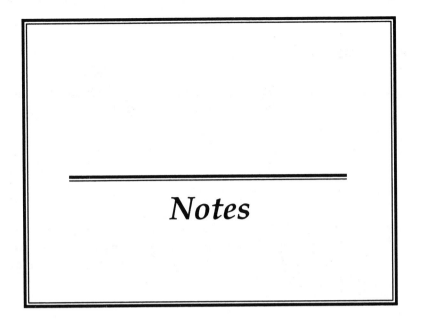

# *Notes*

## LESSON ONE

1. Erving Goffman, *The Presentation of Self in Everyday Life.* (New York: Doubleday, 1959), pp. 71–74. Copyright © by Erving Goffman. Reprinted with the Permission of Doubleday & Company, Inc.

2. Brian Bates, *The Way of the Actor.* (Boston: Shambhala, 1987), p. 7.

3. Ibid., p. 9.

4. Ibid., p. 16.

5. From an unpublished letter.

6. Constantin Stanislavski, *My Life in Art*, trans. J. J. Robbins (New York: Theatre Arts Books, 1952). Copyright © 1924 by Little, Brown & Co., and 1952 by Elizabeth Reynolds Hapgood. Used with the permission of the publishers, Theatre Arts Books, 153 Waverly Place, New York, NY 10014, and Geoffrey Bless Ltd., London.

7. From David Mamet, *Writing in Restaurants.* (New York: Viking Penguin, 1986), p. 116. Copyright © 1986 by David Mamet. All rights reserved. Reprinted with the permission of Viking Penguin Inc.

## LESSON TWO

1. Frederick Perls, Ralph Hefferline, and Paul Goodman, *Gestalt Therapy* (New York: Julian Press, 1951), p. 134. (Dell paperback, 1964.)
2. Ibid., p. 33.

## LESSON FOUR

1. Mary Caroline Richards, *Centering* (Wesleyan: Wesleyan University Press, 1964), pp. 38–39. Copyright © by Mary Caroline Richards. Used with the permission of Wesleyan University Press.

## LESSON FIVE

1. Raymond Birdwhistle, *Introduction to Kinesics* (Louisville: University of Louisville Pamphlet, 1957), pp. 29–30.
2. Edward T. Hall, *The Silent Language* (New York: Doubleday, 1959), p. 43. Copyright © 1959 by Edward T. Hall. Reprinted by permission of Doubleday & Company, Inc.
3. Ibid., p. 42.
4. Bates, *Way of the Actor*, p. 114.
5. Wallace A. Bacon and Robert S. Breen, *Literature as Experience,* (New York: McGraw-Hill, 1959), p. 32.

## LESSON SIX

1. Margaret Schlauch, *The Gift of Language* (New York: Dover, 1955), p. 3. Reprinted with the permission of the publisher.
2. Edward Sapir, *Language* (New York: Harcourt, Brace & World, 1949), pp. 8–9.
3. Ibid., p. 5.
4. Bacon and Breen, *Literature as Experience*, p. 286.
5. Ernst Cassirer, *The Philosophy of Symbolic Forms*, trans. Ralph Manheim (New Haven: Yale University Press, 1953), p. 148.

## LESSON SEVEN

1. Richards, *Centering*, p. 25.
2. August Strindberg, "Notes to the Members of the Intimate Theatre," trans. Everett Sprinchorn, *The Tulane Drama Review*, 6, no. 2 (November 1961), p. 157. This material is also copyrighted by The Drama Review, 1967.

## LESSON EIGHT

1. Alan Watts, *The Book: On the Taboo against Knowing Who You Are* (New York: Random House, 1972), p. 6.
2. Mamet, *Writing in Restaurants*, pp. 20–21.

## LESSON TEN

1. Constantin Stanislavski, *An Actor's Handbook*, trans. and ed. Elizabeth Reynolds Hapgood (New York: Theatre Arts Books, 1936), p. 8. Copyright © 1936, 1961, 1963 by Elizabeth Reynolds Hapgood. Used with the permission of the publisher, Theatre Arts Books, 153 Waverly Place, New York, NY 10014.
2. Constantin Stanislavski, *Building a Character*, trans. Elizabeth Reynolds Hapgood (New York: Theatre Arts Books, 1949), pp. 218–36. Used with the permission of the publisher, Theatre Arts Books, 153 Waverly Place, New York, NY 10014.

## LESSON ELEVEN

1. This exercise adapted from the work of Dr. George Bach.
2. Constantin Stanislavski, *Creating a Role* (New York: Theatre Arts Books, 1961), p. 62. Used with the permission of the publisher, Theatre Arts Books, 153 Waverly Place, New York, NY 10014.
3. Stanislavski, *Actor's Handbook*, p. 9.
4. Ibid.
5. Mamet, *Writing in Restaurants*, pp. 26–27.

## LESSON TWELVE

    1. Stanislavski, *Actor's Handook*, p. 138.

## LESSON FIFTEEN

    1. Stanislavski, *Actor's Handbook*, pp. 137–38.

## LESSON SIXTEEN

    1. Oscar G. Brockett, *The Theatre: An Introduction*, 3rd ed. (New York: Holt, Rinehart & Winston, 1974), pp. 39–40. Reprinted with the permission of Holt, Rinehart & Winston, Inc.
    2. Ibid.

## LESSON SEVENTEEN

    1. Mamet, *Writing in Restaurants*, p. 76.
    2. Jan Kott, "King Lear or Endgame," *The Evergreen Review* (August–September 1964), p. 55.
    3. Moshe Feldenkrais, *Awareness through Movement* (New York: Harper & Row, 1972), pp. 45–46.

## LESSON EIGHTEEN

    1. Stanislavski, *Building a Character*, pp. 218–36.
    2. Ibid.
    3. Ibid.
    4. Ibid.
    5. Ibid.

## LESSON NINETEEN

    1. Alexander Lowen, *The Language of the Body*, (New York: Collier, 1971), p. 32.
    2. This list is adapted from Nathaniel Branden, *The Disowned Self* (New York: Bantam, 1973), pp. 111–14.

## LESSON TWENTY

1. David D. Burns, *Feeling Good* (New York: Signet, 1980), pp. 11–12.
2. Stanislavski, *Actor's Handbook*, p. 56.
3. Mamet, *Writing in Restaurants*, p. 127.
4. Stanislavski, *Building a Character*, p. 70.
5. Ibid.

## LESSON TWENTY-TWO

1. Stanislavski, *Creating a Role*, p. 62. Used with the permission of the publisher, Theatre Arts Books, 153 Waverly Place, New York, NY 10014.
2. Nikolai Gorchakov, *Stanislavski Directs* (New York: Funk & Wagnalls, 1954), p. 77.

## LESSON TWENTY-THREE

1. Strindberg, "Notes to the Members of the Intimate Theater," p. 157.
2. Quoted in an interview.
3. From an unpublished letter.
4. Mamet, *Writing in Restaurants*, pp. 20–21.
5. Ibid., p. 19.
6. Ibid., p. 21
7. Stanislavski, *My Life in Art*, pp. 217–18.
8. Gorchakov, *Stanislavski Directs*, pp. 40–41.

## APPENDIX

1. From *Death of a Salesman* by Arthur Miller. Copyright © 1949, renewed © 1977 by Arthur Miller. Used by permission of Viking Penguin, a division of Penguin Books USA Inc.
2. From *The Glass Menagerie* by Tennessee Williams. Copyright © 1945 by Tennessee Williams and Edwina Williams and renewed © 1973 by Tennessee Williams. Reprinted by permission of Random House, Inc.

# *Index*